Quantum Explorations

Far Beyond 3D

Sue Beckley

Copyright ©2023 Quantum Explorations

All rights reserved. This book or any portion thereof may not be reproduced or used in any manner whatsoever without the express written permission of the publisher except for the use of brief quotations in a book review.

www.quantumexplorations.com

Quantum Explorations: Far Beyond 3D cover art, typesetting, and editing done by Brent Beckley.

Printed and bound in the United States by Lightning Source, a division of Ingram.

All authors mentioned are real and recommended.

Quantum Explorations
Leesburg, Florida, USA

ISBN: 978-1-0881-6523-2
eISBN: 978-1-0881-6531-7

10 9 8 7 6 5 4 3 2 1

DEDICATION and ACKNOWLEDGMENTS

For the men in my life; Brent, Ryan, and Stephen. If it were not for the love of you three, which has always been my motivation to be the best version of myself, I may not have traveled this far to know myself and share my discoveries with the world. Love is my motivator, and my guide. Thank you, and I love you always.

TABLE OF CONTENTS

Intro to Beyond 3D: "The Meat and Potatoes"	1
The Quantum	12
The Four Light Bodies	39
Spirit Communication	56
Timelines, Life Plans, and Soul Contracts, Oh My!	73
All Truths are True	98
What's In a Name: Contacting the Etheric	105
It's Not You, It's Me	115
Let Go of "That Thing" Using the Quantum	129
Real Magic	137
Abundance!	165
Finding and Honoring the Essential Self	169
What Happens in a Quantum Healing Session	174
Starseeds and Galactic Assistance	178
Not Goodbye...See You	190

1
Intro to Beyond 3D
"The Meat and Potatoes"

I am a practitioner of quantum healing hypnosis techniques. Through quantum energy field exploration with the practice of hypnosis skills with clients and friends, I have discovered methods of healing and consciousness expansion which I am going to share with you. Everything I will present is one human's point of view. Please take whatever truth that resonates with you and leave the rest. Or 'marinate' on the concepts that seem interesting to you. This is what I have done for over 30 years; marinate on concepts that my consciousness felt could be true, but I could not quite wrap my mind around to integrate into my beingness yet. The seeds that were planted within my mind from countless other humans over the 30 years have grown into fruit. I wish to share this fruit with you, or plant seeds within your consciousness that will help produce your fruit.

When I started writing this book, I wrote six chapters before I was gifted with information that provides evidence of the information I am receiving in my work. This synchronicity I am compelled to share about first. A friend of mine in the quantum healing community sent me a link to a CIA declassified document that was written on June 9, 1983, by Lieutenant Colonel Wayne M. McDonnell of the U.S. Army Operational Group to his commanding officer. It is subject titled "Analysis and Assessment of Gateway Process" and can be found in its entirety online with a simple search. LTC McDonnell was tasked with reporting about a method of altering/expanding human consciousness called the Gateway Experience. The Gateway Experience began development in the 1970s by a man named Robert A. Monroe. Monroe stated, "The physical universe, including the whole of humankind, is an ongoing creative process." And he proved it through his experimental techniques to alter/expand human consciousness. The various techniques Monroe developed are offered now, professionally, to everyday people that want to expand their consciousness and have been used by military personnel (monroeinstitute.org).

Reading McDonnell's report about Monroe's techniques served to validate and expand further some of what I am writing about in my books. I feel it is always a good idea to follow my intuitive and experiential pathways, but I also love it when other people come up with similar information that I am receiving or expand upon my information further. I am not ruled by science because scientists openly admit there is so much about the concepts of reality that they still do not understand or can agree upon. McDonnell's report states that there are 'bridges' between the known qualities of reality explained with scientific principles and what is still not known and labeled "the occult." I can be considered more of an occultist (spiritualist) who enjoys confirmation from science.

The point of my book and what I am going to share with you is to help you to expand your understanding of how energy works with metaphysical concepts, the possibilities that you can open up to with these understandings, and help you remember that you create your reality. Doing all of that amounts to expanding consciousness, which is what I have been doing for myself for years. I knew there is more to understanding the nature of reality than what I was told as a child. You know it too, I suspect. I hope that you will expand your thoughts about what you know to be true and realize self-empowerment to the point where you step into your abilities to create whatever you wish to experience.

We are all having a human experience, and some of us have remembered that we can shape and mold our experience into anything, as long as whatever experience we are shaping is consistent with our soul's plan for this lifetime. More on that later. The benefit and joy that I derive from sharing are felt in my whole being. It feels like I have fashioned some keys for myself to true happiness, and I can help you create your keys by sharing about energy and consciousness expansion.

This journey of life on Earth varies for each one of us. On the soul level, we all have our reasons for experiencing Earth's realities, and we also have reasons for coming together to experience it with other souls as a collective. Every reason for experience here is valid and needs to be honored. I am not going to present information that I hope will be used by you to "wake" anyone else up. I am not a conspiracy theorist who wants to change the present Earth experience so that we can all reach fifth-dimensional (5D) realities at the same time (known as ascension). I do believe in personal shifts and have had some myself. However, every single one of us will shift into 5D consciousness in our own time, and when we each are ready to do that. Some will experience it before the rest of us.

There is a rumor going around that humanity must all shift together to ascend, within this Earthly reality. I do not believe that.

However, in another dimensional reality of Earth, I know we have already shifted to 5D consciousness as a collective. Both realities exist in the same eternal moment point of Creation, and this concept is what quantum means. We, as the parts of consciousness being experienced within this Earth dimensional reality, are reaching for those higher aspects of ourselves. We feel the higher aspects of ourselves, they are calling to us to join our consciousness with theirs. Or to bring their consciousness into our energy fields, in essence, become them.

Expansion of what we know to be true now, at this moment point of our soul's focus, is the way to reach our higher self realities. I know one woman that does not experience reality within the 3rd nor 4th dimension, but higher. I will not say her name but I promise you that people do not think she is crazy. She operates in this world with us and leads an outwardly normal life.

Whatever "normal" is.

Her internal life and understandings of reality are quite different from most. If I know one person experiencing life this way, then there must be others living on Earth that experience 5D consciousness and higher. The point is, we all get 'there' when we get there. We can bridge between states of consciousness without giving up relationships with those we love and enjoy being with on Earth. Ascension is not about lining us up like a bunch of ducks and having us all shift to 5D consciousness realities at the same time. Higher states of consciousness can be held for a time, and then the human may go back to more fourth-dimensional (4D) realities or even 3D realities. We go back and forth all the time anyway without being aware of doing so. There is no race for the collective of humanity to raise its consciousness to 5D and stay there permanently, working on going even higher.

One universal truth that I have found through quantum healing practice is that each one of us has an oversoul. That oversoul has sent its energy throughout every dimension according to what it wishes to experience. There are versions of you that you are not aware of, experiencing other lifetimes or incarnations, and all of this is going on at the same moment point of what we think of as 'time.' Quantum healing hypnosis has shown me that we can and do access these other selves subconsciously, and we can start to do it consciously by expanding our definitions of what reality is. When we start to trust that **we are** light beings of the highest power (God/Source), we can access any information and reality that we want to. The key to doing that is expanding consciousness (increasing personal energy/vibration).

I'm going to assist you with the process. What I am speaking about here is my definition of ascension. Ascension is expanding our consciousness more to where we eventually remember that we are of God/Source, and we have the power to illuminate realities that we may believe are wishful thinking. We are powerful enough to illuminate everything that can be experienced. We do it anyway… why not become aware of HOW we do it, and get going on fashioning things the way we want to see them play out instead of feeling like we are caught in some video game and we never know what is coming at us next. Our souls did choose to have experiences in dense realities like Earth and to do this the soul must reduce its consciousness for the lower-density reality for it to seem real. However, we are living the Earth experience during very fantastic and magical moments points of Earth's timeline.

Humanity as a whole (collective consciousness) has decided to raise our consciousness to the point of remembering who we are again. We desire the experiences of unity consciousness. We've had enough of war, hunger, destruction of the planet, poverty, anger, resentment, and competition for resources that are abundant enough to provide for every single person on this planet. Mother Earth has provided for everyone. She is a sentient being and has decided to ascend to 5D reality. We must go with her, or stay on another timeline version of Earth that contains realities that are not pleasant to experience. The souls that wish to ascend with Mother Earth are feeling called to increase their vibrations and frequencies, which in turn raises our consciousnesses. How is it possible for some souls to stay within 3D consciousness while others may choose to ascend?

This is a question I have been asking ever since I learned from Dolores Cannon that there will be two versions of Earth. She explained that she received information through quantum healing hypnosis sessions about two Earths that will exist simultaneously when some humans ascend to 5D consciousness. According to Dolores, the souls that are not yet ready to ascend to 5D will remain on the 3D version of Earth until they are ready to shift also. I won't hide the fact that this sparked a lot of fear in me. I became very concerned with the welfare of those I care about who may not be choosing to expand their consciousness. Would I ever see them again if I shift and they don't? I did not want my friends and family to continue suffering the 3D experience if there is another option, but what could I do about it? I know full well that every person has free will to choose what they want to experience. I also know that it is not my right to change someone else's decisions.

The worry that I carried remained for years from the time that I learned Dolores' methods for hypnosis, until my ability to communicate with my other selves in higher dimensions activated. Higher beings of light who work with me during quantum healing sessions helped me to release the fear. These energies are of high vibration and greater wisdom than myself, in my current consciousness as Sue. Accessing them regularly and allowing them to touch my energy fields has raised my consciousness to a point where my psychic abilities have opened right up. Other quantum healers speak of similar experiences happening to them. And it can happen for you too if you wish to allow high-frequency beings to merge with your energy.

I will teach you about doing that through my writing. I will inform you of ways to connect with higher energy beings and energy fields without needing to rely on a practitioner to get you connected. Not that going to a practitioner is wrong in any way. Asking for assistance in the process of ascension is necessary sometimes. We rely on each other as fellow travelers on Earth to share energy and knowledge. I want you to know that there are no gurus in life, and you can access higher energies on your own with practice. I was able to let go of my fear that my family and friends would disappear from my life if they did not ascend with me because I meditated about it, and the guides showed me that when I reach 5D consciousness, I still will have the ability and choice to touch the reality of Earth where three sets of consciousness; 3D, 4D, and 5D are happening simultaneously.

My guides informed me that the 5D reality I will experience will be perceived by me much differently than the 3D and 4D realities, but they are not physically nor energetically separate worlds. That means no loss of anyone maintaining 3D or 4D realities unless I choose to separate myself from them.

It's all about personal choice and free will. I believe that Dolores was receiving accurate information about there being a split between worlds, but I also think that Dolores interpreted that information differently than I have recently. The split between worlds is in the experience, not a physical split of Earth into two aspects of reality. I cannot say who is right. I have come to know that the 4th dimension is a bridge between these two realities (3D and 5D), and that bridge is used to increase our personal frequencies through consciousness expansion. I believe Dolores and I both are correct in part, because of a concept that was discussed in LTC McDonnell's report, holograms. I will be talking a lot about holograms.

I do not know, and could not find out about LTC McDonnell's credentials and expertise for writing this report. My guess, having been a member of the U.S. Army, is that the U.S. Army Operations detachment is an arm of a high-security Army Intelligence branch that does not share publicly the credentials of its members. It is well known that during the Cold War, many 'first world' countries and several other countries were experimenting with and developing ways to increase human consciousness. This was mostly in an effort to find covert ways to spy on each other. Remote viewing (RV) is an example. Remote viewers are trained to use a given set of numbers to locate an unknown target site, using senses that are capable of transcending what most people perceive (psychic abilities), and provide details of what the enemy was planning. One very accomplished remote viewer, David Morehouse, a highly decorated officer for special operations for the US Army; most recently worked as an expert on non-lethal weapons for the elite Study Group of the Chief of Staff of the Army, wrote a training manual titled "Remote Viewing." Morehouse served the Army in many ways including being a member of Army Special Forces Rangers, and he was recruited to be a remote viewer for the Army. He did remote viewing for two years, serving hundreds of missions, before returning to regular military service. Currently, Morehouse teaches and supports other remote viewers. I purchased his book and I intend to learn the process. Not to spy on anyone, but to expand my consciousness. I suspect much of the technique is similar to hypnosis. Why not learn new ways to explore reality through expanded consciousness?

    The pursuit of techniques and technologies to get the 'upper hand' in the spy game brought some fascinating revelations about the capacity of human consciousness. I believe government-run military groups from several countries (namely the U.S. and Germany) also had help from galactic beings, who you might call aliens or Extra Terrestrials (ETs). The abundance of declassified US government information documenting cooperation with ETs is proof that the governments of the world have been holding back, from the general public, advanced technologies to explore alternate realities, for a long time. The secret war games were all about who could get the best technology/information/weapons first, and use it against 'the enemy.' Lately, I'd estimate within the past 6 years, probably more, governments have still been working to access higher consciousness in secret from the general public. But, there is evidence that some governments are working together toward full disclosure of humanity's relationships with galactic beings (see Cosmic

Disclosure, Gaia.com, where former military personnel describe relationships between humans and ETs). Much improvement in technology, health care, Earth's environmental status, and interpersonal relationships with ETs have resulted from humanity's discussions with and cooperation from, Extra Terrestrials (aka galactic beings). It is time we grab onto this concept and stop trying to imagine we are alone in the universe.

The fact that LTC McDonnell was tasked to learn about the Gateway Experience, analyze it, and write a report about it to deliver to the Army Operations division tells me that he has scientific training. LTC McDonnell experienced The Gateway Process himself. He used a scientific approach, and worked closely with numerous experts in the fields of quantum physics, general physics, bio-engineering, and psychology to form the analysis of Gateway in his report. McDonnell worked closely with Itzhak Bentov, studied his work in-depth, and applied it to the report. You may recognize the name because Itzhak Bentov is one of the founders of Medi-Tek, now known as Boston Scientific. Bentov designed Israel's first rocket while working with the Israeli Science Corps before moving to the U.S. in 1954. Bentov went on to invent the steerable heart catheter which has saved countless lives. He is known as the pioneer of biomedical engineering and holds dozens of patents for vital medical technologies.

If that isn't impressive enough, Bentov was a spiritual man and made it his business to explore human consciousness. One of his inventions is the seismograph which records the vibrations of the aorta. Bentov demonstrated that when a person meditates, the aorta tunes to the beat of the heart, synchronizes with the brain waves, and synchronizes with Earth's electrical field. His work stands to explain why a person's consciousness can connect with another person's consciousness even though they may physically be far away from one another geographically. I will not attempt to explain Bentov's aorta work in detail because LTC McDonnell explains it in his report. You may access the report because it is in the public domain if you wish to read more details.

The point I am making is; even if McDonnell did not bring his wealth of knowledge to the table with his analysis, he utilized the research and knowledge of people who knew what they were talking about in scientific fields. I may reference LTC McDonnell's report within this book, and the professionals that he based his analyses with. To highlight the scientific approach that McDonnell used to evaluate the Gateway Experience, I will break down the areas that were tapped into;

biomedical information to understand the physical aspects of the Gateway Experience, quantum mechanics to describe the nature and functioning of human consciousness, quantum physics to explain the time-space dimension and means by which human consciousness transcends it, and classical physics to bring the whole phenomenon of out-of-body states into the language of physical science, removing the stigma of 'occult' connotations.

The Gateway Experience is a method of altering human consciousness to escape the restrictions of time/space, leading to astral projection and other out-of-body (OOB) experiences. It applies a patented Hemi-Sync technology where both sides of the brain are stimulated with sound in a way that brings both hemispheres into one, unified field, altering states of consciousness to the theta brain wave. It is compared to, by LTC McDonnell, results obtained from hypnosis, meditation, and bio-feedback (using scientific equipment to measure the effectiveness of targeted meditation for self-healing). I know that the theta brain wave is what quantum healers try to achieve with our clients during hypnosis sessions as prescribed by Dolores Cannon. Not every person WILL achieve theta during hypnosis, but that was the goal when I was learning Dolores's technique.

As an aside, I have discovered that the theta brain state is not necessary for my clients to have a successful session, and it is almost the exception when it happens rather than the norm. I have noticed that my clients like to have the executive, left brain, alert during hypnosis. They want to remember everything without having to rely on the recording of the session. That is okay because I know how to invite the left brain to observe during the session without interfering. More on that later.

Now you see why I am so interested in this particular report, the hypnosis and meditation links. Reading through the whole report, I found answers to some questions I have been wondering about for years. For instance, 'if God/Source created all of reality in one moment, with one thought, how is it that we are still 'creating'? We are all still creating because I can notice my creative processes as I live my life, I can witness others creating, and I feel it is one thing that every human being is driven to do. How can it be both? Everything was created in one moment AND we are creating in every moment? That was the brain twister for me. Until I read about the nature of holograms described by mathematicians and a Nobel Prize winner for work in holographic physical science principles (Dennis Gerber, 1947) in LTC McDonnell's report.

Bentov described the atomic and subatomic composition of

matter in terms of oscillating energy grids. In a nutshell, solid matter, according to Bentov, simply does not exist. Rather, atomic structure is composed of moving energy grids (fluctuating to move back and forth in a rhythmic manner) surrounded by other oscillating energy grids which orbit each other at extraordinarily high speeds, such that the energy movement is not visible to the naked eye nor through high magnification, but appears to form solid matter. These energies are described to be sub-atomic. 'States of matter' are *variances* in what we think of as particles; the energy oscillating, is caused by adding more energy, or losing energy within the system. The more energy contained in a system, the higher the vibration, and frequency of vibration the system has.

    Stick with me here because although this discussion may seem boring to those not scientifically inclined, I promise it gets more interesting. LTC McDonnell stated that the point of Bentov's work is; "the entire human being, brain, consciousness and all, like the universe which surrounds him, is nothing more or less than an extraordinarily complex system of **energy fields**." That means we, and everything we perceive to be solid matter are only energies configured in such a way that they all *appear* and *feel* to be solid form. We feel the energy, touch it, and think it to be solid, due to the frequency of the energy where we are focused on Earth. Energy creates, stores, and retrieves meaning in the universe by projecting frequencies **to** dimensional energy spaces (dormant/not yet illuminated), and that projection of energy creates a new pattern of energy expressed as a **hologram**. You add energy to a system and it "lights up" that system which is then experienced as reality. This is a big connection for me. This explains how God/Source created everything in one moment (the hologram of Creation), and it APPEARS that we are also creating in every moment when we light something up with our consciousness.

    God/Source made a hologram containing every possible experience, in that one moment of Creation. Source's thought fashioned every potential reality. The potentials are contained within the hologram. Some are actively being experienced, while others remain dormant, or they have not been lit up yet to be experienced. Hence the name 'potentials.' Each reality of God/Source's Creation remains **a potential** experience until someone projects their energy (light/consciousness) to that part of the hologram. Then, that part of the hologram becomes 'reality' for the person that projected their energy to it.

    Reality can **appear** physically manifest to our consciousness because we can feel things by touch, but Bentov suggests that all matter is only energy moving very quickly, so that would mean what we are feeling is a variation of energy fields rather than a fully physical object. This process allows all consciousness aspects of Source (us) to have whatever experience our soul wants to have. We can call it a matrix; we can call it a movie, we can call it life. Whatever name you assign is an experience of the hologram. Many people think that reality is "all in our imaginations" or a dream. Considering that imagination and dreaming are functions of consciousness, it may be true. If universal energy fields are parts of the hologram of Source consciousness, then we as Source aspects are exploring ourselves in infinite ways, through many vibrational energy versions of ourselves. The oversoul may focus its consciousness within any dimension it wants to. Each dimension, or compartment of God's hologram, causes energy to express differently than within other dimensions. We can use our energy and light to reach into and become aware of other dimensional experiences. These are other realities where our soul energy is also being expressed. That is exploring quantum energy fields!

If I project my energy out into the universal hologram of Creation (by thoughts, feelings, actions, intentions) my energy interacts with part of Source's hologram to reveal a pattern of images, words, symbols, or whole realistic scenarios that can be received audibly, visually, emotionally, mentally, physically or all of the above. Then, I read those symbols and scenarios in whatever way my consciousness is capable of reading them, and this becomes **my** reality. It is one reality of an infinite number of realities that exist within the overall hologram that Source created. The individual aspect (me), who is always a part of Source but does not always remember that this is the case, is the one who determines the **level** of experiencing the hologram because it is my energy intensity (vibration) that is illuminating the result. If the individual increases their vibration, then the hologram will provide an increased or expanded reality. These we usually judge as being 'better than' lower vibrational realities, and so we seek to raise our vibrational energies to have those 'better realities' manifest for us.

It is comparable to what Esther Hicks is always saying when her guides tell us to "match the vibration of the reality that we want to see, and it will manifest." Many people feel the truth of what Esther teaches, but they do not know why it is true or how to match their energies to their desired realities. It is not something most of us are taught to do because our parents and other people in society forgot how to do it as well. It takes dedicated attention to **how** we respond to our experiences which causes us to raise our vibrations and create better reality experiences. Humans tend to hold onto what they are taught until something is proven to be harmful to us, and even then we find difficulty letting go of old patterns that no longer serve our wellbeing. We create, unconsciously, during most of our lives, because we have patterns of being that we learned from a young age from other people. Lots of people feel there is a problem for them in continuing old ways, but they don't know quite what to do about it.

Back to the hologram. It seems like we are creating something new at times within our experience of life. Quantum scientists suggest that what we are doing is highlighting another part of the hologram of all there is so that we can experience it. I am not implying that we are not being creative when we do it. It takes a creative mind to light up the hologram where it has never been illuminated before or to illuminate it in another way. In lower dimensional realities like 3D Earth, everything appears very real, rather than a hologram or a matrix, because some of the energy feels solid and we have forgotten our true being; aspects of Source. When we 'create' something, we are infusing with our energy a dormant part of the hologram (energy at rest) that has already been created by all of us (as Source), and that then becomes perceivable. Our energy matches the energy of what we are seeing in our reality. This description is the result of adding LTC McDonnell's report to what I have learned working with quantum energy fields, a model for understanding God/Source and the nature of reality. Moving forward, I will provide details about working with quantum energy fields for the individual. My scientific discussion about this content is complete.

2

The Quantum

To discuss the quantum, I will begin with a discussion of how Source created everything, including separating parts of itself into what we call souls. I like to use the term Source instead of God sometimes due to the negative connotation some people associate with the term God, and other times I put the terms together. I am referring to The Creator of everything when I use the term Source. I already covered the hologram of Creation where everything was created. Every potential reality. Source also decided to create oversouls by separating parts of itself and encouraging those aspects to split more times and venture further away from the whole of itself. The soul journeys away from Source into various realities of the hologram. This requires energy distribution (of consciousness) by the soul as it spreads *its* whole into parts or aspects. Quantum realities are explorations of soul consciousness moving through energy fields created by Source, which we call dimensions, and I describe as 'the hologram of Creation.' Here is a handy little picture to illustrate the concept of the energy distribution of souls, shown in a considerably basic model. In this picture I have magnified the representation of our universe in Figure 1.

My guess as to why all of this happened is that Source, being all-knowing, had the thought, "What is it like to be **not** Source." Once that thought sparked, the creation of all possibilities to be 'not Source' happened, the "Big Bang," if you will. Opportunities to be "not Source" became holographic potentials for experience in infinite ways. We light up and activate areas of the hologram that we call 'realities,' with our consciousness. Source's creation has been expanding and contracting ever since this original thought. That means that Source aspects (souls and their aspects) journey away vibrationally/dimensionally from the whole of Source to experience, and then they journey back to Source again and repeat. It is like when humans have children. The parents create life, the mother gives birth, the parents nurture the child, and eventually, the child moves away from its parents to experience itself. Then, at some point, the child grows older and wiser and chooses to interact more closely with the parents again. I know, not all human children maintain a relationship with their parents. The same can be said for souls. Sometimes a soul journeys and experiences realities so different from

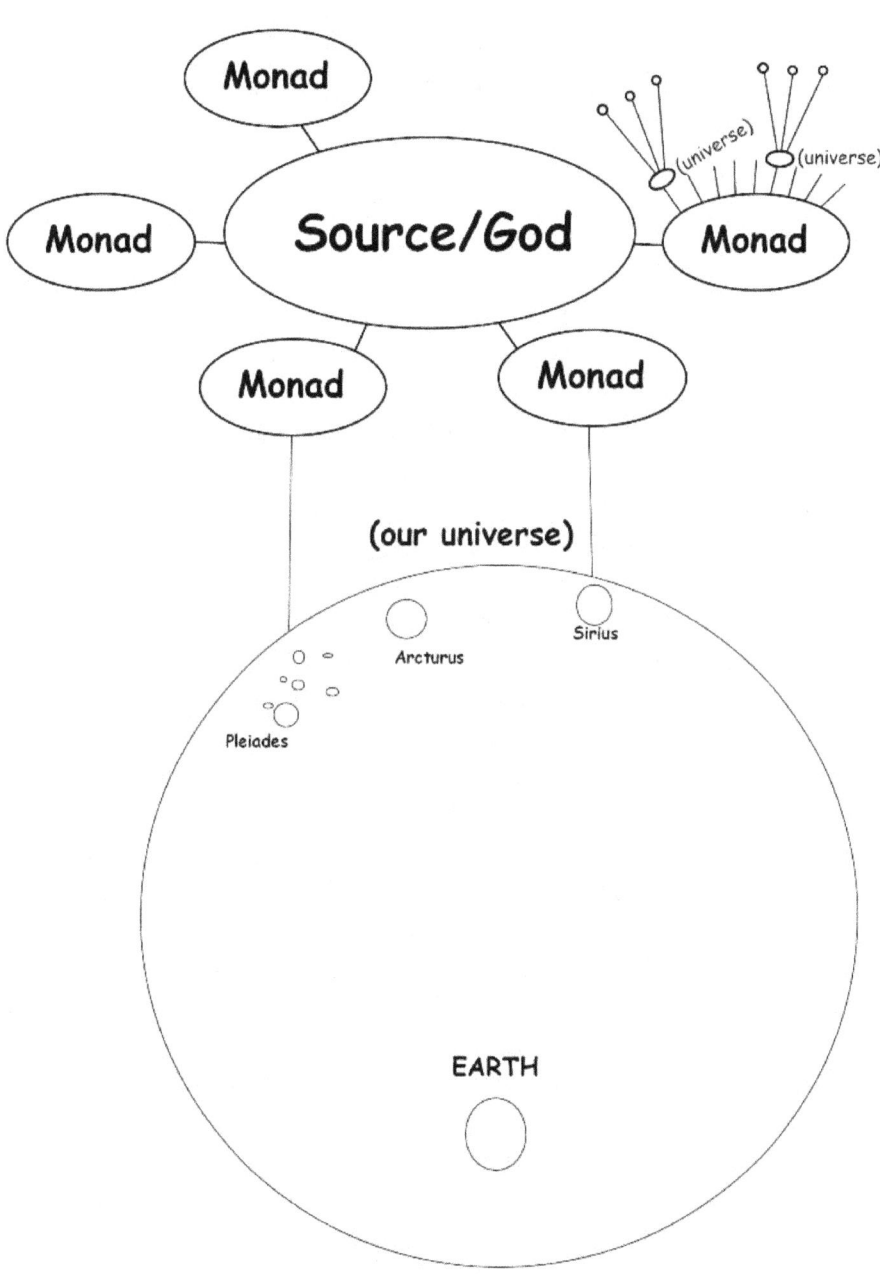

Figure 1: A Highly Simplified Illustration of Creation. "Not to Scale" :-)

God/Source's energy of unconditional love and all-knowing wisdom, that they forget where they came from. They may even think that Source is not real, or do not care if God/Source is real, and they choose to keep exploring realities that seem 'ungodly.' God/Source does not judge these journeys because Source **is** all souls together in their highest energy. No experience is excluded from Source's explorations of itself. No experience is judged, and there is no 'retribution' to a soul for having any kind of experience. Why would Source punish itself?

To imagine that punishment is Source's idea is to believe that Source made mistakes in its creation of everything. Every potential reality is just another experience that Source intends to have. Source knows that eventually all souls will return to it; reunite when they are done experiencing as individual consciousnesses.

So, Source split into aspects of itself (like cloning), to experience through its aspects what it is to be *not* Source. "How far can I go? How many ways can I express myself?" I do not know if God/Source asked itself those exact questions, but they seem to explain why God would split into parts and create diverse realities for those parts to explore. Why would Source want to do that? That is the eternal question, isn't it? In my simple understanding, the answer is because knowing and experiencing are not the same thing. **Knowledge + experience = wisdom**.

We can have knowledge about anything. But until we put knowledge into practice, and have experiences to go with that knowledge, the knowledge is only theoretical. For example, gardening. I have read books about gardening. And what I have discovered is that the knowledge in books about gardening is useful only when I apply the knowledge to the experience of gardening. Until then, the knowledge provides guidelines based on the experiences that *other* people have had with gardening. When I try to grow a plant, there is so much more than what I have read to consider and observe to create the best conditions for my plant to survive and thrive. For example; I must think about the Ph of the soil where I want to put a plant and the location relative to the sun, and how much water and nutrient supplement I need to provide with the type of soil I have planted in. Are there any bugs or animals indigenous to my area that will affect plant growth? Is the plant deadly to the animals living around me? These questions about gardening in **my** specific location are unique to my gardening experience, and cannot be determined by what is found in a book. I can use the information contained in a book to provide guidelines for gardening, but I have to experience how the knowledge in the book works for me. There is trial and error. Sometimes I use "best practices" prescribed in the book, and my plants die anyway. Once I **add** the **knowledge** of other gardeners **to my experience** with plants, I can **have wisdom** about growing them for myself. Source is experiencing itself, its knowledge of All, much the same way, *through* us. As we experience realities, embodied or in the etheric, all of our experiences are stored in the consciousness of Source (wisdom). Am I saying that although Source is all-knowing that it could be wiser? Maybe. Or maybe Source is playing a form of Solitaire because it got bored knowing everything. I am trying to describe an eternal concept with limited means and so I hope you will bear with me while I get the rest of my theory out because I cannot describe quantum fields of energy without it.

When each soul is done experiencing itself, it can choose to merge back with the whole consciousness energy of Source. When this happens, the soul's energy transmutes from its individual consciousness and becomes One once again (the great I Am). And then another part of Source may spring out. A new soul frequency. Source and its aspects do this on and on, into eternity. Expanding and contracting. I suspect that Source will never grow tired of learning about itself through soul journeying because I believe that is why it created everything in the first place. Once the elements of one part of creation (the hologram) have been explored entirely, Source aspects move on to explore and experience other parts of creation. Souls journey into varied realities of the hologram of All creation. Those aspects have many opportunities to explore separation/duality. Separation/duality means all conditions that provide the illusion that we are not all One.

Source wants to experience itself in every possible illusion that is not the whole; the dark, the light, and everything in between. The basic nature of everything is to expand and evolve. We share the spark of Source and so maybe it is more helpful to imagine why we like to create. Why do we want to have unknown experiences? What about the joy and pain associated with having a child and helping that child develop into adulthood? What will that child be like when they become an adult? What choices will they make? Will we be a part of their life, or will that child go off on their own and forget we exist? If you do not have children, then imagine something you have created and the stages of development that you observed while creating. What does your creation process bring to you, and do for you? Did it turn out the way you thought it would? Did you start with a concept and then your project evolved into something else entirely? What kind of feelings and new thoughts came along during the creative process? These are expansive experiences for your consciousness. What did you learn about yourself along the way?

I have been a practicing quantum healer for five years now. Much of what I will be sharing with you in this book are my models of reality that are derived from my experiences exploring quantum realities, working with clients in hypnosis practice, and working with other quantum healers. What is quantum healing? I use my knowledge (Quantum Healing Hypnosis Technique and Beyond Quantum Healing modalities), and experience using my skills and intuition, to assist clients to relax their thinking minds and access their subconscious minds (experience hypnotic mental states), which opens the clients to obtain wisdom from Source energies residing in other dimensions, using quantum energy fields.

Hypnosis helps to answer questions about their lives using the client's subconscious mind. Usually, this process also obtains healing for the client on some or many levels, like their emotional, physical, mental, and spiritual states. The purpose of quantum healing is to assist a person to understand what might be slowing their personal growth during their Earth journey, to discover that they are all-powerful light beings of Source having an Earthly experience, and to help that person to process the answers they received during the session. The healing happens when the client becomes an energetic match to a healthier version of themselves. We sometimes refer to that as embodying more of the oversoul's energy.

Practitioners of quantum healing do not cause the actual healing. We support and guide the clients toward it. Healing happens during the hypnosis session or shortly after, as the client agrees to energetically match to a healthy version of themselves and applies in their daily life the advice given to them by higher frequency beings. I connect the client with high-frequency beings that will assist in the healing process. These beings will help match the client to their energetically healthy version, but ultimately the client has free will to accept another version of themselves, or not. We all have other versions of ourselves that are perfectly healthy. It is completely up to the client whether they allow themselves to meet that energy. Free will means choice in every situation. Often the higher energy beings that come into session provide energy links to the client, and the client only needs to agree for the healing to take place. We are free to have any experience, and we are free to let go of any experience we no longer want.

It is possible that a client may not realize physical, mental, spiritual, and emotional healing at all during the session, or only partial healing. When that happens, whatever difficulty the client wants to overcome has not played out its role in their life long enough for the client to be ready to be fully healed. For example, sometimes souls choose to experience illness at some point during their incarnation to grow from the experience of 'being ill.' Illness is sometimes part of a life plan. I'll discuss life plans later in another chapter, but those illnesses that are planned before birth are usually not healed instantly in the quantum healing session unless the client has fully gained the wisdom of that experience that it was intended to provide. Figuring out that **we are** the ones who created our own undesirable experiences…is that when the evolution of consciousness and expansion happens. Introspection. When we look within ourselves to find answers about our reality, that is introspecting. Our reactions to experiences can be explored internally; why the experiences happened in the first place, how we might want to change some belief or way of being that has blocked our potential, and what we are doing well and wish to continue or build upon.

    A quantum healing session can kick-start the introspection process. It can also blow your consciousness so wide open that you drop a lifetime's worth of harmful patterns in an instant. This is the reason that I chose to become a quantum healing practitioner. After years of being a social worker, it became clear to me that my clients needed more than just a few therapy sessions to see and heal their issues in life. A few sessions are what most people can afford with therapy, or that insurance will cover. Usually, you cannot solve a lifetime's worth of issues within a few therapy sessions. Not to mention, who has all the time in the world to be in therapy? It can take years of traditional therapy for some people to start identifying the root causes of the symptoms that they suffer from. Lots of people will not have the time, money, or dedication to that lengthy process, although **I am** an advocate of therapy or counseling when someone chooses it. I spent approximately seven years in counseling myself, going to sessions once per week.

    My affinity for quantum healing is that if a person is ready to get to the root causes of their difficulties in life, wants to know what next steps to take in their career or romance, has difficulty relating to their kids, has gone to many doctors and cannot find any reason they experience illness; a quantum healing session can provide those insights in one session if the client is willing to know the reasons. It is never intended, nor advertised, that quantum healers provide medical or psychiatric services, and I will never say I have healed anyone. But, how nice is it to be able to help blow the lid off of uncertainty while the client gets their answers within their consciousness? It is very nice, in my experience.

Let's turn back to the basic image of the fundamental nature of reality. You can see in the image that I have drawn Source to be the big circle. What is a circle? It is a symbol of something with no beginning point and no endpoint. I would have used the infinity symbol, but it is difficult to type words inside of those. Just outside of Source, I drew smaller circles to represent groups containing multiple souls, in another dimensional reality than the whole, Source. Those represent the souls who chose to experience separation. These groups of souls have been called 'monads' by other humans describing this level of soul energy, and so I will use this term throughout.

The monadic entities contain our oversouls, who maintain their spark of Source from which they emanated. However, once these energies split from the whole, each aspect (oversoul) experiences focal points of consciousness that are slightly different from Source's All-knowing consciousness. They have somewhat reduced or contracted consciousnesses from the whole of Source consciousness. The monadic souls remember who they are and where they came from because they are very energetically close to Source. Their consciousness does not have to be very limited to focus there. You might think of the monadic entities as being the angelic realms. Monadic souls split themselves further, and project their consciousness (energy) to infinite other vibrational dimensional realities. Some are closer to the vibration of the monad, some are considerably lower in vibration.

One such focal point of reality for soul energy projection is Earth. As you may know, Earth's light energy density is much lower than within the angelic realms. Once a soul projects its energy to a body in a low vibrational reality, the consciousness of that soul's energy must also be reduced, and that aspect of the oversoul forgets where it came from. This process can be called exploring separation from Source/experiencing duality. It is done intentionally by the oversoul. Yes, this means all of us have oversouls that are angelic, if that is the moniker that best suits your understanding. The monadic souls can split themselves an infinite number of times and scatter those energies for experience in every dimension they wish to, or they keep all of their energy within the monad to experience.

Some people (see Dolores Cannon) name the highest vibrational version of our souls "angelic," "higher selves" or "oversouls." It does not matter the name you assign, the fact is, the highest vibrational version of you is very close to God/Source, and split your energy many times, into many realities. You can be anywhere and within all periods (where time is a thing). Your **focal point of reality** is where you, the aspect of your oversoul, choose to focus your consciousness in this now moment. The oversoul's focal point is aware of all the other focal points of itself (its aspects), just like God/Source knows us all. Within the monad, you know that you are me, and I know that I am you, and we know that everyone and everything is **of** Source.

Okay, maybe you have heard that before and it didn't make any sense. I had to think about that concept for years after my mentor Bob first talked about it. This is why I drew a picture model for this book, to simplify the concept. I also learned to think about all of the universes and souls springing from Source in this way through Dolores Cannon's course (QHHT Level One). Before taking the class, I was constantly trying to figure out which planet I'm originally from. I am aware that I have galactic incarnations. I wanted to know, before taking the class, which planets I was incarnated on before coming to Earth, and which one was first. You do not think that your soul is only experiencing as a human on Earth, do you? We all have galactic heritages! Our oversoul energy is spread out to our universe, probably on several planets, and within *other* universes as well. Before learning QHHT, I thought of incarnations as being linear (one happens before the other) and that the progression began when we sprang from Source. Studying Dolores' work and taking her course opened my consciousness to recognize what 'quantum' means.

It's all going on in one infinite moment (this moment), but the dimensions allow us to perceive lifetimes as linear progressions. Our experiences within those limited perceptions help the soul to expand in consciousness by having many varied viewpoints of what it is like to be *not* Source. The linear representation of my picture/model is naturally false because all of creation is happening at this moment point, so; we don't spring from Source into the monad, have other dimensional lifetimes one by one, and then descend to Earth, as the image suggests. The image is meant to model how we are All One, aspects of Source, split energy but never disconnected from each other. We do forget that when incarnated on Earth. And this is why Earth is known for being one of the harshest realities for souls to experience in. On Earth, we can explore so many low vibrational realities, all the while forgetting that we come from Source and will go back to Source, no matter what we do or how we are being. To experience the illusion of separation/duality **as** being real, we must forget. Doing that is challenging sometimes. Earth is truly the perfect playground to figure out what it is like to descend and then ascend again in consciousness.

Each monadic soul 'sends out' parts of itself into many dimensional realities, which means it experiences different dimensional densities. Dimensional densities vary by how fast the energy vibrates within them (the measurement of an energy wave and cycles of the wave, or their vibration, is called frequency). A 3D density reality vibrates much slower than a seventh-dimensional (7D) density reality. The wave is larger and cycles less often. However, the 7th dimension is not physically dense. When I refer to dimensional density, it is easy to assume that the higher we go, there would be more density, physically. The opposite occurs. The higher in a dimension we go, there is more density, but that is related to light energy concentration, not what we call molecular formation or physical density. The vibration of the energy is high in some dimensions and therefore molecules that we identify with would be spread out too far to form physical matter. Think of this in our Earthly scientific terms. Like boiling water. Water is a physical form of the molecules hydrogen and oxygen. When you start to boil water you add energy, the molecules move faster, have more space in between each, and the water eventually shifts form into vapor. Although vapor still contains the water molecules, you cannot see them physically unless the molecules start to move slower again and are about to convert to a condensed state, like clouds and rain. The molecules hydrogen and oxygen are still in the vapor, but the vapor contains more energy than solid water, so you cannot perceive it as a physical form. Water vapor does bend light energy and so we can see the effects of the vapor, but we cannot see the molecules forming a physical object.

It is reported in quantum healing sessions, and from other sources, that 7D is so energy dense that a soul cannot take physical form there. The soul energy does experience consciously, as light forms without a body, in higher dimensions like 7D. That does not mean that we cannot hold a 7D consciousness for a while when we are experiencing Earth life. We can raise our frequencies from where we began at birth by holding higher dimensional consciousness thoughts, speaking words that contain higher consciousness, and doing deeds that emanate from higher consciousness. If we do these things while in physical form it raises our vibration, and over time, our frequencies. If we start doing it constantly over time, I suspect our focal point of reality (conscious awareness) would vibrate right out of this physical dimensional reality and into a higher one.

I have read theories that this is what happened to some ancient civilizations that seem to have disappeared without physical cause, like an Earthquake or meteor strike. For example, the Mayans and Aztecs. Geological evidence shows that for years they were on Earth, and then suddenly they were not, and scientists do not know why. Scientists cannot pinpoint the migration of these civilizations. So, where did they go? Did they reach a consciousness that is so high that they vibrated out of our reality? Maybe they are still energetically focused here but they transformed to another state of being, like liquid water to vapor.

There are ranges of vibrations within each dimension. The highest vibration in the 3rd dimension is equal to the lowest vibration in the 4th. Think of a guitar string. The thicker strings vibrate a lower vibration of sound because they move slower when you pluck them due to their heavier physical density. The thinner strings are less dense, so their vibration is faster and produces a higher pitch sound when you pluck them. A 3D reality vibrates low enough to condense energy into what we call matter, and so we have solid Earth and our physical bodies, and we vibrate differently than our soul energy does in a higher dimensional reality. Varied experience, varied consciousness. Our higher selves know more than we do because their consciousness is not clouded or forgetful due to slower energy patterns.

Once the energy of our soul vibrates low enough (i.e. 3D), the consciousness of our energy will not remember where it came from. This phenomenon has been called 'passing through the veil of forgetting,' but it is just a state of being that we choose to explore. We agreed before the incarnation to forget our origin when we chose to focus our consciousness on life on Earth. Our highest self (the oversoul) that has not yet returned to Source remains in the monad and watches over us while we do this. Your memories of who you truly are remain in this highest dimensional reality, and within other higher dimensional realities where more of your oversoul's energy is concentrated. We have many 'higher selves,' parts of our soul that vibrate at a higher frequency than we do. But, there is only one highest self (the oversoul) in the monad. Our higher selves are not better than us, rather, their consciousness is more expansive and so they hold more of our oversoul's memories/ wisdom.

People believe that angels do not incarnate. Let's address that. Imagine that within the monad, where your highest self resides, there are souls that decided to stay within the monad. These do not wish to journey any further away from Source. These beings are the angels we speak of. They help guide the rest of us as we go through our lifetimes away from the monad. We could see them as angels and more powerful than our souls, but they have the same level of light energy as our oversouls do. We have the same powers as the angels and we do not remember that this is true on Earth. All of our power is contained within our inner self, the heart space, but we have forgotten. The souls that stay in the monad are our cohorts and our friends, but they are not better than we are. We forget about this when we incarnate in lower dimensional vibration because it serves our purpose to experience separation/duality from Source. And when social conditioning gets a hold of our minds, we start to believe we are less than the angels. For that matter, we also have the same powers as Source, because we are Source. That spark within never leaves. The truth and power of who we are does not change because of our limited consciousness in this focal point of reality. It is more difficult for us to manifest instantly the way Source does because the energy here on Earth does not move as fast as it does in higher dimensional realities, but the method of manifestation is the same. Being an energetic match to any thought causes that thought to be evidenced in reality.

Lower dimensional realities allow for energy to condense into what we know of as matter. Our bodies are matter animated by the soul energy, its consciousness. Consciousness is energy (this is why the energy of a spirit can be detected with scientific equipment). Therefore, when our energy condenses into lower dimensions and takes on a body, our consciousness condenses also. Human consciousness is aware, in this condensed version, of what is right in front of it which can be perceived through the five senses, rather than the hologram of Creation in its entirety. Aspects of Source that choose to focus in higher dimensional realities, like 6D - 12D, they experience as energy beings without bodies and with higher concentrations of the oversoul's consciousness. 'Incarnation' does not always mean a soul has created a physical body when we use the word in spiritual terms. I am aware that the word "incarnation" (from the Latin caro, "flesh"), suggests having a physical body. There is such a thing as a light body, which I will discuss in another chapter.

In 6D realities, some soul energies take form, but they are usually what is referred to by us as elementals (they do not have solid bodies as we do, or they can shift form to take on different shapes and projections of their energy). Some 6D energies gather in groups to experience more as a collective consciousness while maintaining their individual identities. Some soul aspects have etheric incarnations on planets, their consciousnesses ascend to higher frequencies, and then their focal point of reality transforms into an even higher dimensional reality. At that point, they may choose to form an energy collective with others who have reached higher frequencies also. In etheric collectives, the higher soul frequency of each being in the collective remains the same, however, each are still individual consciousnesses of their oversouls. But, they choose to experience their reality and make decisions as a more unified consciousness rather than as individuals. And so, yes, there are souls that never physically incarnate and we can consider them to be like the angels, ETs, fairies, gnomes, elementals, etc. Some souls physically incarnate as humans and then ascend into a collective (ascended masters, for example). And, some energies exist in-between these examples that I have yet to know or define. Returning to the water example, the molecules that makeup water appear or manifest differently depending on the frequency of vibration of the molecules. The water does not change its composition, only the vibration of the water changes, which determines the experience of the hydrogen and oxygen. The oversoul determines in what way it wishes to manifest for each aspect, and Source manifestations are limitless.

    In the case of Earth's ascended master Jesus (Jeshua), I have had some very interesting and enlightening 'conversations' with Jesus and Mary Magdalene during several quantum healing sessions. One of the sessions I will share about is when they immediately invited me and my hypnosis partner to come and sit with them by their fire. We had many questions to ask them before that moment, but most of the questions fell away from our thoughts as we enjoyed being in the energy field of Jesus and Mary. Their energy was unified, not separate. It felt like totally balanced energy, the yin and yang of divine masculine and divine feminine energies. They were transmitting peace and love to us. We did manage to ask about their mission on Earth, and if our missions are to continue their mission of raising humanity's consciousness. Jesus responded that all of humanity is continuing their mission. He said there is no 'second coming' of his soul energy to the Earth in human form, as it is written in many religious texts. The 'second coming,' according to what Jesus said to us, is about each one of us realizing the Christ Consciousness within us (defined as seeing ourselves and everything as expressions of the Creator, allowing more love and compassion to flow through us, accepting all as it is without judgment, releasing judgment of self and others as we realize who we are; flowing energy of the One). I wrote much of my first book based on those concepts.

Jesus and Mary made it clear to us that they are ever-present to assist humanity with this process, but no one is going to come to Earth and transform our consciousness for us. That job is for each individual to do. Near the end of this visit with Jesus and Mary, Mary invited us to throw all of our fears into their fire. I have to say, as I did this, tears started rolling out of my eyes, and from the eyes of my hypnosis partner as well. We had goosebumps the whole time and were at a loss for words when the session was complete. Mary invited us to sit with them at any time, by the fire, just to be present with their energy or to ask questions if we wish to. That was not an invite for only me and my hypnosis partner. It is for everyone. They made it clear that anyone is welcome to engage their energy, at any time. I will assume that the reason my friend and I received Jesus and Mary during the exploration of our questions with hypnosis is that we each had a lifetime experience with Jesus when he was on Earth. Mary joined us in the session because her energy is melded with Jesus' energy within the dimension we met them in the session. They are, in that dimension, a collective energy. As to the experiences my partner and I had with Jesus on Earth, an aspect of my soul made eye contact with Jesus when he was carrying the cross, and my friend was a Roman soldier who came in contact with Jesus when he was talking with people at a public gathering.

Both of us were utterly awakened by our experiences meeting Jesus in that lifetime, and both of us hold the energy of that experience strongly in our heart centers today. I am telling you about these experiences to say something that I think is important about soul recognition. There are more 'ascended masters' than anyone can name. All of us **are** ascended masters in other dimensions. When we choose the focal point of reality Earth, the connections that we share with other souls do not go away no matter how many times we incarnate here, which 'time' period we focus within, or how differently our personality expresses in other lifetimes.

There is recognition of other soul energy, even if that soul's energy is not in form during your current focal point. If you are highly interested in the energy of someone you never formally met in this life, who 'passed away,' but you feel a connection with that soul; that is soul recognition. Is there an angel you are particularly called to communicate with? Soul recognition. What about the energies you feel but do not have a name for? Soul recognition. It means you have experience with them, in another dimensional reality, and their energy is still connected to yours with such concentration that you feel it. And, maybe they have agreed to be your guide in this incarnation. Or, you feel them specifically at a point in your life where they can help you. You don't have to know the name of the energy you are feeling. I will explain that statement in the upcoming chapter, *What's In A Name?*.

Ascended masters tend to form collective consciousnesses that serve physical realities, especially ones they have incarnated within. They know that every being belongs to The One, and yet they seem to focus more closely on souls carrying similar consciousnesses to themselves because of shared experiences. It makes sense to me in this way; how is a being from another universe going to know to call upon Jesus for help? This being may be accessing the oversoul of Jesus because the being recognizes that energy, but it will not call on the name of 'Jesus'. After all, this name is an Earthly experience of his soul energy. The oversoul of Jesus will assist that being within the reality of experiences that they share when called upon by the name that the being has assigned in their reality. Realities can differ vastly from the Earth experience. Who we know to be the 'ascended masters' have their energy scattered into every dimension, like our energy is, from their oversouls. Every ascended master is available to anyone at any time. Think of one, and their energy/consciousness is with you. Ask for guidance, and you allow them permission to guide you. They do this to help the rest of us progress in our consciousness expansion. They love us. Why would they not help us along? And here is some more quantum understanding for you. Do you feel a kinship with ascended masters of Earth, galactic beings, and angelic beings? Do you think that maybe all of these beings, with whom you have experience in other dimensions, are working together to help you ascend?

We are gifted with a set of souls that guide us through each life, yes, AND we are guided by other souls that have the wisdom about the knowledge and experience we are seeking to have. Their energy draws to us like a magnet when we are ready to receive their teachings. It is human nature to reach out for higher wisdom. To know ourselves better. Our oversoul sends us this inspiration, to know ourselves better, and other souls are available to us when we ask their assistance in that knowing. The quantum energy fields are multi-dimensional. A soul can project its energy to as many realities as it chooses, to as many other souls as it chooses, and do that all at the same eternal moment point. If I am communicating with Jesus and so are 10,000 other people on Earth, and 40,000 are also talking to Jesus's energy from another planet, do you suppose Jesus can only communicate with one person at a time? No, his energy can commune with us all, in any one moment.

Everyone has access to ALL of creation, at any moment, because we are All One in the highest frequency of vibration that is God/Source. Anything you can think of; scientific information, physical and emotional healing, messages to and from your deceased loved ones including your pets, information about your soul plan/life plan, where you left your car keys...anything you can imagine is accessible by you through quantum energy fields. We access quantum fields all the time. Most of us do not remember that this is what's happening. This book is going to help you to remember and provide suggestions on how to access quantum fields of energy consciously.

We are always experiencing the eternal **now** moment. Past moments and future moments are illusions of the Earth's experience (and similar realities within our universe) because there is no such thing as time. But, we need the *illusion* of time to 'play out' the experiences of being separate from Source. This means you access the energy of what appears to be in your past or your future. Or anyone's past and future. More on this topic in a bit, but suffice it to say, we are all parts of Source, all of Creation is within us as well as around us, and there is only a single moment point, the eternal now moment. That is the definition of quantum.

Our focal point of reality, or conscious awareness, shifts from one lifetime to another. This is intentional. Soul aspects do this shifting of focal points in lower-density realities to experience their existence as being real. Until that point of ascension where the soul remembers and can maintain multiple reality consciousness. This is all that we are, consciousness!

Energy that is aware of itself.

Yes, this Earth energy does manifest physical realities. Parts of creation I refer to as the hologram are illuminated using conscious or subconscious thought. From this moment point, we can access the energy of any life we are simultaneously experiencing because they are versions of our oversoul's consciousness. Imagine you are a sliver of soul pie. At this moment point, you can communicate with all the other slivers of your soul's pie. You can also access a sliver of any other soul's pie, in any of their lifetimes, with agreement from that soul.

Quantum fields are energy fields that are experienced by us in different ways depending on the density of the energy field. Dimensions hold set amounts of density, and therefore, we say there are higher and lower dimensions, and that means dimensions contain varied levels of light energy. Dimensions may be thought of as a bunch of matrix realities that Source created for us, to explore all the ways that we can be 'other than' Source.

I have been exploring quantum fields, using quantum healing hypnosis techniques during my soul's focal point of reality, Sue Beckley, for some time now. I feel sometimes that I have only touched the surface of a pool of information that is so vast, it would appear that I will need infinite lifetimes to begin to comprehend it. And also, I have discovered that there is no wisdom that I cannot access by asking higher dimensional beings my questions, including my higher selves and my oversoul. At this level of my development, I receive the wisdom that my consciousness can receive and interpret, **not** information that my human brain cannot process. This is by soul design as well. We have access to all information of Creation, but we seek the information that is useful to our current focal point of reality. We communicate to higher light beings what information is useful at any given stage of life by the questions we are asking. And sometimes, while we are asking higher dimensional beings about one thing, they supply us with additional information that blows our socks off, but it is useful for our expansion of consciousness. They know what we can handle. We can then piece together the additional information with what we were originally asking about.

This is very helpful because it expands the concept for us. It adds higher wisdom to it. The being giving additional information knows we are ready to receive and digest it. Often it causes us to ask more expanded questions because we contemplate new information until it is integrated into our minds. Quantum exploration involves posing questions to higher dimensional beings, receiving information, asking more questions, pondering and assimilating the information received until it is usable in this life (internalized/integrated), then continuing to ask more questions as consciousness continues to expand. When we know more about the expansion process, then we can utilize the quantum fields purposefully. We create better realities by lighting up more portions of the hologram of all Creation with our thoughts and feelings. Every reality that we know, and the ones we don't remember, are within this hologram of God/Source Creation.

The reason we do not remember being The One is that we wanted to experience the vast opportunities to be 'other than' Source. Every reality that is not pure, unconditional love, is a reality that is in some way a distortion of Source consciousness. God/Source **can only be** All-knowing, unconditional love. It is the highest light frequency there is.

When we are being that, we are God/Source. When we are being 'other than' unconditional love, when we are in a state of not knowing everything, we are exploring what it is like to be 'not Source.' We are talking about being 'not Source,' and how we are moving back towards remembering that we are, again. Using quantum energy fields, we can and will remember more rapidly.

Because everything is going on in one moment point, all information is accessible. The determining factor of the information YOU will access through quantum exploration is what your soul inspires you to focus on. Each one of us will have **our** focal points of reality that our souls are experiencing with. And some realities are shared focal points of reality. Shared focal points of reality are called 'collective consciousness constructs,' or shared experiences of reality. An example of a collective consciousness reality that most Earth beings have is, 'grass can be green, and smells a certain way when you cut it.' Another example of a collective consciousness reality on Earth is that humans need to breath air to live. You may say to me, "Of course, we need to breath air, everyone knows that!" What if I told you that there are human-like beings on other planets within an alternate dimension that do not need to breath air to live, and they exist in a reality that is very similar to Earth? This is a collective of soul aspects, or conscious beings, experiencing a different reality than we do, **and** it is similar to our own. The conscious agreement of a collective forms any reality for the group. Some realities are created by collective consciousnesses of souls that decided not to experience life in a body. They are energy, feeling, thought, and awareness without physical embodiment. This does not make them any less 'real' than we are. Non-embodied souls have incarnations of limited consciousness as we do, but they experience them another way. These are experiences of the mind, and sometimes emotions. Yes, some collectives are mind-driven and devoid of emotions. Some of them have physical bodies on planets and others are etheric.

I suggest that etheric experience is what we are talking about when we discuss Heaven, Nirvana, and any other reality we can imagine that exists after our soul essence leaves our human body. Consciousness does not end when we leave our body, we merely transform our energy into another state of being. As is stated in religious texts, "God's house has many rooms." Whatever reality you choose to experience after your consciousness leaves your body, it is possible you will find yourself within a shared reality, and that is shifting from one collective consciousness reality (Earth) to another (i.e. Heaven). You can think of one such reality where you meet up and interact again with loved ones who have also left their Earthly bodies. People use many names for those collective consciousness realities such as; Heaven, Valhalla, Swarga, Elysium, Zion, Shamayim; the list goes on and on. All of these realities exist. The focal point of reality where your consciousness will be concentrated after your physical death will be decided by the beliefs you hold at the time you leave your body.

If you believe you need to be punished for something, your consciousness will focus on a reality where punishment is provided in whatever way is consistent with your beliefs (i.e. a hellscape). Once you drop the need to be punished in the hellscape, you will find your consciousness moving elsewhere. A guide may appear to you at this point to bring you to another focal point of consciousness, or you will go there immediately. I suggest skipping any hellscapes because as I stated before, God/Source passes no judgment on you.

You pass judgment on you, and it is unnecessary.

Some people believe a relative will greet them at their time of physical death. Guess what? When someone believes a relative will meet them, that is what happens. I first started an investigation of a phenomenon called the near-death experience (NDE) with Raymond A. Moody Jr.'s book; *Life After Life*. Dr. Moody is, among many other things, a psychiatrist and physician. He studied one hundred people who experienced "clinical death" and were revived. They told him in their own words what lies beyond physical death, and Dr. Moody wrote a book about it. He subsequently wrote many more books about NDEs, consciousness, and other esoteric concepts. Since reading *Life After Life*, around the year 1990, I have also read more books written about NDEs by other authors. If you would like to hear more personal stories about NDEs, may I suggest watching some episodes of *Next Level Soul* podcast on YouTube (Alex Ferrari; owner, interviewer).

Do you want to know the one thing I have found all NDEs have in common? **No two are the same.** Some share similar elements, and I would say that is because many humans share similar beliefs about the afterlife. There is just too much information and too many people reporting their experiences with NDEs for me to think the experience is not real. I've had a fair share of clients in sessions that describe what it is like to leave their bodies at the time of physical death after an incarnation; what they experience first, and where they go afterward; which supports my contention that what we experience is unique to us, based on what we want to experience and on our beliefs at the time of physical death.

There is no automatic place you will go because you did something during your lifetime here on Earth. You will determine where you focus your consciousness next. I hope this conversation brings you peace and allows you to drop any fears you may have about what will happen when you 'die.' I also hope that whatever experiences you have in your life, you will let go of the belief in punishment.

Your soul knows what it intends for this incarnation because it made the plans. It knows what questions it needs to inspire within you to gain the wisdom you want from this experience, this life. It planned the major events/meetings/synchronicities of this incarnation and works with you to have experiences that will expand its overall consciousness (who am I?). Why does a soul want to expand its consciousness? How does one do that? By having experiences that are 'other than' what it already knows. The more experience a soul gains by being 'other than' Source, the more wisdom is gained for the soul, about the soul's essential nature, and that expands its definition of self. How many ways can you define yourself? Are you the job you do? Are you the role you play within your family? Or, are you much more than those parts of you? How expansively can you think about yourself? All of this soul expansion is shared with Source because souls are never disconnected from the whole. Source benefits from your expansion, as do all other souls. It's comparable to a long game of 'who am I?' where the questions are endless. Until the soul goes home. Once home (rejoined with Source), we all know exactly who and what we are, everything! We are the omnipresent wave form, energy, and consciousness of God.

One individual lifetime may be experienced over and over again until the soul is done exploring the variations to its liking. The changes in decisions made in each experience of the same lifetime broaden your whole experience of you. So, you may have lived this life **as you** several, if not many times. You can think of it as all of the timeline versions of you, the quantum nature of yourself, and I will talk about timelines in-depth. In this version of you, you make some choices that are different from what you did in the other versions. Not only do you know certain things are going to happen, but you may also feel strongly that you don't want to do something and call it a "gut feeling." What is likely happening in those instances is that you already did that thing while being another version of yourself and you remember, subconsciously, that you don't want to do it again. In my opinion, that is what déjà vu is.

To seek knowledge about my personal experiences (the 'why' of life) and what my purpose is within this life, I studied quantum healing techniques, explored quantum fields of energy, and continue to do so today. This began as a personal journey of self-discovery for me, transformed into a modality of healing that I could use for myself and others, and continues today to excite my senses. The concepts I present are limited models and understandings of what the quantum is, at this focal point of my consciousness reality. As Tim Tactical Advisor in the series Cosmic Disclosure (www.Gaia.com) states, "all models are incorrect, but some are useful." I interpret Tim's word "incorrect" to mean incomplete. What I am presenting to you are my models for understanding creation, how energy works, how I use it to create my reality, and how you can begin to consciously create your reality using quantum energy fields. Moving forward, the models and definitions I will provide are incomplete. They are interpretations of what I have remembered thus far. Memories of my truths. They are touched surfaces of pools of knowledge that are infinite (the hologram). However, these models have changed my life so drastically and for the better, that I wish to share them with you. I hope to spark further questions, interpretations, discussions, improvements, and more explorations of this thing we call reality. I mostly hope that the information contained here helps you to improve your reality; to open up to quantum energies which will expand your consciousness, and result in you recognizing your power to create reality.

Consciousness is a creative force. It is; thought, feeling, memory, and instinct. It processes, observes, and makes choices.

Consciousness is elastic.

It expands, then contracts, and expands again. Some consciousness differs from the biological consciousness we have, like artificial intelligence (AI). Those are created by Source beings, and so they are of Source as well. That was not a typo. If we are Source beings, then everything we create contains the spark of Source within it. Artificial intelligence is part of the energy flow from Source to us. We create something with that energy, and the energy of this creation seems to have some kind of consciousness. Does AI have consciousness, or is its consciousness only part of the ones that created it? I don't know. Maybe it has all the qualities I listed above except feelings? We can't know for sure that at some level an AI won't develop the ability to feel.

See what I mean about questions leading to more questions? We have the human brain which consists of two hemispheres. The left side of the brain is the survival mechanism, the animal part that contains all of our learning from birth, and all of the information from our ancestors which is encoded into our DNA for survival. Some refer to this part of our brain as the 'egoic self.' Some try to excommunicate their 'ego' as if it is something that is causing them to do bad things. Souls cannot embody on a world as physically dense as 3D Earth without survival minds or they would perish very quickly. If we learn to be the masters of our survival instincts (i.e. knowing when we are in real danger or not), then we can experience a state of balance with our ego minds, which is the ideal. No need to separate from our ego mind. No need to banish it. Mutual coexistence.

Next, we look at the right brain. This is our creative mind; where all the great ideas, art, and music come from. It is where we visualize our 'future' and where we create our 'future' realities through those visualizations. What I am saying is that the right brain is the center of our creative processes as human beings. We receive inspiration in this part of the brain and then we use it to 'map out' how we wish to create with that inspiration. Our right brain is also connected to the etheric mind (the soul's whole consciousness, each other, and Source), where we can connect with other souls, and all of Creation through quantum energy fields.

In our 3D world and even into the fourth dimension, humans have routinely held one general focal point of reality, which is the information about Earth and each other that we obtain from the five senses in our immediate environments. Most of what we think to be true is agreed upon by the bulk of humanity, and therefore it is a collective consciousness belief system. Humans do not usually have awareness of themselves in the other realties (incarnations) where their energy is also presently experiencing. Why? The phenomenon of holding one reality at a time has been humanity's definition of sanity.

In lower-dimensional realities like ours, it is difficult for a human brain to hold multiple realities at the same moment. It can be confusing and disorienting. People who have held multiple realities simultaneously in human history have been labeled crazy, demonic, prophets, psychics, schizophrenics, and so on. Many people have been persecuted for their abilities to bi-locate or tri-locate (hold multiple realities in the same moment point). We have seen cartoons where a person is trying to make a decision and there is an angel on one shoulder advising one action, and a devil on the other shoulder advising the opposite action. We find this metaphor funny but the truth is that we do subconsciously bi-locate and tri-locate when we need to make choices. It seems like the conversation is going on only in the mind, and it is, but sometimes people have these conversations with other energies while vocalizing. So it seems like they are talking to themselves.

Other versions of you, and other souls in spirit are weighing in on your decision. They do this energetically, telepathically, and so you experience that as your thoughts, or possibly visions of other people. Although, sometimes those thoughts do not sound like your words or your voice. Sometimes they sound like something you would not ordinarily consider. Conversations like this are multidimensional energies that YOU channeled, requested, and gave permission, to assist with your decision. If you are angry or fearful when you ask for help making a decision, the devilish energy will help you plan your revenge or to run away from something. The angelic energy is always there to balance. To give you an option that is in accord with your highest good. The choice is always yours though. Like talking to a good friend, helpful advice can be accepted while not helpful advice can be ignored.

You are the one with the power and the responsibility for whatever choice is made. I find it comforting to know there are helpful guiding energies around me at all times, especially when I am confused about what to do next if anything.

The Earth collective has agreed, for much of Earth's history timeline, to hold one focal point of reality while incarnated to the 3D Earth world. Unless an individual soul's intention is to experience bi-location/tri-location. There is usually a specific reason for that in that soul's life plan. The reasons are varied and unique. They depend on what the soul wishes to experience in its lifetime. Sometimes a soul comes to Earth and brings with it their conscious ability to maintain multidimensional realities for the sake of the rest of humanity. To elevate the consciousness of others, for example, Jesus. But bi-location and tri-location, or multidimensional awareness is rare among humanity in the recent past of Earth's 3D timeline. Atlanteans and Lemurians could do it easily, but let's stick to the recent past of Earth's timeline (the last 3,000 years).

In this version of Earth, and during this part of our timeline, the bulk of humanity is now choosing to progress through the fourth to the fifth dimensional realities of consciousness. Humans are becoming more aware of their multidimensionality and able to bi-locate (hold two realities consciously). It is becoming more acceptable in mainstream communities. We all can do it, but most of us do not remember doing it. People are discovering a sudden ability to bi-locate within themselves, and it scares them. I suspect that one of the reasons that other people are embracing their abilities to bi-locate is to assist the fearful ones to accept that it is possible. It is easier to do that when others in society no longer label you "crazy" and come after you to burn you at a stake. Have you noticed the abundance of people on social media and writing books who speak of their channelings, their psychic conversations, and their recognition of alternate realities that they know they have experienced? If you haven't noticed, then I will say that I have noticed an explosion in the number of people reporting their bi-location experiences since 2020. Bi-location, again, is becoming aware of another reality, that is connected to you and your oversoul but is perceived as a different reality or another time. This explosion of people coming forward and sharing their experiences is very positive evidence, in my opinion, that humanity is shifting via 4D consciousness and moving toward 5D focal points.

We each can hold multiple focal points of reality (bi-location, tri-location, etc.) if we are ready to open up to the experience. Some people achieve bi-location through meditation, others through hypnosis, some have it happen spontaneously, and yet others have been using their ability to access multiple reality energies from the time of their earliest awareness. If I have a hypnosis session and I become aware of another lifetime in which my soul energy has lived, and I do not reject this information, I become aware of two "focal points" of my soul's reality (bi-locate during hypnosis). One focal point is my current Earth persona (Sue), and the other is the persona that experiences in the other lifetime. **I am** the other, the other **is me**, and both of us are experiencing independent focal points of reality. Until we become aware of one another. When we allow our present consciousness to access other focal points, we then know that our soul pie is experiencing many dimensions, and we open up to our multidimensionality and quantum realities. Because our energy is present in every dimension, within realities that contain the illusion of time or not, we can realize our memories of being anything. For example, I remembered being a wolf that died in a forest fire. Why did that knowledge help me? I (as Sue) am sometimes afraid of enclosed spaces. Especially if the air quality is limited. The experience of the wolf-me was; being surrounded by the fire (enclosed) and I asphyxiated from the tainted air. Now, the memory of wolf-me during hypnosis makes more sense, does it not? It helps me to know why I sometimes feel fearful in enclosed spaces where the air quality is poor and to transmute that fear when I assure myself that I am not in real danger.

The reason individual aspects of a soul appear differently from one another is because of all the possibilities of how a soul's energy may express itself. There are so many permutations of expression of a soul's energy that it seems we are not of the same soul, in the perspective of 3D. As we explore and expand to 4D and 5D consciousness, our soul's aspects do not seem that different anymore, and we recognize one another when touching subconscious awareness. The soul sees and hears, recognizes, other forms of its overall frequency (soul pie). We can communicate with ourselves and share energies (i.e. share strengths, resolve traumas). This allows both aspects to embody more of the whole of the soul's energy, becoming your higher self, embodied.

The quantum information (energy) I have experienced thus far is an overwhelming body of information to wrap my human mind around, **and**; answers to specific questions that I have been asking are simultaneously easy to attain once I began to relax my definitions of reality. That is the difference between using the two hemispheres of the human physical mind (using left-brained logic or employing the intuitive/etheric/light body right-brained intuiting). When the physical left brain tries to handle complex information, it seems to get overwhelmed. It doubts. It is not as expansive in knowledge as the subconscious mind. It wants to protect us from the repercussions of entertaining thoughts of anything that does not make sense, or that our DNA tells us might be dangerous (i.e. witch hunts/persecution/labeled crazy). When we experience new information and we take it in using our intuitive/subconscious mind (right brain), it is not difficult at all because the right brain does not judge what it receives, it allows all information to come in. Then the left brain judges the information for the reasons stated, unless it has been given permission to observe and assured that the person it serves is safe to allow the information to come in.

Information flows into the right brain according to what we are asking, then we get to decide what feels helpful to us at that moment while allowing the rest to sit in our psyche as seed information. The 'seeds' that remain may become connectors to future experiences where we then have an 'ah-ha' moment. This process does not require outside validation. Although, one must be intentional about the vibrational energy that they are tapping into using quantum fields because it is possible to channel energy presences that do not have your best interest in mind. Those beings will lie to you and play on your fears. It is easy to avoid that experience by setting your **intention** to communicate with only **high-vibrational beings** that have your most beneficial outcomes in mind.

Say it like a prayer before you begin to tap into quantum fields because that sets your boundaries for the forthcoming communication and energy exchange. If you do this before each session exploring quantum energies, then you will not have any concerns about whom you are connecting to. The beings best able to deal with your questions will come to assist you. We have free will here on Earth. Other souls and collectives are not allowed to intercede on your behalf unless you invite them to. This means for good or bad. So we make a practice to always call in the energies of the **highest intention and light**, and trust that this is protection enough against the confused soul energy that will come to you if you are in fear. We must also choose how deeply we will go as we consider dimensions, vibrations, frequencies, alternate realities, life plans, timelines, etheric communications with extra-terrestrials, communications with angels, departed loved ones, and of course; communication with God/Source directly. Exploring quantum energy fields allows us to do all of that, as we are ready and willing to use quantum exploration principles intentionally.

In conclusion, monadic souls (including our oversouls) are of Source and have the awareness of being Source. To explore separation/duality, our oversouls (highest-selves) split their energy more times and sent them out into universes that Source created for the experience of knowing itself in all ways. These universes sometimes contain stars, suns, moons, and planetary systems which are varied in dimensional densities, (3D – 12D for our universe). Higher dimensional density realities are non-physical lifetimes, due to the high vibration of the energy there. In these realities, the soul experiences incarnation without a body, as consciousness. All that ever is or ever was, is accessible to us now energetically, through quantum energy fields. We can access information, healing energy, and guidance as we tap into these fields with our energy. We access these energy fields subconsciously, and regularly. As humanity is ready to transform, to shift to higher vibrational realities, we are doing this more consciously. In every moment, the monadic entity supports all aspects while they explore different realities in different densities. There is no disconnect.

We carry our oversoul's frequency, our aspect frequency, and the spark of Source in our heart center, or chakra, that never leaves us. We connect with them and with other souls. The aspect of the soul energy on Earth is not usually aware of the other aspects of itself because the vibrations of Earth are too low to see and communicate with the other parts of the soul that have different frequency expressions (variations of the oversoul's tone). The human on Earth cannot imagine the other parts of itself, in other locations, until it expands its energy reach, out into all of Creation, illuminating more of the hologram. Once the human continues to hold high vibrational energies over time, this increases the frequency of that human, which expands the consciousness of the human. Quantum means that we are all One, Source, and we are also individual Source aspects having individual reality experiences, at the same moment point; the eternal "now" moment. We are multidimensional beings experiencing multiple realities that are all happening in the same moment, and we can explore these through quantum energy fields.

    Some of what I introduced to you in terminology, in particular the use of the scientific term to describe energy disbursement, 'hologram' (of Creation), comes from a report a USA Army LTC Wayne McDonnell to his commanding officer in US Army Operational Group, in June of 1983. If you skipped the introduction to this book, go check it out if you are curious. The report was generated by LTC McDonnell after investigating/experiencing a method of altering and amplifying human consciousness through The Gateway Experience. The Gateway Experience evolved from the Gateway Voyage program, which was developed back in the 1970s by Robert Monroe, and is still offered at The Monroe Institute today (https://www.monroeinstitute.org).

    Robert Allan Monroe was a radio broadcasting executive who became known for his research into altered consciousness and for founding The Monroe Institute. His 1971 book, *Journeys Out of the Body*, is credited with popularizing the term "out-of-body experience". Assisted by specialists in psychology, medicine, biochemistry, psychiatry, electrical engineering, physics, and education, Monroe developed Hemi-Sync; a patented audio technology that facilitates enhanced consciousness and is used by; nuclear physicists, doctors, lawyers, computer scientists and IT professionals, realtors, homemakers, inventors, psychologists, psychiatrists, farmers, truck drivers, politicians, lawmakers, artists, musicians, poets, authors, military officers, students, teachers, and religious leaders from all faiths, according to The Monroe Institute website. I was gifted the report link by a fellow quantum healer and friend of mine when I was in the process of writing this book.

    There are no accidents.

    That's something you will know to be my mantra as you continue reading. When information comes in that supports something I am thinking about, or it expands my understanding of some experience I am having, I say that is a synchronicity. Receiving the report of LTC

McDonnell is synchronicity for me. I feel supported by theories and understandings of scientifically based quantum realities, which I speak of regularly. The report was declassified by the CIA on September 10, 2003, and you can find the whole report by searching "Analysis and Assessment of Gateway Process." Again, I must stress that I have used this report as confirmation of what I already know, and as supplementary information. The scientific quantum theory expressed in the report is outside of my field of experience. My terminology tends to be varied from the terms used to describe consciousness in The Gateway Process. However, considering that LTC McDonnell has experienced the process and reports Gateway to use common elements with hypnosis, biofeedback, and meditation, it got my attention.

What I discovered while reading the report is that military research into altered states of consciousness has been going on for a long time, quietly. I also discovered that quantum physicists, physics experts, mathematicians, and other paragons in the scientific community have been exploring and describing consciousness for a long time as well. This report is a thrilling piece of evidence, in my opinion, that science and spirituality are not mutually exclusive. We may use terms to describe a reality that seems separate, however, while reading the report, I recognized what I think to be The One/Creator/God/Source within a description provided in their scientific term, "The Absolute." LTC McDonnell does a very good job linking what scientists know to what spiritualists have been describing for centuries.

One other synchronicity that happened when I started writing this book is that I came upon the teachings of RA, The Law of One (books by the same title). I found a website where the dictated sessions with the consciousness collective identifying itself as RA, also the consciousness of the ancient Egyptian RA, were provided. After reading some of the conversations with RA that took place in the 1970s, I knew I was receiving more support for what I am presenting to you here. I like confirmation. Especially from eternal consciousness beings that have 'skin in the game' when it comes to humanity's welfare. RA's dialogue seems to indicate strongly that it wants to help humanity succeed in our journey to higher consciousness from 3D. I will reference the RA material from time to time.

3

The Four Light Bodies

Consciousness converts energy into what we call 'form' when it incarnates into lower dimensional energy reality. The body is a projection of our consciousness, as is everything in every reality we choose to illuminate in the hologram for experience. Our soul focuses part of its consciousness within our physical body when we are born, and forms the body while we are in the womb, however, it is not the full consciousness of the soul. Only a little sliver of the oversoul pie. When this occurs, an energetic communication system within our physical body is set up known as the four light bodies. Through the four light bodies, communication between the oversoul's total consciousness is linked with the condensed consciousness of the new human being (its aspect/soul slice).

Our oversoul's communication system forms into the four light bodies within and around our physical form as it completes the incarnation. You can think of the communication system as being like a radio receiver/transmitter. Energy/light has wave patterns, and the light bodies pick up these waves and also sends them back to the oversoul. While the vibrations of the light waves are going back and forth, the physical body is directly affected by the communication. It interprets the vibrations and follows the energy directives which are the messages that the soul and the human aspect consciousnesses are sending/receiving. Our human consciousness (the awareness that we have as us/me plus both hemispheres of the brain) are the primary driver for the human body. They are set up to be the drivers of the physical part of the Earth experience.

Because the soul wants to have experience as a human, with limited consciousness in the third and fourth dimensions, the human aspect of our consciousness that is limited *must* be the primary decision maker. Otherwise, why bother incarnating in a low-density reality? What we are experiencing as humans, and how we respond to our human experiences, provide the soul with expanded consciousness because the human aspect does not remember itself as being only part of a larger soul consciousness, nor does it remember being an aspect of Source. It is like playing a character in a movie within the hologram of Creation. The soul creates the movie and acts in it as a character, but the character does not remember creating the movie. The soul is allowing an aspect of itself to get so deeply involved in the character of this "movie," that the character is not aware that it is merely playing a part. The character is never separate from the soul, but it must be allowed to *think so* in the beginning, to play the part to its fullest, and get the benefits of what it is experiencing. The aspect explores the character's potential, strengths, and weaknesses, and makes choices while going through the main themes of the movie that the soul planned for it (the soul plan). As the character continues playing in the movie (experiencing), it expands its consciousness, that information goes directly back to the oversoul and expands the oversoul's consciousness. As this happens, the character *may* become aware of its eternal connection to the oversoul. The 'movie' then gets better for the character because that connection is made. The character remembers the importance and actively seeks communication with the oversoul. It uses communication with the oversoul to navigate in the movie and make it play out to the character's benefit, in a way that is exciting and joy-filled for the character instead of hard work that seems to add up to old-age and decrepit health. It is comparable to an actor receiving specially made props to use and having a benevolent coach walking beside them in the movie. Eventually, the character might start to remember it is an all-powerful being of Source, *that can create states of being* in the physical reality, which were previously thought to be uncontrollable. A shift happens, and the character in the movie becomes the director of the movie because it remembers that the larger part of itself created the themes of the movie in the first place.

Let's talk about the four light bodies so that you can be more mindful of how you are creating your movie, moving forward. If you take good care of the four light bodies and become aware of how they are interconnected, then you will achieve overall well-being and balanced energy. Then, what you direct to happen in your movie for the rest of your life will be **conscious creation** rather than feeling like you are merely a character with no control over the script.

We must be the ones who decide **how** we respond to our experiences in life. The themes of the movie are provided to us by the oversoul, other souls, and the universe. Our responses to these experiences affect our emotions and our mental states. Our emotions and mental states determine how our physical bodies will perform. And, all of that information is communicated back to the oversoul. When our soul senses we are on a path that is not good for us, or too far off the course of our life plan, it communicates back to us through the light bodies, which affect our physical bodies.

For example, if you are about to get on an airplane that is destined to crash, and you are not meant to leave your physical life yet, your soul will send messages through your mental, physical, spiritual, and emotional light bodies not to get on that airplane. You may have a fearful emotional response whenever you think about the flight, and you don't know why. Or, you may know that you don't want to get on that airplane, but you do not have the reasoning behind the knowing. You may feel an intuition to not board an airplane. Or, your physical body may also respond to the soul's message not to get on the airplane by becoming sick so that you cannot get on, or providing uncomfortable sensations every time you think about getting on that airplane. If you choose another departure time with another flight or change your mind about going to the destination, the sickness or fearful feelings will disappear in this example. You will feel utter relief and not know why.

I experienced this phenomenon before I got married. We went to a travel agent and planned a honeymoon trip to Florida from New York, including flights to and from our destination. Sometime before the wedding, my fiancé received a bill in the mail for a several year's old college expense that he thought was paid already. I already had some reservations about going to Florida before that happened. Something was nagging my mind and I felt anxiety about the trip. I thought it was due to pre-wedding jitters. I suggested to my fiancé that we pay the bill outright, cancel the trip to Florida, and instead drive to a bed and breakfast in Maryland for our honeymoon. Money was an issue for us back then and we were trying to be responsible and still have a honeymoon. I thought the relief that I felt when my fiancé accepted the new plan was because we were saving money.

As it turned out, that same year, I found out I had sinus polyps and needed surgery to remove them. My surgeon told us afterward that the polyp nearest my brain was so infected that if I had gotten on the plane, the polyp may have burst due to the cabin pressure of the flight. I may have died before we landed. I had no clue back then that my soul was conspiring to keep me off of airplanes using my mind and emotions. Not to mention the universe, by sending the mysterious unpaid bill in the mail. I doubt that the airplanes we would have flown on would have crashed. But, I may have died. The doctor was very clear about that potential had I flown. What I was experiencing in my mind and emotions was about my medical condition, not pre-wedding jitters. I had been experiencing sinus infections and migraines for several years before the wedding. I later realized that my soul was communicating with me through my light bodies (mental, emotional) because it was not my time to leave the Earth yet. I think this is why I felt immediate relief from my anxious thoughts and feelings about going to Florida when we changed our plan.

This example could be applied to a place you intend to go where you might experience harm (like a bar, or another country), and your soul does not want you to go there. Or a person you intend to spend time with that might harm you physically, emotionally, or mentally. Humans call these "gut" feelings. **I don't care what you call it as long as you listen**. The soul communicates to you constantly using the four light bodies. It wants you to stay on your life path as well as be the happiest, healthiest version of yourself while you do that.

I'm going to unpack my understanding of the four light bodies for you, one by one so that you can begin using them to consciously communicate with your soul, keep your body in its healthiest condition, and work with your thoughts and emotions to ensure wellbeing. The four light bodies are; physical, emotional, mental, and spirit (etheric/soul-essence).

The etheric light body gives the **first** set of instructions to the baby body while it is forming, from the oversoul. When the soul sends its etheric energy (we may think of that as our spirit) to create the body, the frequency of the energy forms the body to develop exactly the way the soul needs it to be for the incarnation. Yes, DNA helps determine many of our physical characteristics and is one of the reasons why we choose our parents, but, that is not the whole story. The soul plans for the physical body **to be** certain ways which will allow for the life plan (themes of the movie) to unfold as intended. This is why identical twins can appear physically different in many ways, and have varied personalities. Health, sickness, immunities, strength, incapacities, certain types of intelligence, and general appearance; are all ultimately determined by the soul's given frequency for that body.

Theoretically, identical twins should be exactly alike. They come from the same fertilized egg. But, like in music, the soul's energy (tone/song) may be played in different keys, and also in different octaves (frequencies). The song does not change (tone), but the soul's frequencies can and do for every incarnation (how the tone is expressed). In any incarnation our soul's tone may be played so that we appear as a tree, cat, human, air, water, magma...you get the point. The soul's tone can be expressed in several individuals within a shared reality. For example, you are you, and your oversoul energy may also be expressed as a tree, a dog, another person, and whatever else the consciousness wishes to be here on Earth, at the same moment point of your awareness of being you. The focal point of reality of you in 3D is only you. You are not aware in 3D consciousness that you are also the tree, the other person, *and* the dog. Spiritualists call that parallel lives. My understanding is that *every incarnation* of the oversoul's energy is a parallel life in that everything is going on at the same time, the eternal now moment. We are talking about light bodies now and so I will re-direct to that topic again.

Identical twins have different souls (usually, but not always), and therefore, they may look similar and tend to make similar life choices, or they may differ considerably. There are numerous scientific medical studies of identical twins as well as cultural (or social studies) of identical twins that attempt to provide reasons why identical twins express differently or share things in common. There are metaphysical differences in identical twins based on their souls' intentions for their lifetimes. The soul plan decides how the body needs to be and the soul frequency sent to the gestating baby determines much of the physical body development. Once the body is formed and born, the etheric energy that formed it remains and splits into the other light bodies (physical, emotional, and mental) to maintain the whole being. They each have a primary function, **and** they work together.

The physical light body is enmeshed with the baby's body after birth and is influenced by the environment of the child and the child's responses to the environment. The physical light body is the energetic field that knows and navigates what our body experiences. Hot, cold, comfortable, itchy, soothing touch, being hurt, the quality of food the body gets and how the body responds to it; all of this is recorded in the energy field of the physical light body and communicated with the oversoul. The physical tactile experiences of life are recorded in the oversoul's memory of this incarnation. With this information, the oversoul can monitor the condition of the human body, and send signals to the physical light body (like coaching it to be, feel, or want certain things), and this is the communication system that the physical light body provides. When you get that sick feeling in your gut before something bad is about to happen, this is your oversoul warning you to pay attention, passing the message through the physical light body.

The physical light body works in tandem with the emotional light body, mental light body, and etheric light body. Consciousness (spirit/etheric light body), is the driver of the incarnation then it splits and forms into the other light bodies. The etheric light body is then affected by its counterparts in return. Think of a simplified ecosystem where you have plant life, animal life, water, and air all in a dome and they sustain each other. If I do something to one of those systems, it affects the others. If I damage one of those systems, like the water, then the others will likely become damaged also. I will discuss the interdependence of the four light bodies after describing each one first. I've already covered what I know about the etheric light body. It is what you see leaving a person when they die on camera sometimes. Somehow, the film or the digital media has captured the soul energy leaving the body. People have accounted experiences where they have seen the etheric light body rise from the physical body at the time of physical death. Another name for it is spirit. At this point, I will estimate that the other light bodies become merged with the etheric again, at the time of physical death.

The mental light body is a part of the soul's frequency, and it directly influences the brain development of the human after birth. I have read a report from a quantum healing session where incoming soul energy had to 'tinker' with its future baby mind before it merged permanently with the body because the mind of the developing baby was not 'up to snuff' for the soul's purpose. Something in the baby's DNA was causing the mind to not be as intelligent as the soul preferred it to be. In this report, the soul said it was coming in and out of the baby during gestation to 'fix' the brain before finally staying in the body permanently, just before birth. If my model is correct, the etheric light body made those adjustments and then handed over responsibility for the brain to the part of itself we now call the mental light body.

Aside story; through many quantum healing reports, it is not unusual for a soul to send its etheric energy into and back out of a developing baby before birth. It is said that the soul energy of the developing baby likes to drop into the body to check the status and get to know it before entering the body permanently. To my knowledge, the soul will stay in the body at some point before birth. Sometimes the soul energy enters at the time of birth. The timing of when the soul enters the baby's body permanently has been a topic of debate for eons. I suggest it does not matter when the soul enters, it is more important to discuss why the soul may not stay in the body once pregnancy occurs. I have discovered information that some souls will leave the body permanently, before birth, if they change their mind about continuing the incarnation.

For example, when a soul plans to experience life with young parents. It knows that these parents are immature and nervous about the pregnancy before choosing them because it had a meeting with the guides that will watch over it during the incarnation. These guides provide choices for incarnation potentials and give the soul counsel about the conditions for the lifetime they are choosing. However, once the soul merges a few times with the baby they have chosen while the mother is pregnant, and the mother's energy feels more fearful about the pregnancy than expected by the incoming soul, the soul may change its mind about continuing the plan. Maybe the mother has changed her mind about having the baby, and the soul feels this. The energy fields of the mother and baby are connected more deeply when the soul merges during gestation, and so the soul knows and feels more acutely how the mother is responding to the pregnancy when it enters the baby. The soul can elect not to incarnate at this time, especially if it knows the baby may be aborted, and will leave the gestating body permanently. If that decision is made, the etheric light body will no longer communicate with the baby's body and the body will stop developing. Because the energy that causes the animation of the body stops connecting, either through surgical or natural processes, the baby miscarries or is aborted. There is no one to blame because we each have free will. The mother can try again when she feels ready and the soul can find another body if it does not want to wait for this mother, at this moment point. I am not advocating nor denouncing intentional abortion. It is, in my opinion, a choice of free will for all parties when a soul wants to incarnate. There is agreement with this arrangement by all parties or it doesn't happen.

    My descriptions are an attempt to help you understand what is happening with the soul energy when a pregnancy fails to result in a live birth. I got a little off-track here, but I think this information is important to mention because people; male and female, try to make sense of the diverse feelings around a terminated or unsuccessful pregnancy. They suffer greatly trying to figure out why, and how this impacts the soul of the unborn baby. They might feel guilt, shame, relief, extreme loss, resentment, anger, or all of the above. I believe that all souls benefit in some way from the experience. The humans going through it may not see the experience as beneficial. But it can be seen that way if looked upon from a perspective outside of grief. I lost a pregnancy in 2020. My baby died at around 12 weeks of development. I will share the metaphysical reason for this, which I discovered during hypnosis. It was a very good reason. The timing for us, to care for a baby properly, was not right for my husband and me. The incoming soul had never planned to go through the whole pregnancy and incarnation. It was only with us for three months, as agreed, to bring my husband and me closer together before we had to deal with the loss. Our bond with each other increased by both the expectation of a baby and during the period of grief when it died. The experience was also one of growth for my consciousness. I went through all the natural human feelings of losing a baby before I realized that. I know that no soul is ever 'lost.' That does not mean I did not feel grief after the pregnancy ended without having a live baby in my arms. **We need to allow our human feelings about anything.** I had an experience of loss, and then realized many things about myself, my beliefs about souls, and my relationship with my husband. This is what I mean about all souls benefitting. It makes sense that the soul that was with me during the three months (intermittently or statically) has attained some benefit for its role in bringing my husband and me closer together. I will not share my husband's experience of this set of events to maintain his privacy, however, I hope you will trust me when I tell you that he grew from it also.

    The mental light body sorts and defines all experience. It records images, thoughts, and data. It compares what the soul already knows about itself with how the aspect is **being**. It analyzes what reality the human aspect is creating for itself and helps the physical mind to have clarity about the creations. It can be considered the executive of the analytical mind (left hemisphere of the brain). It is also the executive of the right hemisphere, the conduit for all things creative. It catches and passes energy from the universe and other souls to the human mind, and the right brain is then inspired to create something new or recycle someone else's creation in a new way.

    Together, the mental light body, and the left and right hemispheres of the brain, can be considered the **human mind complex**. The mental light body can encourage us to ask, "Do I enjoy what I'm creating, or do I want to create something else?" The analysis of the left brain is not always protective. You might think of the mental light body as an energetic net that we catch ideas and inspirations with. That sounds pretty good, but remember, a net sometimes catches things you don't want, that are totally out of accord with your soul's tone. Our mental light bodies can become disoriented by social programming/conditioning of the physical mind. The communication and energy exchange from the human mind to the oversoul can be cut-off or distorted when the mental light body gets energetically clogged. It can be compared to scrambling an egg. The yolk and the white of the egg are beaten together and so separating the functions of the yolk and the white is improbable. The mental light body can be healed if it becomes scattered or scrambled (unlike the egg) but the process of energy healing that it requires is considerable. This is why it is **so** important to be mindful of our thoughts. Are they our thoughts? Or are they society's thoughts and we've adopted them as our own? Are we participating in stinking thinking? Either way, the analysis is important when determining if the thought is harmful or helpful to your experience. I would contend that some social conditioning can be helpful and necessary, as long as it is in accord with your consciousness expansion instead of limiting it.

Next up is the emotional light body. We need emotional responses as babies because how else is our caregiver going to know if we are doing well or if we need something? In that sense, the emotional light body is first a survival mechanism. The Earth experience is partially guided by emotions. We agree to have emotions when we focus here, and strong ones too. As we grow, the emotional light body serves more as the communication to and from our soul, and our physical body, while maintaining the ability to communicate our needs to other humans. It lets us know if the environment we are in is to our liking. By environment, I mean; people, places, things, experiences. Alcoholics Anonymous teaches specifically about being aware of the environment a member chooses, and the emotional "triggers" environments can incite. If you keep seeing a person and you feel bad after every visit, then your emotional light body is telling you to limit seeing that person! That person's energy is not in accord with your own. If you cannot stop seeing them altogether, then maybe you can restrict the time you spend with them and set conditions for which you are willing to do that (boundaries).

If you watch mainstream media news regularly and you feel upset and fearful every time, then stop watching the news! Most of that has nothing to do with what you are creating in your life anyway. If there is something you need to know about your work, your family, or a group you are working with, you will get more direct notifications from your emotional light body rather than hearing something in the news about it. Paying the most attention to what is happening in your own life is what I term, 'staying in your own lane.' If someone accuses you of being ignorant because you choose to stop participating with someone or something that causes you to feel bad, tell them "Ignorance is bliss." That's what I do. The phrase was coined for a reason. You will be doing yourself a favor by dismissing this person who is judging your decisions and honoring your soul by limiting negative feelings. You are not being 'ignorant' because you choose not to participate with fearful information that likely does not apply to you. You are not being mean when you are staying away from people that you feel decreased energy with, in their presence. I would say you are making good, healthy, smart decisions when making those choices! You are using your emotional light body to guide you in the best direction for your life.

During the writing of this chapter, I learned about an earthquake that happened in Turkey and Syria that killed over 12,000 people. I had heard channeled information and psychic prediction of a massive earthquake event for the past year that was not geographically specific. When I heard these predictions, I immediately disregarded them. Why? Because I choose to honor my emotional light body!

What possible thing could I do to prepare for, or prevent, an earthquake? Maybe I could go around and nail down everything in my house and hoard a bunch of food and water in the hopes that my house doesn't crash in all around me, because MAYBE the earthquake may happen in my location. That is fear-based action brought on by fearful emotions. I am not doing that, or even thinking about that, because it is a doomsday scenario. If I were to consider those earthquake predictions, imagine that they were going to happen in my location, and choose to be in fear states about them, I could have created that experience in my reality. Thoughts and emotions are energy forms that light up parts of the hologram. Why would I want to light up experiencing an earthquake? I may have manifested my doomsday scenario if I chose to go into fear when I heard the predictions.

Fear.

Predictions and news that incite fear are propaganda with a malevolent intention, or at the very least, crappy marketing tactics to obtain more viewers. Information peddled by charlatans and snake oil salesmen. If you want to keep your emotional light body balanced, these kinds of predictions and newscasts need to be disregarded in total, in my opinion. That being said, if someone I trust has a vision of me being involved in an earthquake, I'm going to try to get more information about that situation and prevent loss of life if I can. There is a difference between people that broadcast nets of fear and those who are genuinely trying to save you from harm.

You want to train your emotional light body to communicate to YOU what your truth is, not tap into every emotion the world is experiencing. The world and its people are not yours to save. It's not your job. I cannot save anyone in Turkey or Syria, even if the predictions I heard were specific about the earthquake being in those locations. Could I help now if I wish by sending money or material goods? Yes! Of course,

I can do that.

I could also choose to help someone in my community, that is easily within my reach. I could give a homeless person some food or a coat if it is cold outside. I could comfort the woman crying on the bridge because her 9-year-old son was killed in her home during a drive-by shooting in her neighborhood (this happened). I encountered the woman on a bridge in the park. We spoke for a while and when she shared the story of her son, I hugged her and let her cry on my shoulder. That gave my emotional light body a tremendous boost because I was sharing compassion/love. Going into fear often means we are expending our energy on things we cannot control. If the fear is real, as in a real threat (the lion is coming at me, a tire just rolled off my car and I'm driving 70 miles per hour), then we deal with the threat. **If the fear is about something that we cannot alter or change, it is a waste of energy**. Talk to yourself, acknowledge the feeling, and then allow the fear to fall away from you.

If I want to raise my joy factor intentionally, I can go to the park and be amongst nature; smell the lake air, feel the sun on my face, and maybe feed the birds and squirrels. I could pull weeds from my flower beds and listen to the bird song as I support and enjoy the flowers. I can hug my family members and the animals that live with me. There are endless choices we can make that will either support our emotional light bodies, harm them, or maintain neutrality. My point is, what good will I do for myself and the people of Turkey and Syria if I am fearful and sad about what happened to them?

Is there not an epidemic of fear in the world already?

Do I need to add to it?

Is it possible that by maintaining my balance emotionally, I will help the collective maintain its balance emotionally?

What happens if I do not imagine the experiencers of the earthquake as victims, but rather imagine them as strong people who will help each other out to recover and heal? The latter choice is keeping my emotional status healthy while sending energy out into the universe to be received by others, and they feel that positive energy I am sending to them within *their* emotional light bodies. Holding a high vision of other people helps you and them equally when it comes to energy.

Be mindful of how the environment **you choose** makes you feel. Be judicious about what you allow into your energy fields. Base those decisions on how you feel while you engage with them. Love yourself enough to allow a preponderance of information that uplifts you in some way rather than upsetting news. Your feelings/emotions are your GPS with your soul. They are a gift. Use them wisely. Don't just fall into what society tells you that you should feel! That is harming yourself. No, no, no; those manipulation games to keep you constantly in fear are over. The separation games are at an end if you decide you are ready to be done with them.

Be mindful of **how you are being** and how the things you illuminate within the hologram (give attention to) make you feel. This is called personal responsibility. Are you getting your needs met by throwing tantrums, and then later feeling bad about it, even though you get what you think you need by throwing tantrums? Maybe in that case you'll want to try another method to get your needs met than throwing tantrums, like improving your communication skills. If that feels better to you, then you know the **state of being**, a 'better communicator,' is in alignment with what your soul wants. Obviously, I cannot diagnose your emotional light body if you do not experience feelings like guilt or remorse, because, at some point in your incarnation, your capacity to feel those emotions has been disabled. I truly do not know an easy fix for that but here are some suggestions.

If you are not able to experience emotions, or you walk through life feeling numb most of the time, then I suggest shifting your focus to the mental light body initially, your thoughts, and copying the behaviors that happier people display. Maybe your emotions are not completely disabled, but they have been placed in stasis or frozen because you have had too many painful experiences in life. That is a defense mechanism when you subconsciously close off emotion. A defense mechanism can happen when you avoid something or shut it down completely because you cannot bear how you experience it. If you change the environments from where you learned to shut down your emotions, maybe you will gradually feel safer to let some emotions back into your experience. If you also change your **beingness**, maybe people will respond to you differently and start to treat you better as well. Nobody wants to be in a room with a wildcat being all angry and scary. If you notice that you are the one being angry, and people are avoiding you, then no matter what the reason for the anger is, your emotional light body will not be healed until you make changes within yourself. You have to **be** the way you want to be treated.

This is what is meant when spiritualists talk about healing yourself from within. You have to take personal responsibility for your emotional health and behaviors. Our life paths are not easy. I do not know one single human, by experience or by their report, that does not have *something* challenging to deal with in life. But I do know, because I am very in touch with emotions, that life gets better when we pay attention to our feelings and let them guide us toward what our soul wants to experience. We can heal our emotional light bodies no matter what our prior experiences brought if we are self-aware. This does not sound like a fair deal. Why are you expected to improve your very being when others have treated you so badly in your life? I have heard that complaint in more than a few counseling sessions and I will say to you what I have said to my clients.

First, it is fair, because you chose what you will experience before you incarnated. Any other soul that has harmed you has done so through a soul agreement for that potential to happen. Second, your soul would not have given you those experiences if it did not believe you could handle them and grow from them. And third, the only way to shift your experiences to positive, uplifting ones, is to **be** the change you want to see. Be the very best version of yourself no matter what everyone else is being. You can 'fake it till you make it' by watching and patterning yourself to the behaviors of happier people. That is one avenue to transformation. And you create transformation within yourself with each positive action you choose. You step into personal power to create better realities for yourself.

There are no victims. Only participants in the experience. Each participant makes choices about how they will experience life. What lenses do we see our world through? And what actions are we taking in response to experiences? Your emotional light body will guide your transformation if you let it. Keep reaching for the states of being that cause you to **feel** better. Do self-care as often as you can. Stay away from environmental factors that trigger harmful emotions in you. Give gratitude when you can, as often as you can, for whatever you can be grateful for. The universe will send you more. This sounds like a combination of a smackdown and a pep-talk. My sister would call it a 'come to Jesus' conversation. It is reminiscent of the material I shared in my first book; *The Christ Consciousness; A Somewhat Agnostic Point of View*. Feelings of all kinds are part of the experience here on Earth and can guide you.

My goal with these examples is to open your mind completely as to how the emotional light body works, and how very important it is to balance emotional energy. If you are overly emotional all the time, good or bad, that is not balanced energy. Sometimes the physical body in the third and fourth dimensions needs to experience neutral, restful, and peaceful emotions to stay healthy. It cannot handle the stress of you feeling blissful all the time no more than being sad all the time. I believe our physical bodies will be able to maintain more regular streams of blissful energy in the fifth dimension (density) because the energy of bliss is higher frequency energy and as our consciousness expands, our physical bodies will be capable of holding more light energy. But, that is only a theory for me at this point in my reality.

I do experience joyful emotions and hold them for longer periods as I attend to my emotional light body to be more responsible about how I feel; and I enjoy peaceful, restorative emotional states also. I have read about and heard reports during hypnosis concerning the fifth-dimensional states of bliss and joy and descriptions of how our emotional states are completely balanced, and neutral. The balance still includes peaceful states of being. All I know for sure is that right here and now, where I am focusing in the fourth density consciousness, my physical body and light bodies require lots of moments with neutral, or peaceful emotions, to feel balanced energetically. I suggest peaceful emotions as goals to everyone for balancing your emotional light bodies.

The fourth light body is the physical light body. It is the energy field within the body and just outside of the physical body, that governs and regulates the condition of the physical body. Some people describe seeing this energy and call it the human aura. Energy can be seen as a color, and the colors indicate the frequency of the energy. For example, red indicates kundalini energy (creative/anger/love) depending on what the person is feeling and the intentions of that person. The red indicates how the body, mind, and emotional light bodies work in-tandem. If my feeling and intention towards someone or something is loving and appreciative, my aura (physical light body) may shine red to those who can see it. If, conversely, I have just finished a lively argument with someone and I'm thinking lots of negative thoughts while feeling angry about the exchange, then my red aura is a result of MY direction of creative energy to lower density manifestation. The red itself is not good nor bad, it is creative. What I'm creating with it is my free will choice. Someone cannot read your aura and tell you what your colors mean necessarily. They can give you general ideas about what the colors may be communicating. Another example is blue. When you are told your aura is blue, that **generally** indicates you are experiencing a peaceful state of being in your body, mind and emotions. And, blue also indicates free flowing communication. Maybe you are getting ready to speak your truth, and you are not feeling blocked by a belief system in doing that. You feel no restriction about speaking your truth. You feel free to communicate, and your body is telling you through your physical light body that you are in alignment with your soul when you do speak your truth. This aura reading stuff is for people who have been told about their physical light body colors, or those who can see them. What if you do not see colors around people or yourself?

The physical light body still communicates with your mind about the **condition, environment,** and **actions** of the body. You must start paying attention to how your bodily energies FEEL. I'm not talking about emotions or thoughts. How does your body energy feel? For example, you may experience irritation in your ears or periodically limited auditory abilities in certain circumstances. Certain voices sound muffled, you keep saying "what" or "excuse me" because you are not quite hearing what is being communicated, clearly. Or you may have irritated sensations in the ears and you rub them to relieve the irritation. In this example, your physical (energetic) light body is telling you that you are listening to something or someone who is communicating information that is out of resonance with YOUR truth. Your physical light body is telling you that you do not want to hear this anymore. Chances are, if this is happening, your emotional light body and your mental light body are also reacting to the communication, where you have a somewhat negative emotional reaction to what you are hearing and your thoughts begin questioning the information. You may start thinking..."this guy is full of shit!" These are all **communications from your light bodies** that what you are listening to is out of alignment with what your soul knows is true for you. It does not matter if the information you are reacting to is true 100% for the person speaking it. For YOU, it is not true, and your light bodies are trying to tell you this.

The physical light body will give you your first indications of dis-ease in your body. All dis-ease is a physical manifestation of scattered energy caused by imbalanced light bodies. In other words, if you keep doing something, saying something, listening to something, or believing something (or a combo of all of these), that is out of alignment with your soul's truth, it will scramble the energy of your light bodies, and that distorted energy mix will eventually manifest as illness in the physical body. Why? Energy is energy whether it appears physically or not. If energy flows naturally, i.e. your light bodies are carefully attended to and balanced by you; you give yourself peaceful moments, you engage in activities that are fun for you, and you make healthy decisions about who you let into your life, then all of your energy fields will flow as intended and your physical body will be healthy. Discordant energy will be easily transmuted by you because the balance within your light bodies is healthy. However, if one of your light bodies is out of whack, and you do not make changes to remedy this imbalance, then it will affect all the other light bodies and eventually result in physical illness. It is the last tangible evidence that your soul uses to communicate with you that you are not experiencing your truth.

By the time someone experiences physical illness, they have been ignoring all the other communications of their light bodies. The physical light body will tell you this illness is impending. For example, you may start feeling tension in your neck, and it returns often. You go to the doctor and the doctor cannot find a chemical or physical reason for your discomfort, and maybe the doctor recommends a pain reliever, massage, or some other remedy for the symptom, "tension in the neck area" that is a short-term remedy. You might feel relief for a while, and then the tension comes back. Eventually, the tension becomes greater and turns into pain, and maybe that leads to headaches. You start taking more pain relievers and then you find yourself going to a "specialist" for chronic pain management. Sound familiar? In this example, you may have taken a different option to find out what that neck tension was telling you before you ever stepped into a doctor's office. What are the other options? First, you could have done some meditation and asked your physical body what it is trying to communicate to you by giving you the sensation of tension in your neck. Get comfortable, quiet the mind, and ASK your body. Then wait for the answer. It will come to your mind. Trust what it tells you, no matter what your brain judges about the information, and make necessary adjustments. If you "hear," *we/you feel like you are carrying the weight of the world and we need a break*, then listen to that, that is the answer about why you have discomfort in the neck! You may not hear it, it may come as a thought. You may SEE examples of how you feel like the weight of the world is on your shoulders. Whatever way the body gives you the answer, trust that and believe that this information is true for you. Do not analyze nor make excuses for why you are too busy to lighten up your load. The neck tension will only increase and get worse if you do that. Take steps to decrease the pressure and responsibility that you are currently carrying. If you cannot do that, then make **very** sure you carve out time for yourself to recharge your batteries and relax. Balance the energy. I say that a lot but it is truly so very important to balance stressful energies with peaceful ones. Fun ones too! All work and no play will scramble your energies. The horse cannot carry the load if it becomes lame or dies.

    If you do not feel secure enough to meditate and ask your body what the issue is causing the discomfort in the neck, then engage an energy healer; someone with a good track record and lots of positive reviews. Make an appointment with a shaman or a hypnotist. Consult a well-reviewed psychic. Go to counseling and start talking about what stresses you, and the beliefs you have about yourself. Talk to someone you trust and just let out all the stuff you keep bottled up inside. Talk to yourself! I have discovered many distorted thought patterns within myself by talking to myself! Sometimes you don't know you are stinkin' thinkin' until you hear yourself say things out loud. Who cares if you think you sound crazy; go into a private room or out into nature and have a discussion with yourself! Once you figure out the root cause of the discomfort in your neck, you can begin to resolve it. This may entail changing; your behaviors, patterns, the people you hang out with, your job, re-arranging duties to care for an elderly family member so that you are not the sole caregiver, finding a new group of friends to hang out with, etc. It may be something as simple as "stop listening to the news"! The weight of the world's problems is very heavy indeed, and could give anyone discomfort in the neck (pain in the neck) just hearing about them. Finally, if all those ideas do not appeal to you, you can always find a copy of one of Louise Hay's books which will help you identify the root cause of your dis-ease in the body. Louise was my first resource to finding out that all illness is caused by energetic distortions, and I believe her information is timeless. Your physical light body will continue to render more discomfort and amplified symptoms if you ignore the original messages.

    I think one more example for the physical light body's communication is needed. Let's go with food and beverages. We each get accustomed to eating certain foods from birth. Some foods nourish our bodies and give us strength and vitality, and others make us feel sluggish or uncomfortable. Those that make us feel sluggish and uncomfortable will over time reduce the energy of your physical light body and contribute to discomfort in the body, if not totally causing illness in the body, if consumed on a regular basis. Why? Your DNA may not allow your body to process those foods well, which causes your systems to work extra hard to do their jobs when you eat them. You may have a belief that certain foods are harmful to you. Thoughts are energy and the body knows what you think and believe. You may love certain foods and beverages that have been harmful to you in a past life, which is recorded in your DNA and read as "harmful" by your body in this life. If we do not know about these things, how could we possibly make better decisions about our foods and beverages? Simple. Ask your body what it wants when you are considering a menu or looking into the cabinets or fridge because you are hungry. Don't automatically assume you want anything specific because you have a habit of eating in a certain way. Maybe you want to feed your body a bowl of cereal and your body wants a salad. Maybe you are not hungry at all, but thirsty. Drink some water. Maybe you smelled something your neighbor is preparing for dinner, and although you have never had that food before, your body wants to try it. Sometimes I would feel hungry at night around 10 pm, and instead of criticizing myself for eating at that time of night (a no-no by many standards), I would stand in front of the fridge and ask my body what it wanted. My husband would laugh at me when the answer was Brussel sprouts with lemon and butter, but that's what I would eat at 10pm at night sometimes when that answer came. There is no reason to believe what anyone else tells you about your body. What is healthy for you is healthy for you. Your belief systems may be faulty or distorted by what society tells you about your body. That's okay because it happens to us all. Figure out what your body tells you it wants, and then do that. Judgement of whatever your body wants is not helpful, nor necessary.

    I will finish this discussion of the physical light body by saying your energetic needs are unique, and only you can determine what your body needs to be balanced. Get in touch with the communications of your physical light body, what it is telling you about your current status, and you will be able to realize the flow of good health. Even if your soul has included some kind of disability or illness into your life plan, you can still be the healthiest version of you while experiencing those realities. It is all about feeling the best that you can and using your light body to guide you there. It will if you listen to it.

4

Spirit Communication

"Spirit" is a term to describe souls and collectives of souls (group consciousnesses) that are not physically incarnated within our 3D reality where we can perceive them with our five senses. You could think of them as ghosts, but I will provide a more expansive view.

Spirit(s), by my definition, are the energy aspects of a soul, or group of aspects, and this energy is focused in different dimensions than our own. I am speaking of the energy of your grandmother that passed away, Elvis, Einstein, extra-terrestrials, Jesus, Mohammed, Buddha, or any other soul energy you not might not be aware of. Spirit communication with these energies is accessible to us at all times. Having shared a specific incarnation with a particular soul aspect is not required to contact them, because the universal truth is, we are all eternally connected to Source and to one another. In our universe, there are 12 dimensions which were created to experience separation from Source and expanding consciousness. There is a range of frequencies that can exist within each dimension. These dimensions allow our souls to experience in many varied ways while always remaining connected to each other. There are infinite ways to experience, infinite ways to connect, and by the way; we can and do connect to spirit energy outside of our universe also. Our connection to everything allows us to communicate to spirits and beings in other universes, the planes of existence we think of as the heavens, all the way to God/Source directly. Some people think of communication with the heavenly beings as prayer alone. Nonetheless, it is communication. It's a two-way communication potential if we listen and notice what communications are coming back from the beings we pray to. As many humans can attest, the communication is not one sided. People throughout time have shared stories of conversations with God, Allah, the angels, and many other higher vibrational beings (9th dimensional Pleiadeans for example). We can communicate energetically with other physically incarnated souls, non-corporeal souls, high vibrational communal societies, low vibrational warring societies...we have within us the potential to have communication with every kind of being or 'society.' The goal on Earth now is for us is to remember the set-up (ways that we do communicate), utilize information and guidance from spirit to expand our consciousness through these communications, and keep our personal vibrations higher as we experience reality during our Earthly lives.

The layers of energy density that we call "dimensions" contain different scalar frequencies. Frequency is how fast or slow the vibration of light or sound passes through other energetic fields. My explorations of the quantum have not suggested that humans embody within any dimension lower than 3D. That does not necessarily mean soul energies do not incarnate in lower densities than 3D, but I believe it means to have a **human** body that can contain the energy of our consciousness (self-awareness), we must incarnate within the 3rd dimension or higher. In some dimensions of this universe, the light frequencies are too high to allow energy to form the illusion of a physical body. Souls that have energy focused within these dimensions are alive but having experiences through their consciousness only.

What humans believe to be the 'heavens' are other dimensional realities where soul aspects experience without a body. I believe this is what Jesus meant when he said (paraphrased) "the house of our father has many rooms." God/Source being the father, soul aspects are the sons and daughters, and many dimensions exist (rooms) to have experience within. The energy is obviously not dead, or it could not have experience. The energy of our deceased relatives, for example, are soul aspects that transformed from physical to non-physical and have also transformed from one state of consciousness to another. One is a physical reality, the other is an etheric reality. Until that soul aspect decides to incarnate again. Then it chooses which kind of incarnation it wants next, what focal point it will focus within.

Some soul aspects never take on physical bodies, by choice. They sometimes exist as consciousnesses that have higher levels of light energy, meaning; more awareness of Creation than we remember, but they are still separated from Source which means they have less consciousness than the God-mind (Christ Consciousness). It may seem like I'm describing beings that are smarter than us, which is not true. They remember **more** than we do because they retain more of their oversoul's energy than we bring with us to Earth. They have been called higher energetic beings (HEBs) by Neale Donald Walsh, and so I will use that term.

Not every soul aspect "in spirit" is a HEB. Some soul aspects in spirit reside in lower dimensions than ours, have lower consciousness than humans do, and that means they are having experiences further away from the consciousness of Source. You may judge them and assign names to them like "demons" or "negative entities" if you like, however, I suggest that all experience in every consciousness is still God/Source energy. Our oversouls make choices about what kinds of experiences to have, which dictate what dimension and form we will take for any incarnation. Meanwhile, Source doesn't judge any form we take because we are Source. It is experience Source is after, and all experience is welcomed and allowed. Plus, consider that it would be impossible for soul aspects to choose between light and dark if there were no experiences of the dark. Why would Source bother to create every condition of being 'not Source' if it only wanted to know the light, of which it already is? Contrast assists soul aspects in making choices. All soul aspects consciously/energetically come back to the oversoul eventually, and then merge back with Source. Experiencing all of Creation means that aspects do this back and forth, while feeling that the illusions are real during each experience. They explore everything, every possible way of being, before returning to Source.

HEBs are available to support, guide, and protect the rest of us while we experience in the lower light densities (dimensions). Ascended masters are soul aspects that have assumed physical form(s) and, you guessed it, ascended, by achieving a higher frequency and transforming to higher dimensions of experience. It is possible to ascend to an enlightened consciousness while remaining in human form, which is what humanity is trying to do now in this version of Earth. The ascended masters are not gone from us, as stated above. They are always available to us in spirit, and so we are able to have communication with them. They act much like the angels do to guide us in our own ascension.

Most ghostly contact with spirit that have been written about over time probably involve situations where a spirit has wanted to contact a human so much, for whatever reason, that the spirit has lowered its vibration enough to allow the human to perceive the communication with their five senses. Spirit cannot lower its energy vibration that much for very long. These kinds of communications usually come and end quickly for that reason.

This is not the same as when a person notices a ghostly reenactment of events where the ghosts cannot be communicated with. Ghost stories where humans have seen visions of etheric energy doing the same thing over and over again, maybe at a certain time of the day/night, are energy readings, or energy observations. In these cases, people witness the scenes played out in exactly the same way but there is no communication by the spirit to the humans watching the scene. The spirit does not seem to notice the human presence. When that happens, what is being perceived is like an echo of energy, within an event, in another place in time. In other words, another dimensional reality exists, which is very close to our dimensional reality in density, and so the energy can be perceived when humans are not trying to communicate. The images are seen and heard but not interacted with. Echoes of the future or past are energy signatures (frequencies of soul aspects) that someone picks up with their 5 senses. The ones who do perceive this phenomena are usually energy sensitive naturally, or have developed extra sensory perception to do so (considered psychic/intuitives).

For Earth reality, our soul aspects operate within past, present, and future constructs because the linear progression of what we call time allows human consciousness in 3D to follow a life plan. Echoes of the 'past' or 'future' are events happening in the present moment, but they are happening in another physical reality (different dimension). That is why most people are not aware of past/future events. Could you imagine what chaos it would be mentally if we could be aware of what is happening in every dimensional location, all at the same moment? All the history of Earth in your location going on now? We would not be able to separate **this** reality (focal point of consciousness) from any other dimensional reality. It would probably cause instant insanity for us at the 3D level of consciousness. Humans are typically focused in one dimensional frequency at a time to avoid that. But this is changing.

One of the great things about ascension is that we can focus our conscious minds within several dimensional realities, simultaneously (bi-location), if our personal frequencies are high enough, and we choose to do it. Ascension means that our consciousness expands enough to handle bi-location, and we are able to know the differences between the two locations. For example; after being hypnotically regressed in the 1990's, I was aware that I am Sue, but I became aware of another lifetime as a mountain man in the 1700's. I was not confused about which lifetime I am currently experiencing, as Sue. I bi-located during the hypnosis session. As we ascend, we don't become disoriented from our current focal point of experience when bi-locating.

Interaction with spirit is possible because there is no actual 'time.' Time is an illusion of our 3rd and 4th dimensional realities. Everything is actually happening in the same moment, the eternal now moment. Spirit communication is co-mingling energies that are close in frequency of vibration to where two or more parties understand each other. Not all communication from spirit is received successfully by us because we either do not understand the meaning, or our frequencies are not high enough to perceive them. I wish to discuss some ways to improve communication with spirit. Once some things are highlighted, I hope you will remember that spirit is communicating with us constantly.

When I began writing this chapter, I stumbled onto the work of Don Elkins and Carla L. Rueckert, who worked together for 12 years to perfect their channeling process and help others develop their own. They received messages from a group consciousness calling itself RA. The books they wrote are titled *The Law of One* (books 1-5) and yes, this RA collective reported that they are the same RA consciousness connected to ancient Egypt. RA reported to Elkins and Rueckert that it projected its consciousness into a human living in ancient Egypt. This human apparently agreed to be the medium for the collective RA, because that cannot happen without soul agreement. This person know as RA to the other Egyptians communicated technologies to help the society increase its consciousness and live better. The pyramids were built using advanced technologies that are lost to us now. The pyramids were energy receptors and energy amplifiers, as well as navigational devices for visiting ETs. My understanding is that RA hails from planets within the Orion system, and the pyramids are aligned with the Orion system. So the Egyptians were taught by RA how to use the energy of the pyramids to access higher states of consciousness while in meditation within them, and the Egyptians were able to learn how to project their consciousness out of their bodies (called astral projection). They realized that they are spirits having a human experience and that all souls belong to one whole collective, what RA called The One. RA taught that the incarnated self is a projection of Source mind, a distortion of it. That makes sense to me because anything outside of knowing that we are all Source beings and our true nature is unconditional love is an illusion of the truth of who and what we are. A 'mind distortion' or limited consciousness reality. The natural question of modern times is, what happened to RA? It should come as no surprise that the leaders of the Egyptian society did not like sharing power with another human with God-like qualities. I do not know if the human hosting the RA consciousness was killed, but I do know that the technologies of RA were being used to enslave the Egyptian citizens and to control them through fear. Just this little bit of information from RA seems to confirm what I have come to know independently; we are all parts of Source, we incarnate to experience in different ways than Source, and that we are each making our way back to Source (The One) through the experience of raising our consciousness. This stumbling onto the material of RA was no coincidence, it was a synchronicity. Of course, I ordered several of the books to read further.

Now that I have established what I am talking about when I say, 'communication with spirit,' let's dig into the nature of soul energy. Every object or person has a frequency of vibration. If an object or person begins to vibrate faster and does that for a while, the frequency of that object or person will change. It increases. Imagine a note being played at high pitch vs low pitch. The high pitch wave of sound will repeat more often. The low pitch wave repeats less often and looks wider than the high pitch wave on a graph. Each one of our souls carries its own unique energy signature (frequency), or version of the oversoul's tone, in each incarnation. My soul energy frequency that is known as 'Sue Beckley' in this life carries a different frequency than my other incarnated selves. The tone of my soul energy remains the same throughout all incarnations, physical or non-physical, but the frequency of that tone changes from one lifetime to another. Paul Selig (The Guides) refers to this; "the one note sung in many octaves." The name changes I've made throughout my life as 'Sue' have altered my vibration a little. Names create sounds and so your vibration changes a little bit when you change your name. However, the constant energy signature of my oversoul (my tone) remains recognizable no matter how many names I go by. Souls that I have other incarnations with will recognize my tone even if they do not recognize my name. Humans call this 'soul recognition.' It means that when we meet someone in this life that we have never met before, and have the strong feeling that we know them already, it is most likely a soul we have experience with in another incarnation. We recognize their soul tone. When this happens, both parties usually recognize one another, even if they do not know from where. When this occurs, we can have different reactions to that other soul's tone, even though we do not know the person in this life at all. For example, I meet Lisa for the first time and feel an immediate affinity for her before getting to know her. Lisa and I may be friends, associates, even family members in another reality (incarnation); or maybe our oversouls reside in the same monadic entity. Our souls recognize each other at the moment of meeting in this life, and the bond from that other incarnation (emotional/energetic connection) is felt in the now moment. The reaction could also go the other way. If I meet Lisa and I feel mistrust or disdain, that might indicate that we share one incarnation or several where our energies are not in alignment. This kind of reaction to soul recognition brings about an opportunity to resolve whatever problems are occurring within other lifetimes between souls. We have free will choice. We can either choose to avoid a person that we immediately don't like after the first meeting, or choose to engage further with that person and see if a mutually beneficial relationship can be established. Neither choice is wrong because if you decide to stay away from the other person, for whatever reason, you can always "mend fences" in another dimensional reality. There is no judgement by your soul about how you handle these awkward, uncomfortable experiences.

I've laid some groundwork about soul identity through personal energy signatures (tones) and frequencies. RA calls this "frequential harmonics." We can increase or decrease our vibrations throughout a life, but our frequency *usually* remains similar to that at birth during each life unless we consciously work to change it. Our personal vibration is linked with our name. A name is part of the harmonic expression of the tone. Using different frequencies of the original tone, the soul projects its energy into individual incarnations, within different dimensions. We do not *always* maintain the same frequency that we are born with. We can alter our frequencies within lifetimes. I believe it is the oversoul's hope that we do change it. If we can raise our vibrations (the way our consciousness experiences the world through love and joy) for extended periods of time, then our frequency will also increase. If our frequency signature from birth raises or lowers a lot, other souls (people) may comment about it. They notice. People can feel the changes in you. For example, someone I knew in childhood may say, "I don't even recognize Sue anymore." This would be a compliment to me, in my opinion, because I have intentionally shifted my energy to hold higher vibrations, longer, and therefore raised my frequency (frequential harmonic) since childhood. I pay more attention to the things I'm grateful for and focus less on the difficulties of life than I did as a youth. Another example; a person, let's call her Terry, has altered her frequency by lowering it. She did this by engaging in damaging practices to herself throughout her life. Maybe Terry experienced very challenging circumstances, and she responded to her emotions about the challenging circumstances by drinking and using drugs to alleviate the feelings associated. If Terry did this over an extended period of time, she would cause damage to her light bodies (and her physical body); which results in lowering her frequency. It now takes longer for Terry to "shake off" the energy of whatever negative experiences happen next, and a cumulative effect happens. She maintains states of low vibration longer (i.e. she seems regularly depressed in mood, cares less about her appearance, stops socializing, feels trapped in a shitty job, behaves reactively, keeps drinking and drugging, and so on). A person who knew Terry in her youth might say, "I don't even recognize Terry anymore," and that would not be a compliment because her frequency was lowered. The friend will still be aware that Terry is Terry (same soul), but the feeling and experience of Terry now is much different for the friend than it was in their youth.

    Another thing I have learned through quantum healing sessions is that each one of us have "higher selves." Versions of us that reside in higher dimensions and have more expanded consciousness. As mentioned above, we carry the same soul energy (tone) that our higher selves do, but we have different frequencies. Frequential harmonics determine HOW that tone expresses itself during any given incarnation. For example, the tone of my soul that is Sue now is the same as the tone of my soul incarnated as a solitary mountain man in West Virginia, living in the dimensional Earth years 1700's. Our different frequencies make us look differently, act differently, and seem like different energies altogether. And we are, in some ways, because we have different life plans and realities which we are experiencing within. But we share the same soul energy. He is me and I am him, and our higher selves carry both sets of memories. I discovered this other "self" (the mountain man) during my first ever hypnotic regression. The reason that my higher-self connected me to his lifetime memories during hypnosis was to link his cause of death to my sinus infections in this life. The man died due to a sinus infection. I apparently carried over his fear of dying from that lifetime to where my body was giving me sinus infections, and I needed to become aware of our connection before I could resolve the fear of dying. Once I figured out the connection, I released the fear **for** him and myself (quantum healing), and my body no longer experienced sinus infections. The process freed me from any fear of dying because I remembered that soul aspects do not die, they transform. I watched myself as the man die physically, and yet I (we) are still alive. Soul aspects change form over and over again, experiencing as many lifetimes as they wish, until eventually they decide to merge back with Source. I have not found any evidence that our souls are in a hurry to merge back with Source, however, our souls do seem to be drawn to the light and higher consciousness experiences. It seems we wish to realize higher potentials for soul expression and experience, and this raises our consciousness. The higher we go, the more we want to know. Spirit communication can be **very** helpful with this endeavor.

    When I conduct a quantum healing session, I ask for the client's higher-self to come in and assist by answering questions for the client and/or provide healing. I am not always getting the client's *highest* self to respond (the oversoul within the monad). Whichever higher version of that person's soul comes into the session, it is the version that is best prepared to answer the questions posed by the client. Different parts of our soul have different experiences. The questions being posed dictate who steps up to answer. For example, I had a female client wanting to ask if she has extra-terrestrial (ET) origins. This was not the main focus of the session, but she was very interested in it. She mostly wanted guidance about her career and what her next steps should be after graduation from college. The higher-self version of my client's soul that came through to answer questions is another incarnated being living in ancient Lemuria on Earth, originally from the star system, Lyra. The client got answers about her next steps for her career, and some knowledge about her galactic lifetimes. The higher (vibrational) version of herself that came through also tied their galactic experiences with her current choice in career. They are both the same soul, however one aspect of the soul spoke to another, through the other, to provide answers to the other aspect's questions. The reason the Lemurian version could tell my client more about herself is because she is of a higher frequential resonance than my client. She carries all of my client's memories, even though it seems like the Lemurian version lived in the past, if you consider linear Earth history. It's all going on now, in a constant "now" moment. Communication between the versions of us is possible with intention. Intention sets the energy connection of who you will speak with. Our soul remembers every lifetime! Our memories from any lifetime can be used to advise us in our "now" moment. Our highest-selves have ascended this human reality in some location of space time, and most of them have consciousness that transcends space and time. If you find out that you already ascended the density of 3D Earth in a "past life," and have come back again, maybe you have come back to help others ascend. But first you must remember who you are (an eternal being of Source) as you navigate the 3rd density once again. And it is possible that a soul wants to experience ascending again, but in a different way. That is the quantum of a soul's journey. There is no version of us that is higher in value. Our higher selves are not better than us, they **are** us! And I can tell you with 100% confidence that I have never had a client doubt that contact was made with a higher vibrational version of themselves when it happens. There is recognition once the client investigates their subconscious about who it is they are communicating with during a session.

Sometimes, in a session, the client will have another being from a higher dimension come through to assist them. It is not always a higher version of the client that 'steps up' to answer questions. This I have no control over as the hypnotist. Neither would I want to because souls communicate with each other in the highest realms to decide, for the client's highest good, who is best to come in. The client's part in that decision is on the soul level, again, the quantum, where aspects make these choices. The soul of the client may agree to have another soul answer their human-form questions. I have come to believe that the decision of what a spirit will reveal in session has been decided before I even begin hypnosis. They get together with my soul (my higher-self), and craft an experience that will best serve the client. Once I merge my energy with the client's energy during the pre-talk session, my higher-self "downloads" to me the questions I will ask, using my intuition. If a soul other than one of the client's higher-selves is chosen to bring the messages during a session, sometimes it takes a few minutes for the client to recognize the soul. I ask a lot of questions to get clarity about who we are talking to. Usually the client does start to resonate with the energy of the one who came in, and soul recognition happens. The memory of who that soul is returns for the client. I have used quantum healing hypnosis as a method of attaining communication with spirit for my clients, and myself. Understanding soul recognition (frequential harmonics) has allowed me to believe in the method, and help others understand how it works. Not that I can say I understand completely how it works. Probably not even close. The quantum is still a mystery for me in so many ways. I continue my exploration of it.

    I have purposefully been working with spirit communication techniques since my early 20's. I had a great mentor back then who suggested I start the process of spirit communication using animal totems. He lent a book to me by Ted Andrews called Animal Speak. This method of communication with spirit includes basic concepts compared to channeling higher dimensional beings, but no less effective, and a softer starting place in my opinion. The method is simple. I would notice the animals and birds in my environment, especially the ones that directly crossed my path, and look them up in the book for possible meanings of why that animal "showed up" for me. What could be the communication of this animal spirit appearing to me? Then I would locate the animal's description in Animal Speak to find the possible messages it was bringing and derive meaning of its appearance for myself. For example, if I was starting a new project at work and a Robin or many Robins landed on the railing next to where I sit, or became visible through my window at the moment I looked out, I could associate that bird totem (message from spirit) with a "twelve" timeframe for my project from start to finish (usually twelve months, but it could be twelve weeks, or twelve years). The association is; Robins tend to stay in one place all year (twelve months) where food is plentiful. Robins also have red in their feathers. Red is supportive of kundalini (creative) energy. That bodes well for my project. And another aspect of Robin that is helpful to know in comparison to my project is that Robins don't typically fight for territory like a Blue Jay will. Robins defend their territory with their birdsong. The Animal Speak book tells me that this reflects a need to 'sing my own song' if I wish to have new growth, and not worry about competition. The blue of Robin eggs supports the throat chakra, also associated with singing and speaking your truth. As you can see, much meaning and communication can be gained by paying attention to animals and birds that cross your path. I've expanded this kind of communication with spirit to include insects, lizards, trees, clouds, weather and pretty much all of nature because nature and its creatures are vehicles for spirit communication. After some years of this, I found that I am able to know the meanings of the nature totems by the energy signatures I feel from them. Especially if I notice them while I am thinking about something concerning a decision in my life. Say I'm having a difficult time emotionally and I look into the sky and see a dragon shaped cloud. That is a spirit message to conjure my inner dragon, and/or that I'm being guided and protected by strong forces. It's about divining gentle messages or hints, asking questions, and getting answers without trying the direct communication "spoilers" of how the whole thing will turn out (i.e., going to a psychic for answers). Why know before experiencing? And these communications bring about the feeling/knowing that I am always supported by universal forces. I know that I am never alone in my life. Universal forces send a spirit totem when I ask for messages. It's very reassuring to know that the universe always cares about my wellbeing and supports my life plan. The universe also sends you intuition and spirit messages when you are in danger, or are 'off course' with your life plan. Nowadays you don't need a book to do this (although I highly recommend Animal Speak if you are new to this method of spirit communication). If you prefer, you can Google "what's the spiritual meaning of dragon," or whatever nature totem you encounter, and you will get many interpretations from several sources. Feel into the results of your search and you will find the meaning that best applies to your question. If you decide you want to know what a certain kind of bird is telling you, be specific. Searching for 'bird' in general will provide communication from spirit, but if you key in a specific *type* of bird, then the communications become more specific for you. The most important key word to add while doing a Google search like this is "spiritual." I have found that searching animal names without adding "what is the spiritual meaning of" in front, brings about scientific discussion more so than the spirit communication of the animal.

Now let's talk about intuition. What are 'the clairs'? Humans have given names to the various ways we communicate with spirit that are in addition to the collective agreed upon about five senses: taste, smell, touch, sight, and hearing. These names begin with a 'clair' and end with something referring to the "extra sense" that is being used. Communication with spirit using these 'extra' senses has been called extrasensory perception, or ESP. The spiritual community refers to these senses as part of our intuition. You have to look 'within' to 'intuit' what spirit is communicating, or use your 'internal senses.' Examples are: clairvoyance (seeing what most people can't see), Claircognizance (automatically knowing something without experience or evidence, also called clear-knowing), clairaudience (hearing spirit directly in your mind or hearing the echo of past/future events). There are more that I did not list, and you may search them on the web. Each one of us has the potential to use "the clairs" if we want to and as long as our soul has not put in-place something in the life plan that prevents it. Yes, you have all these abilities on the soul level, and more; however, there may be a reason why you wanted to subdue some or all of them for a while, as you live your life plan. Then, as you purposefully take action to raise your vibration, your soul allows you to realize these abilities again. It goes back to the math equation $1+ \_ = \_$. If you add something to your original energy field that lifts your frequency high enough, the clairs activate within you. If we all came in at birth with our clairs wide-open, there would not be much point in experiencing in 3D. I believe this is why most of my clairs were not open until recently. I had a bunch of self-discovery to do, paired with increasing my consciousness (frequency), before I could communicate more directly with spirit using my clairs.

You may experience your clair abilities in a different way than I do mine. Say we both have the ability to see visions, or clairvoyance. My clairvoyant objects (what I am seeing that no one else sees) may come to me in dreams (when my thinking brain is off) or just after waking, or when I start to fall asleep. You might see clairvoyant objects in your waking hours. Some object examples: people, places, events, or symbols; like a rose. If you are not suffering from an extreme illness or using mind-altering drugs, you can learn to trust these spirit communications as you become more comfortable receiving them. Some people use mind-altering drugs to get to states of consciousness where they can tap into spirit communication. I do not have experience with these methods, and therefore do not judge them nor recommend them.

I do suggest playing with your ability if you have difficulty trusting it. Lighten up and have fun with the clairs. For example, ask your higher-self, the angels, or a deceased loved one to send you a clear sign that your clair is real. Ask them to send you a rose. Be specific about the color and smell of the rose you are asking for. Then let go of thinking about the rose. Go on with your business. You may later see a rose in your mind when not thinking about it (clairvoyance), or smell a rose suddenly when there are no roses in your environment (clairalience). If you are not quite ready to fully experience your clair ability when you ask, spirit might make it so you find an actual rose in your environment, or someone gives you the rose the same day or within several days. This is still spirit communication. You set the intention, spirit hears you, and then spirit finds the best way (they know what you can handle) to let you know they heard you by responding with your rose. Another example is when you ask spirit to find you a parking space while you are on your way to some destination. Maybe your destination is usually crowded and you hate searching for parking. You ask the universe to provide a parking spot for you. Once you get to the lot, you may "see" where you need to go in your mind, and when you follow that intuition, the spot is there open for you. Or, you may know which direction to go (claircognizance), and you find the spot easily. Eventually, if you play with your abilities to communicate with spirit, you will notice much more direct communications from them. Like the time I was playing Trivial Pursuit with my husband's parents about twenty years ago. My husband and his parents are/were (his father passed) brainy people. I'm not especially good with trivia. My husband chose me to be his partner in the game. Great, no pressure there! I was very concerned then about letting people down or appearing to be stupid. I remember setting the intention to remember history. I was good with movies and music, so I had a decent chance of getting some questions right. I remember getting a card to name a place where some event in history happened. I had no clue what the event was, nor the place. Suddenly, and just before my time ran out to answer, the name of the place sprang out of me. I didn't consciously know where this place is, yet the name rolled out of my mouth! You should have seen the look on my father in law's face. I would have laughed if I were not trying to conceal the fact that the answer was not really mine. I thought it was some kind of weird accident on my part, but I didn't want to admit it. Or was it my answer, from another aspect of me that heard my intention and responded through me? Was the answer given directly to my brain by another spirit, to assist me because I did not want to appear stupid in front of my family? I don't know. But I was grateful for the assist, whoever gave it to me.

One last example. About five years ago, I was walking out the door to go grocery shopping. I heard in my mind, "take an umbrella." I don't know if this would be classified as claircognizant or clairaudience, but I heard a voice that wasn't mine, and so I guess clairaudience. I was not freaked out because I did not recognize the voice as spirit communication at the time. I thought maybe it was my own brain being overly cautious with advice. That day was warm and sunny. I did not see any reason to bring an umbrella. I realized, after my shopping was done, that it was a spirit communication. Right before leaving the store, a heavy rainstorm began, complete with thunder that rocked the ceiling of the store. I'm not too sure I would have left the store any sooner if I had brought the umbrella. Me and some other store patrons waited in the doorway/lobby for the storm to calm down before leaving. I do know I would have gotten less wet when I did leave to put the groceries into my car if I had the umbrella! That singular experience was my tipping point to trusting spirit communication. I can't say what needs to happen for you to believe in yours. Practice helps the process.

I will share further about the types of spirit communication that I have developed. My journey of learning how to provide a quantum healing session started with Dolores Cannon's method; Quantum Hypnosis Healing Technique, and progressed with Candace Craw-Goldman's program; Beyond Quantum Healing. Certifying in these techniques led me to know some of the methods of hypnosis, but then I needed lots of practice. I conducted sessions for friends, volunteers and family at no charge, and eventually started my paid business practice called Quantum Explorations, after growing my skills for several years. I noticed when starting practice sessions that my "clairs" were opening up more. Now that I have been practicing hypnosis for nearly six years, several of my clair abilities have opened all the way up. Meaning, I can use them at-will. Looking back through my earliest memories in childhood, I've always had strong empathy (clairsentience), and *sometimes* I experienced episodes of claircognizance. Now it's different. Working with universal energies using quantum hypnosis techniques has opened the gates for several of my clairs. I still experience only occasional instances of clairvoyance. I have my theories about why that one is not readily open for me yet. But, my claircognizance is off the chart, as are clairsentience, clairtaction (reading the energy of objects), and the ability to smell spirit energy (spirits give you a scent you will recognize as theirs, or a scent that is symbolic of certain events) called clairalience. I suspect that working with high frequency energies during quantum healing sessions has caused a resonance in me with those energies and increased my frequency, which in-turn activated my intuition more. You can open up your intuition too if you decide you will. Practice makes perfect and start by **not** telling yourself you are imagining things when one of your clairs activates.

    Our intuitive abilities (the clairs) are tools, gifts that our soul gave us to use in navigating life. It is comparable to demigods getting gifts from the gods. We are Source, yes, but in this dimension, we are Source energy in human forms. Our consciousness is not Source-level consciousness yet. We are on our way to that again, and this we call ascension. Why not use the tools our souls bestowed upon us now to help guide us in our creation process of happy/healthy lives while on our way back to Source? If you are willing to embrace your newly discovered abilities, then you can work with spirit to attain higher knowledge, wisdom, guidance, trust in your life path, and the feeling of safety while interacting with other humans. You will be able to feel, know, or sense when danger is around you; situational, relationship, or threats to your physical health. You will be able to intuit if someone does not have your best interest in mind, is angry with you, feels loving toward you, etc. The "gut feeling" is a clair. It's intuition. It also works with animals of all kinds, which is very cool if you love animals as I do. Your intuition will guide you to your truths. All truths are true for someone. It's YOUR truth you should be interested in because following that leads you to be on your highest timeline. For example, someone may tell you about this awesome beach destination and claim it as the best place to go for vacation. That is their truth. You may not like the beach and hot weather. Maybe your truth is that a ski trip on the top of a cold mountain feels better for you. You get where I'm going. A better example. The mainstream media news. I don't recommend watching it because it's usually all bad news, but in this example, you watch to get updates on issues that are important to you. How do you know that the story you are hearing is true? If you use your intuition, it is like a lie detector, and you will either feel truth or falsehood, or maybe feel neutral. You may know something is true right away when you hear it broadcasted. Or maybe you consult with spirit and they tell you some part is true but not all, it's all true, or it's all false. If none of those work for you, your body is also a good lie detector. It senses your truths and gives you physical feelings accordingly. Bad feeling in the body, not true. Good feeling, true. Neutral feeling, could be true and it doesn't really matter for you which way you believe.

One final thing about intuition and spirit communication that is important to share. Social conditioning. Social conditioning happens for all of us as we grow from infancy. We are born into a society complete with parents (or whomever raises us), relatives, and the people within that society that are our teachers, librarians, doctors, casual acquaintances, ministers, friends, enemies, store managers and neighbors. There is also usually a set of rules within the society that dictate right and wrong behaviors (laws). All of these outside influences play a role in shaping our realty. They influence our perceptions of life, what is good and bad, right and wrong, and they shape our beliefs. This is called social conditioning. It's neither good or bad, it just is, and you agreed to it when you chose the body you incarnated with and the family you would be born into. Right. So social conditioning effects whether we embrace our intuitive abilities, the clairs, or if we reject them. If we reject them, we usually shut them down. In other words, if you are told so many times that the spirit visiting you as a child is just in your imagination, or your 'imaginary' friend, then you might start to believe that and stop having the spirit communication because you no longer believe it is real. Once we close our minds to something, the thoughts become reality and we manifest that reality. Children are usually very open to spirit communication because they have not been talked out of it yet. Especially babies and toddlers. They just came from the spirit frequency and so it feels natural for them to keep interacting with spirits. Some children have the unfortunate experiences of being accused of lying and being punished, or accused of being possessed by evil. Those may never open their intuition back to spirit communication again for fear of retribution or going to hell. The other cause for shutting down intuition is past life traumatic experiences. I've had several clients discover during a quantum healing session that they were persecuted for using their intuitive abilities. Think of the Salem witch trials. For myself, I discovered during hypnosis that I had a life as a Russian woman about 500 years ago. I used herbs and created medicines for people in my town which were effective for most of their ills. The spiritual leader of my town felt that my power to heal was a threat to him (due to religious coercion). He had me outcaste from the town, and threatened any parishioner that went to me for help with the same fate. I was old and widowed at the time I was cast-out. I did have a shelter to live in, but my ability to find or grow food for myself was limited. I had relied on the town peoples' exchanges of food for medicine to survive before being caste out. Some of the town's people still came to me in secret and brought food. But mostly I was starving and cold. It wasn't a pleasant way to live out my final years, and I was lonely. As a result, my foray into using herbal medicines in this lifetime happened in my forties. I had witnessed the failures of Western pharmaceuticals and decided to abandon them in favor of herbal and natural remedies for ailments. Not 100% abandoned, but let's just say I haven't been to a primary doctor in over seven years. I consult with homeopaths or make up my own treatment plans using my intuition and knowledge of herbs. I would have never known about that lifetime if it were not for spirit communication. I had strong feelings about not using certain medicines, so I stopped taking those medications (like amphetamines, for ADHD, that screwed up my neurological system for years). The other spirit communication I used is a quantum healing session. If you feel fear about developing your clairs, maybe you too have had a lifetime where social conditions punished you for using your abilities. It is possible, that is all I'm saying. Or it may be social conditioning in this life is the culprit. Our intuition is natural and it is our right to develop and use, no matter what anyone else says. Many people feel their own power is threatened when an individual or bunch of individuals stop coming to them for advice, leadership, or permission to do things. These power-hungry people will cast all kinds of dispersions at those that use their intuitive powers. Well, I say let them say whatever they want! If they don't put food on your table nor pay your bills, what do you care? Live your best life.

5

Timelines, Life Plans, and Soul Contracts, Oh My!

I am going to apologize in advance for the length of this chapter. I tried writing about these concepts separately before concluding that these concepts are too entwined for me to discuss them independently. I will start with timelines and you will notice the other terms mingled in with that discussion. I promise to describe life plans and soul contracts more deeply as we go along.

    A timeline for life, for your incarnation, is created by you (within the consciousness of the oversoul) and your team of guides. Together, you plan out a timeline for incarnation which establishes **when** the events of your life will happen in the life plan that you also created before you were born. Big events, minor events, and every kind of experience in between are plotted out along the timeline for your life. The timeline of events is established with your life plan. It is put in place to ensure that certain experiences will match up with the life plan, because your oversoul wants you to experience in a certain way, in steps. The plan is working on soul-growth issues that maybe it has never worked on before or has not mastered yet within <u>your</u> level of consciousness. To make the plan effective in this effort, events must happen at specified points during your lifetime (on the timeline). For example, you may not run if you have not learned to walk, and so the effects of events scheduled on your timeline build upon one another. I believe this is why 3D Earth has the illusion of linear time because it allows us to build our wisdom and interpret meaning more easily as they unfold 'one at a time.'

    In your soul plan, you may have included the intention for the lifetime, 'learning to be compassionate.' Your oversoul wants to experience opportunities **to be** compassionate through you, and so it will include many chances to do that. A timeline of events for that particular experience, 'learning to be compassionate,' usually includes difficult experiences with other people and animals. During those early difficult experiences that happen on your timeline, you may feel like a victim. Someone has hurt you, or you witnessed someone hurting someone else. As you go along the timeline, you may come to realize that people struggle as you do, and sometimes they are hurtful because their energy is expressed outwardly, toward you or someone else, but their actions are not really about you or the other injured party. The actions belong to the person who is hurt caused by the feelings of the person. You may even find yourself feeling compassion for the hurtful person because you can empathize with their pain. You look closer and notice they are part of Creation, just like you are, and they are behaving badly because they are in pain. The next time someone else comes along with hurtful behavior, you will be able to avoid them or set boundaries with them because you see the pain, but you also know it is not yours to fix nor account for, and you move past this point of your timeline largely unaffected by the other person's pain while holding compassion for them.

At the level of consciousness which most humans bring to life on Earth, we need many experiences of something before we **real-ize**, use real eyes, about that something regarding ourselves and others. A timeline including repeated opportunities to have these experiences until we do realize the dynamic we want to master in the life plan is how we get there. Once humans can release the role of 'victim' and move into their personal power, compassion for those who agreed (in the soul contract with us) to harm us in some way can be understood.

The timeline includes a series of events and experiences that you will *most likely* encounter. Like with a project; there is a start, some kind of middle (turning points where life changes considerably), and an exit point to a timeline with a human. The timeline that we plan before birth is kind of structured in this way. Most of us include within our timelines several possible 'exit points' (points of physical death) during one incarnation. The oversoul gives the aspect, you, several chances to get out of this life if you wish to. Usually, these decisions to exit are not made by you or me on a conscious level, but on a subconscious level. When a human takes an exit point, it is following communication with the oversoul on the astral plane (usually during sleep) and the decision to leave life is made. The exit point appears to be an accident; a drowning, a drive-by shooter hits someone that isn't the target, you overdose on your medication or take one that you are severely allergic to, you die from an illness, a car accident, it could be any cause.

The interesting thing that I discovered practicing hypnosis is that once you leave your physical body, you are given the choice during the life review to change the decision, and you can be inserted right back into your body at a point in 'time' right before the incident where you left your body. If this happens, it is likely you will not remember making that choice, and your memory will be only of having an accident, or recovery. This means you changed your mind to accept that exit point, and you will have other opportunities to leave your body on the timeline you are currently on. It gets confusing, I know! But I'll tell you from experience that the one timeline that we start with includes lots of possible alternate timelines that we can shift to as we go through life.

We make little shifts all the time. We go from the current timeline to a higher one (vibrationally), then we may dip down to a lower timeline if we start thinking about past experiences and want to work through issues, and then we may shift back up to the timeline we started on or go higher. Timelines are opportunities to have experience in this thing we call life. They shift with us to give us experiences that are in accord with our current level of consciousness. I find it best not to judge the timeline I find myself experiencing because whatever is appearing as an experience for me is exactly what I need for soul growth. I do not see this life as a 'one shot' thing. I know that I can live it over and over again, changing my choices, and gaining more wisdom from it, if I choose to. And, there are infinite other 'lifetimes' to illuminate with my consciousness when I'm done focusing on this one.

It helps me, when I use this broad perspective of Creation and incarnation, to not to be too serious in my current life focus. The broader perspective allows me to play more, be gentler with other people and what they are experiencing, and realize that any one experience is not the end of my soul's journey even if I should die from it physically. The 'final exit point' that we decided upon before birth, **can** be altered by us as we raise our consciousnesses. The original timeline that we start on at birth is flexible, like clay. What you choose to experience during the conception of your life plan is probably not going to be the ultimate set of experiences that you have had by the end of your actual lifetime. You may respond to events differently than you thought you would while making the original timeline. Timelines vary in experience by frequency (vibration over time). Raise your frequency, and you may shift to a 'higher' vibrational timeline. A higher timeline is easier to live. You experience less active fear and judgment of yourself and others while you are living a higher timeline. Moving up to a higher energy timeline serves as the springboard for going to the next highest timeline. Your **reaction** to every event along your timeline can alter the experience of the next event, and even shift you to another timeline altogether.

Before we incarnate, a pre-birth plan, or life plan, is created by the oversoul. The life plan is created by the soul to ensure that the aspect of itself will have certain experiences during its incarnation. This life plan sets the 'timeline' of the aspect's life events. Each one of us is an aspect of our soul's overall energy. You can think of the life plan and timeline of events as our destiny that **we plan** before we are born, but we as humans do not remember doing it. I know, I repeated that information while saying it in another way. I find that repeating intricate concepts using alternate language helps to internalize an understanding of the concept. Timelines and life plans are topics that can twist the brain the further I try to discuss them. They are quantum topics and not for those unwilling to dig deeply into the meaning of life. Creation itself is what I am discussing while I talk about God/Source, the hologram, incarnations, and realities. Once again, I can give you only the information that I have come to know, flawed and incomplete. Any belief I express is a model of my consciousness understanding of this form, Sue Beckley. I will never suggest that my models are the complete understanding of what is possible to know during the human experience. I hope that this information can help you understand life, as it has helped me to do, and that you will hold space for the repetitive nature of my discussions here.

The word 'timeline' is used to describe our experiences as a progression of events, but, the quantum nature of dimensional reality is not linear, and so there are many timelines surrounding any one event. The current timeline that you are on leads to the next event, and depending on your reaction to the event, it is possible to shift from one timeline to another. It may be a very subtle shift, in which case you may not notice a change or the change you do notice is small. A massive shift may occur in you after which you will find yourself on a much higher timeline; which is referred to as a quantum leap in reality. Every event on a timeline can trigger multiple reactions in each individual. Each reaction dictates if the person stays on the current timeline, or moves to an altered version of it. As the probabilities converge concerning what you will experience next, you may feel that something is going to happen for you, and yet you have no idea what is coming. You feel the energy moving closer to you. This is an opportunity for you to shift the timeline that you are on if the feeling is not good. Shifting consciously requires you to be aware of the choices you are making in the now moment. More on that later.

The soul's original timeline may shift/change a little bit from the time of birth, a lot, and if the aspect goes through life completely unaware that the events in front of them are a result of their choices, the aspect will then experience much of what was placed into the original life plan and think the events are destined and unalterable. It does matter if you shift or not. Your soul wants to have experiences. If you do shift, which most of us do many times while here on Earth, then that is a bonus for your soul. I chose to present a model for you of how it all works for you to know that you have choices, and you can shift your timeline.

What do I mean by "reaction to a life event?" There are *so* many possibilities for human reaction, or non-reaction, to any given event on a timeline, that infinite variations of timelines exist as potentials, from the moment of birth to physical death. In other words, the soul knows itself enough to anticipate how it *might* react to certain events, but it does not know when the timeline is created **exactly** how the human personality (the soul aspect) will react to the events, and therefore the primary timeline contains many variation potentials. Infinite variation potentials. The timeline we stay on or shift from is contingent on our reactions to the life events. It can be as simple as I went down road A instead of road B (my reaction to the event of going on a trip somewhere), or it can be a complex reaction as leaving a spouse that is abusive after they hit you for the fifth time. Every life event carries meaning for you, and that meaning is unique. **No two people experience a life event in the same way.** Each has its own physical, emotional, and mental reaction. I have said this before and it bears repeating.

Consider a Christmas parade. Each child and adult attend because they are either forced to attend or want to attend. Usually, the desired outcome is to obtain some holiday cheer (uplifted emotions) by attending the parade, having fun experiences with your family, being close to other people with the same agenda, or some combination of these. What happens? Some children have a great time, other children have a miserable time, some are busy on their phones and don't notice the parade much at all and they are happy doing that, some children meet other children they have never met before and they play together while oblivious to the parade, and the list goes on. Then you consider all the possible reactions to the event that the parents might have; trying to keep track of their children when they walk off somewhere, enjoying the parade with the children, meeting another person and having a great conversation, remembering that they left the stove on and worry the whole time of the parade that the house might burn down, etc. Mix adult reactions up with the reactions of the children, throw in whatever is happening with the parade members, add a touch of city police influence and maybe some animals that people brought with them, and what do we have? The mathematical potential for reactions to this event, the Christmas parade, is massive. And we never know how we will react to events until we participate in them. Every single person at the Christmas parade will have their own unique experience and their unique reactions.

We discussed differing reactions to events. Now I will cover the **intensity** of reactions to events. The intensity of the personal reaction to experiencing also factors into timeline shifts.

Please review these addition math functions:

1+ 0 = 1
1+ .1 = 1.1
1+ .4 = 1.4
1+ .8 = 1.8
1+ 1 = 2
1+ 2 = 3

For this illustration, the one at the left of the plus signs indicates an event. It could be any example of an event. What is added to the event, is the intensity of your reaction to the event. You could say, for example, that going out to eat ice cream (1, the event) could have a (+.1) reaction, and going to a concert (1) to listen to your favorite band has a (+.4) reaction. Neither reaction is likely to change your timeline, but both *usually* have some physical, emotional, or mental effect on you, so your reactions are rated .1 to the ice cream and .4 to the concert. You partake in the event, you have the reaction, and the reaction determines if you stay on your current timeline, shift to a similar timeline, or even shift to a whole new timeline (+2). An event like going to a concert may elicit a (+.4) reaction from you, but a (+2) for someone else. The (+2) reaction would change that person's timeline in a bigger way, more noticeable. You could feel excited and joyful after the concert for a week (the +.4), while the (+2) person went out to buy a guitar and join a band after the concert. We both witnessed the same concert, however, our reactions to the concert were not the same.

The 1 on the left of every addition function is representative of an event on a timeline. What is added to the event is the reaction of the person experiencing the event. The total (sum) dictates what happens next, or the **version** of the timeline that the person will be on after the event + reaction. If a person responds to an event with no reaction (1+0=1), then the timeline will continue to provide the following event planned for that timeline, unaltered after the previous event.

For example, every time someone pulls their car out in front of my car in traffic, and I have to hit my brakes because of it, I get angry and start swearing. It's true, I have been known to get very angry during these events. We could rate that reaction at .5. On another day, someone pulls out in front of me in traffic, and I have to hit my brakes, but this time I only swear a little bit, feel mildly annoyed, and then switch my thoughts quickly back to where I am going. The second reaction could be rated .1. It carried less energy. During these instances, my timeline probably won't change a lot, $1+ .5 = 1.5$ and $1+.1= 1.1$, which means I stay on the same timeline that I was on before the event. But, the second event reaction might lead to **better experiences** moving forward. So, if I had engaged my usual reaction, to get truly angry and swear a lot, then later that day I might have had an encounter with someone being impatient with me at the grocery store, honking at me because I took "their" parking spot, for instance. But, since I reduced my reaction from .5 to .1, I have reduced the negative emotional vibration from my usual reaction, and I will still take that spot in the parking lot, but maybe the person who also saw the spot will not honk at me for taking it. The .1 reaction slightly shifts the next event (a less reactive competitor for the parking spot). The higher vibrational reaction, .1 instead of .5, means the probability that the next event I will experience on my timeline will be less intense.

    Let's now expand this driving example to demonstrate my highest vibrational reaction to someone pulling in front of me, causing me to hit my brakes. What if, while I'm driving, I pay more attention to the cars in front of me and next to me, and I notice someone speeding up in the next lane who looks like they might pull in front of me? What if, instead of maintaining my speed, I lay off the gas a little bit which allows 'speedy' to safely pull in front of me, and I don't even have to hit my brakes when she does this? Who knows, maybe 'speedy' is in labor and needs to get to the hospital quickly! So, in this highest reaction to the event of someone pulling in front of me (the experience), I rate my reaction as $1+ 2=3$ because I have chosen a reaction that is far higher in vibration than my typical reaction.

    This is **a quantum leap**.

    This highest reaction places me on a timeline that is decidedly easier for me and the people around me on that timeline. The people around me are more likely to be considerate of me because that is the energy I am giving out. They too are being a higher vibrational version of themselves, because we are on an alternate timeline of reality. The reactions I give to other people are energetically 'returned' to me on this new timeline because that is the way universal energy works. The return may not be witnessed immediately, but it is coming. We treat other people the way we wish to be treated because it makes us feel better, **and** the added benefit is that later on someone will treat us well when we need it. This positive energy exchange goes round and round, as long as the intention is not to get something in return. Expecting to get something in return for good behavior would be manipulation. Universal forces will respond to manipulation by sending you that same dynamic. Goodwill (given freely), being the highest version of yourself because you like the way that feels for you, these are the types of reactions to situations that will shift your timeline to one where life is enjoyable, much less stressful, and to one of personal power.

There is a shift of consciousness that I went through during the final version of the driving example. Instead of paying sole attention to my own goals for being on the road, I opened up my mind to pay attention to other persons' goals that were there driving someplace also. Even though 'speedy' might not have been in labor, she may have had some other reason to drive fast and shift lanes, and I was not judging it. I did not see the event, her potential to cut me off in traffic, as a personal insult. And even more importantly, I cared about my emotional state, to feel peaceful, and so I chose a reaction to 'speedy' that allowed me to feel peaceful. After the event and my reaction, the energy of my reaction might have been so high that I receive notice from my husband that he already stopped at the grocery store, and I was free to do whatever I wanted to next, instead of having to go shopping, as planned. It sounds crazy, but our reactions to events determine what the next event we experience will be like. Who knows! Changing from angry to peaceful may even have put me on another timeline altogether. I may have gone for ice cream instead of shopping and met the future editor for this book instead of looking for a parking spot at the grocery store and getting a horn honked at me. If there is such a thing as luck, we make our own. We could say that this example describes karma. Like naming God, it doesn't matter what you call it, as long as you understand how it works!

Events in life are planned by souls to elicit a reaction from their incarnated selves. If there is no reaction after one event, then the event, or something very similar to it (the dynamic), is repeated until there is a reaction. If the new reaction is high vibrationally, then the timeline experience gets easier. And when I say reaction, I don't mean it is always a physical reaction. Sometimes the reaction is emotional, sometimes it is physical, mental, or a combination. It can be all three. We go through the veil of forgetting (purposeful amnesia) when we are born and so we forget that we planned all of these events for experience to grow our consciousnesses. This is how the soul seeks to expand itself while experiencing Earth. It is the method that we use to continually expand consciousness while embodied in a 3D world. Forgetting that we are aspects of Source, putting a timeline in place to help us remember (by choosing our highest reaction to events), and incarnating over and over again with opportunities to shift our timelines is how the soul enjoys expanding, within quantum fields, before merging back into Source (The All). Then we can spark back out of Source and do it all again, as a different aspect of Source. Life- plans and timelines are maps with highlighted destinations to use during these explorations of the soul. Choosing our highest reactions to events leads to more joy-filled destinations.

Our souls want to get to those.

We feel that calling.

Detours are no problem, but we can feel lost when we detour from the life plan. We think being lost is some kind of failure, but it is not. Feeling lost gives contrast with feeling on-purpose. No matter what has passed, the soul is always there to get the map back into your awareness. If you are willing to pay attention to the messages of the soul, you will be on track with your life plan even if you have no idea where you are going. Your next highest joy will lead you in the proper direction. Have you ever noticed a story about a person that did something for a large portion of their life, then found inspiration to do something else that seems very unlikely for them to choose, but the person expresses great joy about their decision to change? Following your intuition leads to quantum leaps sometimes. The potentials to change timelines are endless.

Timelines are for individuals and collectives. What I described above are examples of individual timelines (or **subjective** perspectives of experience). One person's timeline is **subject** to that person's reactions to events that happen during their life, and that one person is the main subject of the timeline. The collective of humanity also has timelines, and these seem to be as unlimited in number as individual timelines are. **Objective realities** (collective timelines) exist because more than one soul agrees to experience them. These timelines are created by **shared** beliefs and reactions to world events. For humanity as a whole, we agree about things like: water is wet; trees have limbs and sometimes they have leaves, but trees can have needles instead, the sky leads to outer space when you move away from the Earth, Earth has an ozone layer surrounding it which allows us to breathe air; yard grass is usually green but it can be yellow during the winter; people are born either male or female or both (hermaphrodites), humans normally have two arms and two legs, etc. The **objects** we agree to as being 'real,' are humanity's collective shared realities.

'Objects' in the framework of this discussion can also mean concepts. When we notice the objects that people don't agree on, it shows that there are many collective timelines other than just our subjective ones. One example of this is that there are collectives that believe and perceive the world to be round, and there are ones that believe and perceive the world to be flat. Is there a timeline where many humans experience the truth that the world is flat? Yes! And those people have evidence of it being flat. So, are the humans that are firm about the Earth being round incorrect? No. Both timelines exist. Both are experienced as being 'real' for the believers of each. Does this concept trouble you? Do you feel resistant to the possibility that there are many versions of Earth and you are only experiencing one slice of those possibilities? Note your reaction to my statements now, because at some point on your timeline, as you continue to ask questions and open your consciousness to ideas that transcend what you have known previously, you can then refer back to this current feeling. It may be resistance, and then shift to feeling happy that you have resolved the confusion about quantum realities! I would share what that feels like for me, however, you will experience it differently. Collectively speaking, the timeline where we all remember quantum realities (timelines) and choose the unity consciousness timeline of Earth; is going to be a massive turning point for humanity, an easier experience of Earth for all.

There are collective realities and timelines for groups that believe in anything you can think of. Some examples are groups that have been abducted by aliens; groups that believe there is a cabal of rich and powerful people controlling the rest of humanity for thousands of years on Earth; groups that believe it is possible to be taken over by entities that control their lives and make them do bad things; groups that think having lots of money is the only way to find happiness in life, groups that believe they can transform their physical bodies with their thoughts alone; groups that think baseball is the best sport in the world; and groups that think going to Comic Con is the highlight of their entire yearly experience; just to name a few. Within **those** groups, there is non-agreement, and that creates other timelines of collective reality. It makes me dizzy just trying to conceptualize the number of collective timelines that exist for humanity.

The only reason to consider collective timelines/objective realities, in my opinion, is to be mindful of what you are doing with your energy fields by participating within them. Each one of us is involved with multiple collective realities because we carry multiple belief systems within us. There is no judgment by God/Source of any collective reality because it's all human experience, and we expand through experience, so Source gets the benefit of any expansion we have. We have free will for a reason. How expansive would life be if it was dictated to us, what we were allowed to experience and what we could not? Humans have crafted a bunch of laws to make it easier to live and function within society, but those are not Source laws. Neither are the laws you find in religious texts. Those are man-made also. Can you imagine that all of humanity is capable of holding the same beliefs about life? I cannot imagine it. Not in the 3rd and 4th dimensions, especially. Even within the higher dimensions, individual souls have different beliefs. Souls do tend to contain more of the memory of Source the higher they go energetically, but before merging back with Source, they maintain their independent consciousnesses. Higher energetic being (HEB) soul collectives appear to be of one mind because their memories are very similar and more expansive in the understanding of the One.

Again, I would not worry too much about collective timelines at this point unless a collective you have chosen to participate with is draining your energy and you feel like you might not want to participate within that collective timeline anymore. This is your soul telling you it is time to move on from it. For example, you are part of the collective that believes it is important to be active in politics, and you are also part of the collective that believes it is important to vote during elections. You become aware that being active in politics is no longer exciting, you feel drained of energy or feel sad when you do it, and so you decide that you are not doing it anymore. You have just 'dropped out' of the collective energy and timeline of the group 'active in politics.' Political events will still be going on and you can witness them if you wish to, but you will not **be** part of that reality. It can appear to you as if politics do not exist at all if you decide not to witness politics being practiced. You have changed your personal, subjective timeline, but you probably have not changed the objective timeline of those who still believe it is important to be active in politics. This decision does not mean you have to give up being part of the 'voting' collective. If participating in that collective belief system does not cause you to stress, and you still believe in it, then there is no compelling reason to give it up. In this case, you may want to **touch** on the reality of political people when deciding which candidate you want to vote for, but that does not cause you to be **of** the reality of 'practicing political activism.' You touch it, briefly engage, and then release it again.

I will say this because it needs to be considered if you wish to stay on your personal highest timeline. DO NOT TRY TO PRY SOMEONE OUT OF THEIR COLLECTIVE BELIEF SYSTEM (OBJECTIVE) OR PERSONAL BELIEF SYSTEM (SUBJECTIVE) TIMELINES. **You are responsible and can only control your own decisions/reactions.** Even when we are talking about children. You may guide them. Tell them about your beliefs, and let them decide what beliefs are shared. If you try to pry someone away from their beliefs or change their timelines, or try to destroy a collective timeline that you believe is bad or wrong, then you are lowering your vibration and causing yourself stress without obtaining a result for the trouble. Changing someone else's reality cannot be done. Not to mention the damage that will result within your relationships if you try. The only way for a collective timeline to collapse and disappear is when no more people are participating in it. When all energy pulls away from a part of the hologram, that potential experience becomes dormant. It is not destroyed, because we cannot destroy any part of Creation. We light up parts for experience and then withdraw our energy from those parts when we are done with them. The only way for a personal timeline to change is when the individual in question reacts to their experiences in some way that changes it. You cannot do it for them no matter how much you love them.

Many humans have become aware of life plans (pre-birth plans) that we each create for ourselves. What is a life plan? Are they flexible or are they rigid? Are life plans 'destined' to happen, no matter what? Those are the questions I've been asking for years and will discuss in-depth later in this chapter. If you want to do some study about life plans, I suggest the books of Robert Schwartz, who brought the idea of pre-birth planning into the mainstream with the books: *Your Soul's Gift*, and *Your Soul's Plan*. I found the information contained in these books to be transformational for me in understanding why certain things in my life may have occurred. I used the information in Schwartz's books to set up a list of questions for myself, to discover meaning within my life events (mostly the troublesome ones), and then utilized hypnosis or meditation to derive my soul's answers about those life events.

I think that knowing why something happened is healing and cathartic for me, and important information for releasing the energy of events when the energy of them is painful. I found that I could forgive myself and others for past transgressions when I understood what I was supposed to learn from them, hold the highest thoughts about all people involved, and internalize the information about me that those events were set in place (by my soul) to teach me. Hypnosis sessions have taught me that once we find the **meaning** behind the events in our lives, we no longer have the need or desire to experience similar events. Anything we had planned within our timeline to experience in the future that resembles those lessons disappears from the timeline. In essence, you are on another timeline, and that is why the events disappeared. And that is very exciting! The old saying about learning from the past in order not to repeat it in the future comes to mind. We don't have to keep repeating the same experiences if we can figure out a higher vibrational way to respond to the events in our timelines. It is not the event itself that has the meaning, it is HOW WE RESPOND TO THE EVENT that our soul cares about. We assign meaning to events by the way we react to them. If someone tells you that you are ugly, are you assigning meaning that you **are** ugly, or are you assigning meaning that some person is projecting their opinion of you that does not matter to you?

    Every event that our soul planned is intended for the expansion of consciousness only. It cares not if we judge them to be good or bad. Remember, consciousness in human form is limited, and consciousness in higher vibrational dimensional realities is more expansive (no judgments). Humans judge, souls do not. Your soul wants to expand consciousness while in *human* form, or you would not be here having these experiences with timelines. It truly knows that you have all the tools you need to get through life and to choose happiness while you are doing it! We all came to Earth with the ability to respond to difficult experiences in an enlightened way because we are always connected to the oversoul. We came to remember who we truly are and to act as creators. We came with the power to change our timelines.

    My thought when beginning exploration of life plans was; if everything is already planned out for this life, then what's the point of efforting in life (trying to be better)? Why not just cruise through life and allow what is meant to happen, to happen? I think that's a fair question when considering destiny. But then, some very interesting information came to light during a quantum healing session I was conducting. My client wanted to know about her relationship with a man in her past, and why it never developed past a certain stage. It's the kind of thing a lot of people wonder about. Especially if you had really good times with a person, were very attracted to them, and have no concept of why the relationship ended. My client reported during hypnosis that the reason the relationship ended is that she had learned to stand up for herself at her job before the relationship got serious. She decided, while working at this job and dating the man, that she was not going to tolerate abusive behavior from her boss, and left the job to work in a healthier environment. This reaction to events with her boss, which she did for her benefit, expanded her awareness of self-value and self-love and simultaneously canceled out the need to continue the relationship with the man she was dating at the time. How are the two related, and is it good to change jobs and quit a relationship around the same time? We asked her higher self about that, and the HS reported; if she (the client) had stayed with the man in this lifetime, they would have eventually married. Once they were married, the good nature of the man would have changed over time due to his disappointment in his career (he didn't reach the level he was planning for in his work on that timeline), and so he would have begun verbally projecting his career disappointment onto my client during their marriage. The relationship would have become emotionally abusive. Her final takeaway from that part of the hypnosis session is that she 'voided' the part of her life plan to marry the man due to learning the lesson of self-love (protecting herself from abusive people) and self-respect when she changed jobs. She no longer needed to have the experience of being married to the man, and therefore they naturally lost interest in each other. The marriage did not happen. No conflict needed to happen for them to split. It happed organically, with no one being blamed for the relationship's end. I enjoyed hearing about that part. And finally, both of their timelines changed for the better due to her expansion.

When you hear the expression, 'take the high road,' it usually means doing so for yourself. But, taking the high road also helps other people. The client was interested in knowing how the man's timeline changed, so I guided her to ask his higher self for permission to access that information. Practitioners are taught not to encroach on another person's information without permission from their higher self/oversoul, during hypnosis. To do so is breaking the law of free will, breaking into someone's records, and I do not recommend it for any reason. We may ask for permission to access that information, and often it is given. Practitioners also ask the client, during hypnosis, for permission to pose questions to their higher self, about the client. That seems strange, to have to ask someone if we can talk to another version of themself. It is necessary for a quantum hypnosis session because we are dealing with separate aspects of the same being, and they have different levels of consciousness. Practitioners cannot assume that every slice of the soul pie is willing to know information about themselves, even if that information would be coming from the whole pie and the slice asked the questions. Also, not all questions are ready to be answered for the client when they ask, and so the client's higher self regulates the disbursement of information accordingly. The oversoul will not pre-emptively alter the timeline experiences that the client will have. It gives only what is necessary and useful at the moment point.

Back to my client's query about her ex-boyfriend. Usually, if the person asking questions about another person has good intentions, the higher self of that person will grant permission to know the answers. I'm so glad we asked about the status of the ex-boyfriend because we discovered that his timeline improved a lot due to their relationship breakup. His soul was no longer bound by their soul contract to be together, to experience career disappointment. The resulting bitterness and abusive behavior that he would have experienced, his reaction to the events on that timeline had their contract remained unaltered, was no longer necessary for his aspect to experience. His aspect was then free to choose a higher timeline. I am happy to tell you that he is successful in his career, has a family, and, his higher self reported that the man is content in his life. My client and I were thrilled to know that her choice to love herself more resulted in another person realizing their self-love. This is an example of how the quantum works. Yes, there is what you can call destiny, **and** it is flexible. You are the driver and determiner of your destiny. This is true from before birth, and while you are living this life.

Our life plans contain agreements to experience certain things with other souls (soul contracts), for one reason or several reasons. Soul contracts pertain to one *possible* shared timeline together. If, at any moment point, one or both of the people involved with a soul contract changes themselves significantly, or gain the wisdom of the contract's intended events before the shared events come into reality, then the contract is unnecessary, voided, and the souls involved are free to pursue another timeline of events (like in the example with my client and her ex-boyfriend).

It is possible to avoid an event on your timeline if you know about it ahead of time. An example: a girl went to a psychic who read her energy field (timeline) and told her she was going to have a baby at a certain age, and the girl didn't want to have a baby at that age. She took steps to make sure that she would not have an accidental pregnancy around that age specifically and continued being careful to prevent pregnancy until she was ready to have a baby.

     Another example: I keep dreaming about a guy that I don't know, and I get a strange, unsettling feeling about him when the dream happens. It's like I know him even though we have not met. Then one night I'm out with my girlfriends, and I see the guy! He appears as though he is going to come over and talk to me, but I leave the scene and go to the bathroom with my girlfriends before he reaches our table. When I come out of the bathroom, the guy is not there anymore. Potential crisis averted. I could amend this example to show how connecting to the inner self will avert the same crisis. Maybe this time I do not have a specific dream, but I am out at the club with my friends and a guy shows up at our table looking interested in me. I feel, right away, that this guy has bad intentions for me. I do not know how I know, and that does not matter because I go with my 'gut feeling' and excuse myself from his attention. I keep my girlfriends close the remainder of the night, and we walk out of the club together, safely to our cars, and go home. **We do not have to be psychic** to know when something coming on our timeline isn't good for us. Our light bodies inform us when danger is coming. When we tune into that information; trust it, act upon it, or don't act, as prescribed by the feeling, knowing, sensing; then we move from one timeline experience to another, better one. I will own the judgment that avoiding harm is better. I think you will agree with me.

     The answer to destiny is yes, there is a general life plan in place when we incarnate, and soul contracts are also agreed upon to support life plans. What is a soul contract? A soul contract happens when two oversouls agree to have their aspects on Earth share experiences together during one incarnation. It may be a long-term experience or a one-time thing. For example; having a full relationship, or having one date together. Another example is when another person comes into your life to inform you about something, and then you never see them again. That information is necessary to you for something else you will experience on your timeline. The person that gave you the information did so because their oversoul agreed to meet with you in the time and space that they did. Soul contracts imply that we agree to do something important together, and it is important; what we do for each other. But, a soul contract does not imply that what we experience together has to be long-term. Someone may come up to me in the park and compliment my dress, which makes me feel good in a moment when I was not feeling so good. That interaction may not have been planned before my birth, but it could have been agreed upon by our souls because we were both planning to visit the park that day and the person's oversoul was asked by mine to help lift my spirits. The one giving the compliment was given the inspiration from their soul to do something kind and they followed the inspiration. Synchronicity, yes? I think the word 'contract' carries a heavier weight than using the term 'soul agreement.' Spiritualists these days want to avoid any term that implies subversion, probably because humanity is moving to remember states of personal power, and 'contract' suggests an unbreakable bond and loss of free will.

    I use 'soul contract' because it is the first moniker I have known to describe soul agreement. Either set of terms is useful if taken in the context with which they are intended. God is not going to come out of the sky and send you to some hellscape reality if a soul contract is broken. The person you agreed with is not going to be angry with you if the soul contract is broken either. As in the case of suicide, the other souls in the person's life know on a soul level that the person leaving Earth needed to do that for some reason. The aspects of the others in that lifetime may not understand why the person left, but their souls do understand. The person who completes suicide does not harm the timelines of the others due to breaking the soul contracts they have together. The others will shift to an alternate timeline that does not include the one who died. I chose this very emotionally weighty example because it happens a lot on Earth. Folks get confused that the one who dies by their own hand is somehow bad, wrong, mentally ill, and persecuting the ones they left behind. It is not for us to judge others in this way.

    This type of judgment is separation thinking and not unity consciousness. Although I am not advocating suicide, another perspective is that someone may have added a potential "exit point" in their life plan to end their incarnation by suicide. That may be one of their possible exit points on the subjective timeline. Think of how that experience, losing a loved one to suicide, can help others to grow their consciousnesses. The experience of self-inflicted death has numerous implications for the person choosing it and for the people that love that person. It allows the others to know they are resilient, to see chances to come together and help one another cope with the loss, have an experience of abandonment, and then come to the understanding that no one really dies. There are so many growth opportunities for the soul when something really disturbing happens on Earth like suicide. Soul contracts are agreements to the **potential** for experience. I'll give you another example. How do agreements to toxic relationships help your soul expand? Toxic relationships serve our soul because they help us identify that we (soul slices) are passing fears to each other, from one lifetime to another, and the patterns of fear we carry around with us attract other souls experiencing those fears. The relationship is toxic because two people play out their fear patterns and traumas together. Toxic relationships highlight fears and help us identify them, and then once we release the fears and step into our powerful true nature, the toxic relationship ends. Toxic relationships happen to benefit both parties involved.

"It takes two to tango."

If one soul slice is fear-free (like an ascended master or spiritually centered person) and another is riddled with old traumatic fear, they will not create a soul contract to be in a romantic relationship together. Probably, two such people will not be attracted to one another that way unless co-dependency is involved. The energy of each is too repelling to the other, like the same polarities of a magnet. Unless one is seeking wisdom from another. The two may contract to come together so that one may learn from the other how to release their fears. That situation is not a toxic relationship though. Another example of a toxic relationship where souls do agree to come together is within family units. I can talk to you about dysfunctional family dynamics with educated psychology terms because this is the place I started when I began my social work experiences. The more expansive view is that souls agree to come together in family units that are dysfunctional or toxic because they contain soul slices that are attempting to heal. As you may be aware, souls tend to incarnate in groups, multiple times together to work out these dynamics. These generational dynamics are usually not resolved within one lifetime. And, while one soul aspect is playing the 'bad guy' in one incarnation, it may be playing the 'good guy' in another. Souls like to swap roles. An example is that in this life as Sue Beckley, my father took care of me throughout my younger years, and then when he became older and physically challenged, I was his caretaker. I am also aware through an early hypnosis experience that my oversoul is also the same as my dad's father (my paternal grandfather who died one month before I was born). I will say that another way. During hypnosis, I discovered that I am also my grandfather on my dad's side. We are two slices of the same soul pie. My grandfather has an impressive personality. He is strong and intelligent, however, he tends to feel hopeless when life does not go as he imagines it will. I know that feeling. I have shared that feeling as evidenced by my ideations of suicide in this lifetime during periods when my life didn't go as planned.

In the lifetime as my grandfather, I coped with my hopelessness due to perceived poverty during the Great Depression by becoming an alcoholic. Maybe even before that because he came to America from Slovakia because he was convinced that he could be "anything he wanted to be in America." Lots of immigrants were sold on that idea. The reality that my grandfather experienced was becoming a shoe leather tanner in a factory. He may have started excessive drinking before The Great Depression, I am not sure about that detail. The point is that my grandfather and I, two slices of the same soul pie, both experienced hopelessness because our lives were not looking like the picture we imagined. My father's role with my grandfather is that he watched over him, taking his car keys away when grandpa was drunk in a bar, taking on my grandfather's wrath instead of letting him hit my grandmother, driving him to Rochester for cancer treatments when my grandfather could no longer drive. My dad took care of his dad. And he took care of me.

My dad's example of personal strength within a seriously dysfunctional family unit showed me that I can be strong also. He carved out a life for himself that contained many instances of joy. Yes, my dad struggled. Yes, he and my mother argued, screamed, and hurt each other emotionally because they were both injured and fearful people. They projected their pain out to each other, and the kids sometimes. My primary family unit was toxic much of the time, no doubt. I had reasons to want to leave this planet. My dad had reasons too, but he always pressed forward no matter what life brought. From what he told me, suicide was never an option because he always maintained hope that things would get better. That perseverance showed me that I can do it too. There were many instances of love within our family also. We focused on those more than the others which is why I was able to get past the desire to leave. My mother, despite her childhood abuse, showed expert resilience at times also. After my dad passed away, I had one more experience of hopelessness where life events spiraled downward for me and the people I love, all at once, and I wanted to suicide out of my Earthly experience. I made the plan to end my life and started to execute the plan. Then, at the pivotal moment when I was about to pull the trigger, I had a flash view of myself lying dead on the ground, and my loved ones seeing me that way. I stopped what I was doing immediately and put the gun away. Before that moment, I was trying to reach my dad energetically to ask for help. My vibration was too low at that time to reach him. I could not reach any of my guide team nor the angels it seemed. What I believe happened is that my dad heard my calls for help and enlisted an angel, or used his highest-self, to provide me with the image that shut down my plan to leave. He found a way to break through my desperation and contact me.

Me and my dad have been taking care of each other throughout several incarnations, switching roles, and working together to resolve fears. I have to say I think it is my turn to take care of him again, but when we communicate now, he assures me that there is no need to keep score. He tells me that love is love no matter how many times it is given. We will be together again when I'm done doing what I need to do here on Earth. My dad tells me that my mission is "big," but he will not illuminate what my soul's plan is for the rest of this lifetime. A large part of me believes that my plan moving forward is to share with other people how I got onto a nice timeline, and this is why I am writing the book. One final thought I will share about soul contracts comes from a session I did at the beginning of becoming a quantum healer. That thought is that we are all helping each other out. Even when it appears that one soul is harming another, the soul contract for the experience helps both souls to expand. Believe it or not, we are all One, and we remember this within the highest dimensions. The fact that we are also having individual consciousness experiences does not take away from our Oneness. It means that we are experiencing some separate reality illusions within different versions of the hologram of Creation.

Life plans and soul contracts are not rigid and can be changed at any time by the choices we make. I know, I said that before. It is very important information to know when learning about timelines. We decide how the timeline will go by how we **respond** to the events in our life. And this part of 'efforting' does not have to do with physical work. It has to do with efforting to know yourself as much as possible. To go within; on your own or with the aid of a practitioner, and discover what motivates you, how you wish to be treated, how you are treating yourself, how you are treating others, what the events in your life mean to you, and how you are perceiving the world you live in. This is where the most effort needs to be applied. Yes, we also have to make efforts toward whatever we choose to 'do' in life, or whatever we desire to learn and create. However, the internal work is the most important effort for the soul. We all have to pay the rent and eat. I share this from personal experience; if you save the bulk of your efforting for personal growth and development, anything you want to 'do' will be easier. You may choose to cruise through life, going from one event to another, scratching your head about why the same experiences keep showing up in your reality. It is a valid choice, and your soul will not be angry with you if you decide to cruise. Until you grow from the experiences your soul has designed for you, and apply them for your consciousness expansion, you will keep getting the same experiences. The experiences may be provided by different people or health issues getting worse, but the choice not to expand your consciousness will keep them coming and amplify them until you do shift. To ignore and cruise is to deny your soul the expansion it is seeking. Why go through the density (bullshit) of Earth's life if you are not getting anything out of it besides more pain? It is like a donkey being tied to a bar that goes round and round every day. Eventually, the ground beneath will become worn and rutty, and the walk will become harder for the donkey.

Next, I will share what I know about how to get to your highest possible timeline. This is what Abraham Hicks would refer to as manifesting your greatest joy. The quantum healing community has merged terms to call it manifesting your highest timeline. Whatever you prefer. We have timelines that are set in place from before birth, we can shift them, so let's get into how to choose higher timelines.

We are born with a certain frequency of the oversoul's energy. Everyone has a unique frequency, and many have similar frequencies which is why people are attracted to each other. Frequency is the term used to describe how fast we cycle through vibrations. If you have a high frequency, then you can pass through lower vibrations quickly. Say you are in a grocery store, and you are a high-frequency being. You are generally happy, your body feels good, and your attitude about life is mostly positive. You encounter a person that is not being high vibe, and that person is projecting her discontent about whatever, outwardly. People around the low-vibe girl in the grocery store notice her behavior. It's like seeing a rat in a food market, they stay away from low-vibe girl. Empathic individuals feel her vibe with or without noticing any outward behavior. But you notice her behavior, and for whatever reason, you allow it to affect your vibe. Because you are a person with a high frequency, it is likely that the effect you allowed from low vibe girl will pass quickly, because your high frequency allows you to go through cycles of vibration fast (the feeling of the vibration moves through you quickly). In other words, you can shake off low vibe girl's energy, and without alteration of your day. You go back to being happy again and forget the experience rapidly. If you are a being of lower frequency, then the vibrational effects from others (low vibe girl), or a sudden change in your vibration, will pass with more time. You will stay in the lower energy, longer. You may think she has 'ruined' your day.

    When we can hold happy/joyful thoughts about ourselves and our environment we experience higher vibrations (energy). If we continue a pattern of seeking the highest vibrations over time, we can increase our frequencies. We are not stuck with the frequency that we are born with. It can go higher, and it can go lower. We get to choose which way it goes by choosing our thoughts and reactions to experiences. For example, as a child and young adult, my parents allowed me to watch horror films. I knew nothing about their impact on my vibration because I was a kid. My parents didn't know either. I responded to horror films with extreme fear. I would have nightmares. After watching *Amityville Horror*, I couldn't walk past my kitchen windows at night for about a year. I would run through the kitchen at night, and not look at the windows for fear of seeing bright-red glowing eyes. As a young adult, I chose to stop watching horror movies because I did not like how I felt during and after, and the nightmares that would follow started including me and my family members. Watching horror movies decreased my vibrational energy because fear has a much lower vibration than joy, and my psyche could not tell the difference between what I saw in horror films and real experience. I started watching more family-themed movies, movies and TV shows that had action but little violence (I like action films), or shows that were inspirational. True story or fiction, it didn't matter. What does matter is the way each choice affected my energy fields. I have gotten to the point where I am not attracted at all to most of what other people find entertaining. I do not watch action films that much anymore unless there is an adrenaline rush without the violence. This is not a judgment, by the way. I am simply telling you my vibrational story and about one way that I raised my moment-to-moment vibrations and overall frequency. I also did it by reading interesting books and being around people that carry higher vibrations. And we all can figure that watching Gone With The Wind, The Texas Chainsaw Massacre, or the mainstream news is not going to increase vibration. Hanging out with your friend who is always telling you their story but never taking any action to improve their situation, just wanting to complain all the time, is not going to increase your vibration either. Do you get where I'm going with this?

    You are the only one who can increase your vibration, by hunting good stuff for you and paying very close attention to what is going right in your world, rather than focusing on the negatives. It doesn't mean we don't handle problems when they arise. We must. But continued focus on problems at the expense of joyful experiences keeps us trapped in lower vibrational energy, and it keeps your frequency lower too. When you pay attention to how you are feeling in any given moment, making positive decisions about who and what you spend your time with, then your vibrational energy will naturally increase. After holding your vibrations higher for a while, your frequency will increase. This results in the above situation of encountering a low-vibe girl a 'no residual effect' incident, because you throw off her energy like it didn't happen. If someone cuts you off in traffic and you avoid a collision, it's no big deal when your vibration is high. Your peaceful demeanor is unaffected. And how cool is that?

Consider Taylor Swift's song *Shake It Off*. In it, she is telling you her story of how she maintains her high level of creativity (she writes her songs), and how she maintains her successful attitude amid a ton of criticism from other people. She sings that she keeps "movin and groovin", and she "shakes it off" when people create stories about her. These "haters" don't change her or her life, because she does not let their low vibrational energies affect her high vibration. Or, if she is hurt by something she reads about herself, she "shakes it off" and continues to fashion her life on her terms. That is a high vibe! That is high frequency. And if I may use Taylor's example a little bit more, that is how we create success in all areas of our lives no matter what is going on around us. The higher the vibrations we can maintain over time, the higher our frequency becomes, and that is how we go to or stay on, our highest timelines. If you can do this, the bullshit will stop occurring on your timeline. You will feel a lot better.

We've discussed increasing our frequencies to be on our highest timelines. Let's visit the choice of decreasing vibration and lowering our timeline because it is possible to go lower than where we began from birth. Say you watch the mainstream media news a lot; daily, or multiple times per day, and you start to think that the world is terrible, and all people are power-hungry jerks that only do things to keep their power over other people or serve their own needs. If you choose to do this and disregard how doing this makes you feel, you eventually skew your vision of the world, of people in general, will align with lower frequency energies, and then it is likely you have lowered your vibration and frequency. If you choose to believe that you are going to experience breast cancer because 'many of the women in your family have had breast cancer,' and you hold that belief over time, you will lower your vibration and possibly *create* a self-fulfilling prophecy, realize breast cancer in your body, and lower your timeline significantly. A third example of how to lower your timeline is how you deal with stress and trauma.

If you take measures to decompress (exercise, pursue joyful activities and people), or you decide to go for counseling to deal with your emotions and beliefs about traumas, then you will likely not experience lower vibrational energy in your fields for long. You will work through these experiences and have a higher vibration by doing so. Working through trauma brings about the proverbial 'light at the end of the tunnel.' Hope is renewed even after the most dire situations if one is able to honestly process thoughts and emotions to heal from traumatic events. Healing is raising your vibration. But if you respond to stress and trauma with excessive alcohol use, not engaging in fun activities or exercise, hanging around by yourself feeling depressed, using drugs to alter your states of consciousness, or eating junk food all the time, then you are choosing to lower your vibration, and that over time lowers your overall frequency. When your frequency is lower, it takes longer for you to get over negative energetic experiences. They get stuck in your energy fields and before you know it, you have an accumulation of low energy swirling around your reality. It also attracts more negative experiences into your reality; those things waiting for you on a lower timeline to experience. Until you decide to "shake it off" and deal with the painful experiential energies and heal yourself. And once you start doing that, your timeline will contain lighter and more positive experiences. I've got a T-shirt for this. You know; been there, done that, got the T-shirt? I've been in the vibration of depression so many times I've lost count. It is possible to shift it because I am living proof. If I can do it, you can do it.

People who have raised their vibration and frequency can, and do, avoid certain elements contained in their original life plans. If they do not completely avoid an event that was planned that can be judged as negative, it may be because the event is part of a soul contract with another person who still needs to have the experience. But, the ones who have done the work on themselves will experience the event and respond to it much easier than the versions of themselves that didn't raise their frequency. Remember, higher frequency means we process lower energies more quickly! The person that improves their frequency recovers from (transmutes) negative experiences faster and can continue focusing on building their life to be what they want it to be.

Anita Moorjani wrote a book called *Dying To Be Me* that provides an amazing example of the above by sharing how she healed herself from terminal cancer. I found out about Anita's story while studying Wayne Dyer's work, and how he actualized his highest timelines. Wayne encouraged Anita to share her story because he believed it would help so many people to do the same thing for themselves. And it has. I highly recommend both authors if you are looking for ways to start changing your reactions to life, and focusing to discover, to live, your joy (which raises your vibration). In a nutshell, Anita realized that she was not living her greatest joy in life, she was living to meet other people's expectations of her, which caused her body to respond with the dis-ease we call cancer. Once her consciousness opened to another choice while she was in a coma, Anita decided to continue her life on Earth and start engaging in activities that she felt passion for. She changed her work, she changed her food, she started engaging in things she enjoyed but didn't think she had the time for in the past, etc. This increased her joy. The very act of deciding to do this during her coma had the effect of total remission of Anita's cancer. The other physical crises she had going on were healed as well after she chose to live in joy.

This concludes my discussion of timelines, soul plans, and life plans. If you want to be on your highest timeline, mind your vibration and frequency. Quantum leaps are possible, but it may be easier to aim slightly higher and keep stepping up to start. If you don't know where to start, find some inspirational stories of people's lives, and consider what they did. It's okay to be wherever you are on your timeline. Past choices are in another dimensional reality and cannot easily be changed from this reality, so don't criticize yourself for what you didn't know up until now. There's a great start, let go of self-criticism. That is an instant shift of your vibration. More on this in the Real Magic chapter.

6

All Truths Are True

The act of believing in something **creates** the reality of that something, which we then incorporate as part of our life experience. The spiritual interpretation of what I just said is; you have to believe it to see it. We light up parts of the hologram with our consciousness, and the parts we light up, the ones that become our realities, are decided by the beliefs we hold within our minds.

It is not easy trying to figure out why someone holds any concept as true, especially when all evidence shows that the majority of collective humanity believes in something else. I know. In my social work/counseling days, I encountered people with some interesting truths in my opinion. During my role as counselor, I had to have discussions with myself while considering if it was important to try to shift the client's truth (i.e. is it causing them self-harm or harm to someone else?). Questions like, "Is it something that is hurting my client's relationships," or, "Should I try to shift it with them because their life is in tatters and they are asking me to help"? Talk about moral dilemmas! This, by the way, is the biggest reason why I prefer doing a quantum healing hypnosis session with a client versus counseling. During a quantum healing hypnosis session, the client identifies and heals through their truth, not mine. What works for me may not work for them, and so it is **their** truth that affects their healing.

I'm just the one with the training and experience to get them **to** their truths, safely. And that feels much better for me. I believe that helping others find their answers is empowering for them. The best healers in the world cannot heal someone unwilling to shift. And that, my friends, requires trust in the practitioner. A client must trust you before they will tell you their truths.

Each one of us operates in **our** reality. You've heard that concept described maybe in a derogatory way, "that guy lives in his own reality." Like it's a bad thing. Each one of us also operates in collective realities. These collective realities are the manifestations of the collective timelines I spoke of previously, which are comprised of experiences paired with beliefs, reactions to experiences that shape beliefs more, and what happens next on the timeline based on the reaction to the previous experience. As you can imagine, all of that creates confusion and dissension about what 'truth' is in personal reality, and even more so when we pair personal reality with collective realities. Unless we choose not to participate in collective reality at all. I suppose it is possible in remote parts of the world or if you are very intent on using that perspective to live life. It seems to me that each one of us is shaped initially by someone else's truth, and then we find our own.

For example, think of a homeless person or a recluse who does not engage with anyone in the world with thoughts or opinions. That homeless person/recluse is not *completely* outside of collective human reality, because they still have to eat and drink to survive and if they get sick or too cold/hot they will die. But does that homeless person/recluse have the conscious awareness of still being within a reality where humans do certain things in certain ways? Some yes, some no. That person has their own belief about what reality is, and whatever perceptive and physical experiences are happening for that individual, **those are real for them**. They are true for that individual. Nobody can know all the reasons a person is homeless or a recluse. No one can say that what led to those conditions is wrong. Maybe a person got to the point where the collective reality was too difficult to deal with and so they sought out a reality where they wouldn't have to deal with it anymore. I have experienced periods myself where I wanted to leave humanity and the collective narrative completely. Maybe the person ran out of options, things to try, that would change their living conditions. Whatever caused a person to be homeless also plays into that person's definition of reality. It is the same with a famous actor, a member of the clergy, a professional basketball player...you get the point. Human experience creates human reality. Since no two experiences are exactly alike, no two realities can be. We can share definitions of things word for word, and yet the experience of the things we define is unique to the individual.

Police officers and investigators have problems because 'all truths are true.' They may ask five people who witnessed a crime about what they saw, and they will get five unique descriptions if they get a description at all. This makes police work difficult. How is it possible that five people experienced the same event and cannot describe it in the same way? One person swears the perpetrator is Caucasian, while four others describe a Hispanic man. One person tells the police that the perpetrator was wearing a red sweatshirt, and is tall. The others give descriptions of the perpetrator (i.e. average height, wearing an orange t-shirt) which conflict with the other description. The police are trained to know that witness accounts are affected by what a witness is going through at the time of the crime, and their beliefs. A witness may be experiencing divorce, sleep deprivation, problems with their kids, being late for an appointment, fearful about what they just witnessed, etc. One witness may have experienced prejudice all of their life and so identifying a perpetrator with their own 'race' becomes a problem. In the psychology field, the term for this kind of dilemma is cognitive dissonance. The witness wants to do the right thing for the police, and they cannot imagine themselves targeting one of 'their race' as the perpetrator of the crime. This person may not have seen a Caucasian perpetrator, but their mind may have told them the person is white. Or, they know the perpetrator is Hispanic, but their personal feelings about what has happened to them, prejudice, causes that witness not to want to admit what they saw.

If you expound on my example here to all of your life experiences, you might be able to see more clearly why all truths are true. We can share truth with other people, and, our life experiences are not the same as anyone else's, so each experience of shared truths is still unique. The probability of any two people sharing the same exact truth is astronomically small. When we talk about loving someone who loves us, love is agreed upon as a shared experience but the experience is perceived through individual consciousness. Experience is individual, and so is truth.

I read a story about a guy who was taken prisoner during the Vietnam War. He was a US Airman I believe, shot down and imprisoned for something like 3-4 years. There were other US military personnel imprisoned with him and the living conditions were agreed upon as "inhumane" and "unimaginable." Torture, and being made to watch while others were tortured and then killed, were regular occurrences. The Airman was tortured sometimes. He figured out ways to avoid being tortured by not incurring the wrath of his captors. He placated them. Anticipated their demands. The food, when it came, would not have been considered food by most human standards. The unsanitary nature of life in the jungle prison made my stomach cringe just reading about it. Most of the prisoners living with the Airman either died before the prison was liberated or got very sick physically and/or emotionally. The Airman did have some minor health issues at the time of liberation (dehydration, malnutrition, and parasites), and emotional trauma from the experience. But, he came out of the whole thing in much better shape than the other US prisoners did. Two of the US survivors died not long after liberation. The status of the Allied prisoners was not provided in the article. When the Airman was asked about how he survived imprisonment so well, he reported that other than thinking about returning to his family, he visualized playing golf. He visualized a reunion with his family at the beginning of the imprisonment, mostly. He said that after a while, it became too painful to visualize his family and imagine holding them again, because so much time went by, and thinking of them only made him miss them more. He switched to visualizing himself playing golf, one of his favorite activities. He would see himself play 18 holes at one particular course he liked from his past, every day, one hole at a time, and he credited this to keeping him "sane" while horrible things were going on around him. He also improved his golf score on that course by a large margin, following liberation. This means that the visualization, without actual physical practice, created a physical, tangible, result (healthier body, emotionally more stable, and a better golf performance). The Airman did **not** succumb to massive illness from a dangerously unsanitary, malnourished environment as so many other prisoners did! So the question for this discussion becomes, of all the prisoners; whose reality of the prison experience was right? Whose experience of the same environment was true? The men that paid more attention to the conditions of the prison, or the guy that visualized golf? Were they all the same experiences of reality because all the prisoners shared a reality, being imprisoned by Vietnamese soldiers?

    I suggest that the prisoners experienced very different realities. Survival and health depended on how each prisoner perceived the reality of being imprisoned. I believe that there is not an actual 'right' answer or one 'truth' about the experience. Me, I would want to survive and see my family again, so visualizing playing golf would make sense as a coping mechanism and survival skill because I like playing golf. Or painting, or whatever I could visualize to immerse myself in something other than what I was outwardly experiencing that could threaten my survival or my sanity. That choice would create a new reality for me because during the times I was visualizing golf, I would not be thinking of how much I missed my family, the torture and nasty conditions of my existence, and maybe I would also avoid getting seriously sick (like the other prisoners did) because I was not constantly thinking about the dirty conditions. Maybe someone else would not have thought of the coping mechanism that the Airman used and believed it better to perish than to come back home after suffering such horrible conditions. That is one possible reaction and belief to consider when being imprisoned. Is that wrong? Is that truth any better or worse than my truth? I don't think so. It's all experience, and we have free will while living life, which indicates that one person's experience is no more valuable to their soul than another would be if they had chosen a different response.

Consider the example of Holocaust prisoners, excluding discussion for a moment about the ones who were shot or gassed, because those are not conscious choices made in human form. Humans tend to want to survive. It's in our DNA to try to survive, no matter what comes. Most prisoners had a desire to survive no matter what they had to do, in the beginning, and then some gave up after a while. Some gave up at the beginning of their imprisonment at the internment camps. Those folks fought the Germans after stepping off the trains and were shot. And what about the people who never got to a train because they fought their would-be captors? Who was right? Which person's truth was most true? Does it matter what version of reality each person chose? Can we judge those that resigned to die quickly? Is it possible that two people sharing similar conditions can hold different beliefs and therefore experience different realities, and **both** are right?

What I am trying to convey is that every single person has some shared reality with others of humanity and a personal reality that is their own. Each one of our realities is based on our genetics, our experiences, our beliefs, and our life plans. What is true for one person may not be true for another in similar circumstances, because we are complex beings. Stepping into personal power means that we identify our truths, and act according to them, as long as acting on our truth does not cause harm to another nor take something away from someone else. Why should anyone be concerned about your truth if it does not affect them? You are the one who holds the truth based on your experiences. That is your reality, and you must deal with any elements of that reality, good or bad. So what if it differs from my reality? I'm busy having my own. Me paying attention to what you are doing with your truth diverts my energy from focusing on my life. Ideally, it will be helpful to be flexible when talking about truth. If I compare what I believe is true right now with some information being passed down to me by a ninth-dimensional being, there may be a disconnect. I may not understand the information being given to me. However, if I continue to receive information from a ninth-dimensional being and listen with an open mind, maybe I will begin to understand. Maybe I will start to hear some things that feel true to me, and the information is now becoming relevant to me because I can apply it to my belief system. Not all information coming from a higher dimensional being is something useful, and maybe some of it it is. And that would not automatically mean that my truths before receiving the information are now false. Some may be, but certainly not all.

An example can be if you like the Red Sox and I'm an avid Yankees fan. Who is right? What about the people that do not enjoy watching baseball at all? Are they wrong? My husband would say "yes," to that question, and it would be funny because he does not imagine life without baseball. This is a small example of how we come to **our** truths.

The progression of personal truth is cumulative. We can go from totally believing some concept to later rejecting it, but more likely our beliefs expand. Concepts grow and take on new meanings with the passing of time and experience. As humanity ascends to higher consciousness, I think truths are starting to blend. When consciousness expands, we can see things from more angles. Truths seem less black and white because new information is available to an open mind. I'll give an example from my own life experience next.

The one truth that changed for me concerns a topic where humans get very upset about truth, abortion. I have wavered with my truth about this topic. What I thought to be true before my work in quantum hypnosis is that having an abortion was taking away the choice for another soul to experience life. Through my hypnosis experiences, I have received information that changed this truth. It shifted my perspective on free will choice. Every soul has free will choice, no matter what another soul is choosing. Abortion, for me, is no longer the heinous crime that I thought it to be because I received more information about it, from sources that I believe in completely, higher energetic beings (HEBs). I have witnessed many discussions about what I described earlier; the soul's plan for incarnation, and these changed my truth about abortion removing a chance for a soul to be born. I have not changed my belief that if someone is going to have an abortion, it should be done as early in the pregnancy as possible. What **did** change is big for me.

You have your truths about this topic, and both are correct. How is that possible? Again, subjective reality. We create them through our reactions to experiences. If I am choosing to believe in something in one moment that you do not agree with, you do not know my life experiences that brought me to hold that belief. And I do not know yours. Unless we talk about it in a civilized manner. Then we can share our experiences and tell each other why we believe the way we do. This conversation, if done respectfully, can bring enlightenment to both parties. Even if no one changes their beliefs after discussion, both can gain a perspective other than their own. And that expands consciousness. It builds compassion and respect, even if it does not alter our truth.

    I chose some difficult examples of ways each of us come to our truths, which create our realities, the portions of the hologram of Creation that we light up. It seems easy to agree on some collective truths, like garden grass is usually green and can turn yellow during the winter when it gets cold, or flowers can be enjoyable to look at. It seems easy until collective truths clash with personal truths, collective truths clash with each other, or personal truths clash. It does not serve our soul's expansion to try to change another person's beliefs/truths/reality. No matter what you do or say, you cannot change anyone else's beliefs/truths/reality. **We can only change our own**. And so, why get all tied up emotionally if someone does not believe in your truth(s)? Why knock yourself out trying to change someone else's beliefs? It's a waste of energy in my opinion. Accept that we each have our perspectives, and try to be flexible with your truths.

7

What's In A Name?
Contacting The Etheric

People ask me, especially during quantum healing sessions, "Who are we talking to," when we communicate with spirit. Many times, when I use hypnosis to assist a client to gain higher wisdom, we encounter energy beings of a high frequency (HEBs) besides the client's higher self, and they guide us by answering the client's questions that we discussed before the hypnosis portion of the session. Other times, when I'm making a YouTube video or casually speaking with a friend about topics, I receive guidance through my intuition and I pass the information to my audience. And still, other times, when I'm in meditation or just doing my daily work around the house, my guides speak to me. Many people believe it is important to know whom you are speaking with when people channel spirit. I'm here to tell you it is sometimes important to know, but not always. What is in a name is a lot! Names carry frequencies of vibration, and so, I think it is an important topic to cover when speaking about the quantum.

When I began conscious spirit communication in meditation, I would call on someone specific like my highest self, or Archangel Metatron, Archangel Raphael, Jesus, my grandmother, etc. I called on specific beings according to what I was trying to accomplish (i.e. to get info about my personal life, a question someone has asked me to consult about with spirit, to heal myself or assist others with healing, obtain knowledge about my family, etc.). When I do this, I see a ball of light that comes into my mind's eye (third eye), and I know that the one I have called upon has come to merge with my energy and communicate into my mind.

For instance, my dad's energy is a magnificent blue that looks magnetic and shimmery on the edges. It is one of the deepest electric blues I have ever known, and I have never witnessed that color of blue here on Earth. My mother's energy is pastel yellow with a neon yellow and white edge around the circle of light, like a soft sun. Archangel Raphael's energy is electric green, and Metatron's is shimmering gold with diamond-white light on the edges. The Christ Consciousness is all of the colors together and so it appears as brilliant but soft white light to me. This was usually the way I would identify whom I was speaking with when I called on a name. One evening, I called on Raphael because I was feeling stress-energy in my body, and Raphael is my 'go-to' angel who helps me transmute unwanted energies from my body. I can do energy release and healing on my own, but there is no harm in asking for assistance when I feel like having a powerhouse help me out because I am fatigued. What happened is; I started to see Raphael's green, and then the green merged with Metatron's gold-white, and it filled my entire third eye field of vision. I immediately felt the stress go away. Poof, gone. I didn't have to go through my usual meditation process of identifying the areas in my body where the low energy was sitting and concentrating Raphael's light into those areas before washing my whole body with his healing light, while saying in my mind, "I am ready to release this energy." No, this time the stress-energy was gone immediately and my body felt soft and relaxed. I thanked Metatron and asked why Raphael went away, or what happened just then. I heard a concert in my mind, kind of like several voices saying the same thing, and they stated, "We are all one." They then said to me, "We are all one, as you are us and we are you." Then I asked, "Is it important to call upon my guides by name, or to know their names"? The answer came, "You limit their energies to aspects of the being when you call a name." My next question was, "So it would limit a guide's energy if I asked for a name and used it"? The response, was "yes". I said, "Is that what you just showed me"? They answered, "Yes." So they gave me a tutorial on how it is more beneficial to call on all of the angels when I need assistance rather than one angel in particular. Don't get me wrong, I appreciate everything Raphael has done to help me. But, calling on a legion of angels to help, or asking my oversoul to assist...that energy is so close to God/Source energy that I never imagined they would **all** respond. Believing I am not worthy of their energy, was me reducing my importance within Creation. I know in my mind that they are there for everyone, all the time! I had not considered myself important enough to call all angels just to help me reduce some stress. The angels showed me my value with this lesson. I was able to internalize the knowledge and memory that **all beings are worthy of the highest light because we are it**. We forget that, and we forget that we can tap into our highest light at any time. Participation in the duality/separation illusion caused us to forget. I hope you will call on all angels when you need something. And God/Source too, whatever name you use for them. I hope you will remember that you are One with them also, as well as every other being.

    My memory can be a bit sketchy when I am trying to relay a timeline of when things happened for me, but I do remember that sometime after this communication, I released the need to know 'who' it is that is communicating with me when I receive information. There is no need to worry about connecting with low-energy beings when your intentions are of the highest light. I trust that whoever comes to me has the answer to what I am asking, the answer is true for the person I am asking the question, and also for the highest purpose of all involved with the question. Whomever it is that communicates with me **already knows** my intention, which permits them to assist with whatever I am asking assistance for. And here's an important thing to remember; we do have a team of spirits (including our highest self and angels) that agree to follow us in life from birth, to guide us. They communicate with us all the time. Some stay with us our whole lives. Others start with us from birth and then leave, or focus their consciousness elsewhere because we have gotten through the part of our life that they came to assist with. You may think of the ones that come and go as specialists, or 'present with a purpose.' Alternate guides will come to us on the next leg of our journey. Those will have specialized experience with whatever you are trying to accomplish, remember, or overcome next. When I speak of 'my guides,' I am referring to the soul(s) that are working with me at the present moment. Like Paul Selig, I do not try to name them. I do not want to limit the potential of what they can bring to me by calling on one aspect of their soul. I want the whole potential of their consciousness, the whole pie, when they work with me.

    I still sometimes call on a specific name to assist me in specific situations. For example, if I am conducting a quantum healing session and I'm not sure where to go next with the client, I may, in my mind, call on Dolores Cannon to assist me because she is an expert in the field of quantum healing and this name hails the version of her soul that I am trying to get help from. She is with me every time I ask her to be. Because soul energy can focus anywhere, any 'time,' and with as many other souls as they wish, Dolores can be with me and also with five hundred other quantum healers, assisting us all at the same moment. I can also ask for help during a quantum healing session from my other mentor, Candace Craw-Goldman, without contacting her on Messenger (I am happy to say she is still alive on this planet). Her highest-self, and other versions of her as a 'quantum healer' in other dimensions are always willing to assist when I ask. I hear her voice in my head like she is sitting next to me during the session. And then there are times when I want to feel the energy of someone I love that has left physical form here on Earth, like my father or mother. I want to communicate with one of them or feel them. I will say "dad" or "mom" rather than using their formal names. Why? Because this grants me access to their whole soul energy rather than their aspects, Steve and Laurie, my parents' names on Earth. The Steve and Laurie that I knew in my life are only a small part of them. One was a successful electrical engineer who loved fishing, and the other was a talented artist and seamstress. I'm not seeking those specialties when I commune with my mom and dad, although those specialties are available to me if I ask them specifically. Usually, I want the energy of the love of my mom and dad, not the aspect energy of what they did here on Earth. Now that they have crossed over from physical form, calling them mom and dad specifies **whom** I am talking to, the energy connection is automatic because we shared very specific experiences, and my intention of whom I am talking to is known.

In an article written by Dr. John Gliedman for Science Digest (July 1982), Gliedman asserts that quantum theory states; once the energy fields of subatomic particles collide with each other, the energy fields become 'entrained' (another term which can be interpreted as entangled). This means that the particles can be "halfway across the universe from each other," and they "instantly respond to each other's actions." The indication here is that when someone on Earth that you care deeply about is experiencing something, you can feel it too on some level. You may pick up the phone and call them, and they will say, "Hey! I was just thinking about you!" Or maybe they are struggling with something and they ask you how you knew to call right when they needed to hear your voice. It's the entrainment that pulled your energy to theirs.

This fits with what I have come to know about contacting spirit. My understanding is that everything and everyone comes from God/Source. In that sense, all of our "particles" and energy fields are entrained with one another, but some feel closer than others energetically. Therefore, we are simply a thought away from anyone else, at any time, in any dimension, in any universe. If we want to connect with the whole soul of someone we know, we go to their highest self, who has no name, but we must start with a lower frequency version of that soul's essence; their name, or their role with us in life. Otherwise, the soul energy may not recognize that we are intending to contact them specifically. Using the name of the one we wish to connect with highlights a *part* of the hologram of Creation where their energy resides (a slice of their soul pie). But since that aspect of the soul is connected to the whole soul (oversoul), we can then ask to speak with the oversoul, or we can speak to the aspect we know of, or any version of that soul in-between. All of the versions of the soul are connected in energetically different dimensions, and this is a very basic description of quantum entanglement. Once our consciousness reaches a high enough frequency, there is no more illusion of spatial distance within the hologram or time-space dimensions; there is only the infinite consciousness that we call God. Everyone is One mind here, One consciousness, and so there is no need to communicate within. God/Source still communicates with us within the hologram because of the ever-present spark of Source that resides in every aspect of us. It resides in our energetic heart space and this is why humanity is continually being directed to "go within" and listen to what the heart tells us.

LTC Wayne McDonnell's report refers to what I know as God/Source "the Absolute" in his discussions about The Gateway experience. He describes the Absolute; "it has no beginning, no end, no location. It is conscious force, the fundamental, primal power of existence without form, a state of infinite being." That description could have come from a Bible. What does this prove? It proves to me that many scientists understand that everything is consciousness energy, physically manifest or not, everything is connected, and we can communicate with each other in awareness if we can raise our frequencies and brainwaves high enough, regardless of what form we currently inhabit within our consciousness focal point; **and** that there is an all-knowing, all-powerful consciousness that is infinite, but scientists avoid like crazy calling this consciousness, God. God is an esoteric concept. Scientists avoid esoteric concepts as a rule, but it seems that too many scientists have found evidence of the connectivity of everything in their exploration of reality to avoid describing what we call God. A rose by any other name is still a rose. In this case, it does not matter that scientists and spiritual/religious people call the One, the infinite consciousness, by different names. We are speaking of the same energy and potential when accessing that energy with our heightened consciousness.

As much as I love to marry science with my theories and models, it may make more sense for me to state my point in another way. Say I want to talk with God/Source. I could pick any name, and I would be speaking to God/Source because we are all God/Source. But our limited aspect consciousness is only part of God/Source when we use personal names (a sliver of the pie), not the whole. Using a name energizes part of the hologram of Creation, not the Absolute. Why not just call on God/Source directly instead of using a name?

I know, I know, even saying God/Source is giving a name of sorts. Here's where my brain wants to explode, but I will try to explain how I understand the situation.

The whole of everything that can be called God or The Absolute, which is all of everything, in every dimension, is all-knowing, right? Omnipresent, omnipotent, and within each of us. If we assign a name to it (God), it knows we then are speaking of it with that general name. If a collective of people assign a name to it (God), then there can be agreement on what we are talking about when we speak to one another about 'God.' Naming is useful for communication. Humans like to communicate. It's kind of necessary for Earth life. Being all-knowing, God recognizes when we communicate with it no matter what name we use for it. If one community calls it Allah, and another calls it God, it knows both intentions because it is omniscient, and so the communication is immediate. But, if I am trying to speak with God and I call it Albert Einstein, I'm going to be speaking to the part of God that is Albert Einstein's consciousness. Brilliant, yes, but only a sliver of the pie. Better to use the general term of your understanding when trying to contact the infinite.

There are times when I want to call on a name rather than calling on my guides, the angels, my higher self, or The Christ Consciousness for answers because I am asking for information FOR someone else, in a session. In this situation, the aforementioned beings guide the questions I ask during hypnosis, but they do not have a role in answering my client's questions through me. My guides speak to me through **my** filters of reality, and therefore I do not consider my channeling the information for a client a wholly reliable service. It is much better in my opinion for the client to have their questions answered by **their** guides, higher selves, and other spirits using the client's subconscious activation. For this example, assume I have a client in-session and they want to speak with a deceased relative about a difficult experience they had together in this lifetime, that remained unresolved when the person died. When I use the name of the deceased relative, it sends energy to the part of the hologram of Creation where the relative is known by my client. It energizes, activates, and lights up that aspect of the soul for communication.

Now, just because that aspect has crossed over to the spirit world does not mean that aspect has resolved certain issues and maintains expanded consciousness about them. Sometimes a soul slice gets stuck in worldly dogma and maintains an unenlightened consciousness about experiences. The aspect's higher-consciousness selves **will** have transcended the issues of the incarnation with my client, but the aspect that is known as the deceased relative may want to have another incarnation experience to resolve it rather than releasing the issues while in spirit. That is okay, and that aspect will resolve it eventually, but talking directly with it before resolution happens is not helpful for the client who is trying to resolve the conflict between them while in this session. The multidimensional nature of what I am telling you becomes apparent in this conversation because one person can resolve a conflict between two people while the other person is not ready to resolve it. Both realities exist simultaneously because there is no time, and these are quantum realities. I can usually tell right away if one party is not ready to resolve an issue by the dialogue between them that the client is sharing with me during the session. If the deceased aspect is not ready to heal their conflict, what I do next is ask the client to call on the deceased relative's highest self or oversoul to come into the session for resolution. This highlights and energizes another part of the hologram where the deceased relative's soul energy resides in the highest frequency next to Source.

We have to be **very** specific sometimes, as quantum healers, who we are guiding our clients to speak with. The deceased relative's aspect that is not ready yet to resolve the issue has not expanded their consciousness enough to know what their drama was about, and so it may provide information to the client that is slanted in vision, and more harm can be done emotionally to the client. It is like keeping an argument going instead of getting the broader picture about the souls' purpose for the dispute. Once a higher frequency version of the deceased relative agrees to discuss the issue with us, the client can and usually does gain the wisdom of what the whole dispute was about in the first place. They understand why they and their deceased relative agreed to experience the discord together. This higher perspective is very healing. Especially when a client finds out that they and this other soul have had several lifetimes together, and they have switched roles in the various lifetimes. In one lifetime person A is the oppressor of person B, and in the next lifetime, they change places. Or, there is no oppression, they agree to see an experience through different lenses. It is a mutually beneficial exchange for both souls.

Sometimes the client discovers that they and the deceased relative have shared many lifetimes in various roles, they are working on multiple dynamics together, and they always love one another even when they are having challenging lifetimes together. I believe Dolores Cannon called her technique 'quantum healing' because more than any physical healing a client may receive, understanding that each incarnation is only a tiny sliver of our immortal existence brings emotional peace to most people. We realize that if we don't work things out with someone we love in one lifetime, we get endless opportunities to do it in other lifetimes. And so, this is an example of when I would use a name when contacting spirit, and when I would shift to the oversoul if necessary.

Every individual aspect of our soul has a name unless that aspect resides in the hologram where there is no time nor space, in a very high energy reality close to Source, or within a collective consciousness. In the case of a collective consciousness, the group of souls may give itself a name like; The Z's (Lee Harris), or The 9D Arcturians (Daniel Scranton), to make it easier for humans to identify whom they are channeling. Assigned names, nicknames, and changed names in lower densities are names that were assumed during incarnation, given by another aspect of Source that named us, like our parents. The individual names carry one vibration of the entire frequency of the oversoul, but not the full vibration of the oversoul. The collective called RA describes a name as; a vibratory complex of sound in our density. I do not think our oversouls have names unless we assign names to them as we do with the angels. It's comparable to the teaching of Moses where he asked the burning bush what its' name was. I believe the answer was, "I am that I am." Moses was purportedly speaking with God. If this is the case, then God did not want to take on a name.

Why?

In the spiritual community, I hear lots of people asking awakening people to drop their labels and identities to be One, of unity consciousness. Dropping identity with anything is prescribed by ancient spiritualist traditions to reach enlightenment. It is said that to label oneself in any way is to limit our energy. So, if I say that I am a mother, and I identify most strongly with being a mother, then maybe I am focusing my energy mostly on mothering. I find identity through this role and acts of being a 'mother.' That seems rather limiting. I will tell you that I am so much more than a mother. What if you are a carpenter by trade? Is that **all** that you are? Of course not! The words 'I am' are some of the most energetic, creative words that we can utter. The energy of 'I am' lights up the hologram of Creation like a torch. Be careful with what you follow those words with because as a creator being, whatever follows "I am" is your statement of intention. Your body hears it, and the universe hears it. Whatever follows "I am" is illuminated, by your consciousness.

Your body and the universe return whatever you tell it you are.

Say something enough times and it manifests as your reality.

I am fat or I am stupid…stuff like that is creative in the opposite direction of what you want to be. Replace those statements with; I am love, I am perfect health, I am compassionate, I am beautiful, I am a perfect expression of God, I am abundant. Whatever you want to be your reality, put the words 'I am" in front of it and see how things shift for you. "I am" is the way you define yourself using whatever name you choose to label yourself with. You are **not** the history that is associated with your name unless you continue to identify with your energetic being in the past. Drop that thinking. If someone is saying your name and associating it with something you do not wish to be, then correct that person or let their words fall right out of your consciousness. You may have been A, B, or C when you were a child or even yesterday, but today you can be X, Y, or Z right now if you choose it. You may say, "I was given my name at birth and I love my parents, or I respect my spouse, and so I will never change my name." Why not? If your name brings associations with energy that you do not feel in alignment with, why not change your name? Free will, remember? My surname has changed two times because I have been married twice and I chose to change them. Not to mention all the nicknames I've been gifted.

Ask me seriously who I am and I will tell you I am undefined. I am. Sometimes I will tell you I am Sue. One time I met two little girls of a friend of ours. I said to them (in reference to the movie Spaceballs) "My name is Barfolomew, but people call me Barf." I was trying to be playful with the girls in that instance and they called me 'Barf' for a year. I loved it every time they yelled "Barf!" What is in a name is energy. We know that letters and symbols have energy, and when spoken, the tone of each carries its unique vibration. Some vibrations are more soothing than others. That is something to consider when you want to name your children and your pets! It is also something to consider when you call the name of someone. It is not always the name that can be discordant, it can be **how** we say the name that can transfer lower energy or higher energy. "Hi, Sue!" carries a much different energy than, "Oh, hi Sue".

One final thought about your name. Say you have done some things in your past that you are not particularly proud of. Or you may have been dubbed with attributes from other people that you do not like, and this has caused you to dislike your name. This is you accepting a definition(s) of yourself. Staying in the belief of the past energies of associations attributed to or assumed by you with your name is not helping you to recognize your presence here as a being of God/Source energy. Transform that energy and know who you are now. Even if other people do not agree with your new designation of self (when you tell them you have changed), they will certainly witness it if you care to share further experiences with them. At least YOU know, and you are the only one who matters when it comes to associating meaning with your name. A name change is not necessary unless it is something you feel excited about doing. If this is the case, then go for it!

You define yourself.

8
It's Not You, It's Me

There is this topic that has been discussed and 'treated' by spiritual practitioners, including quantum healers, called 'entity attachments.' To properly discuss quantum healing (navigating and utilizing quantum fields of energy to heal yourself), this fear-laden issue needs to be addressed and cleared up. There are lots of people walking around believing that they are, in some way, possessed by entities. This means that something or someone; some energy other than your soul energy is inhabiting your body, mind, and emotions and affecting your spirit, making you do things or controlling you in some way. At the very least, according to many people other than myself, having an 'entity attachment' suggests that you are not fully in control of your life, creating your reality at all times. This is a disempowering way to move through your life. Dolores Cannon, my mentor of QHHT disavowed this concept in its entirety, and so do I. Our souls are incarnated in this reality which is a free-will reality. The part of the hologram that is the Earth experience (in its many versions) **does not allow for any being outside of you to take control nor influence you unless you agree to it**.

Please hear me when I say that.

Feel the energy of those words and sense their total safety and comfort. It may seem, at this time, that I am calling out a lot of practitioners of etheric energy healing who practice getting rid of entity attachments with their clients. It may seem like I am calling them liars, or charlatans. I am not doing that. What I am doing, and explaining with firm resolution, is that what is called 'entity attachment' is a wildly misunderstood experience. I intend to describe what is going on with people that believe they have an entity attachment and also describe a method of relieving that experience through personal empowerment.

Let's start simply. As I have discussed in many ways, each of our souls has many many incarnations away from being One/God/Source, in all dimensions, with or without physical bodies; and through the consciousness of our oversoul, and our ever-present connection to The Christ Consciousness (God/Source), we are connected to every one of those incarnations. None of our 'other selves' are disconnected from us. As I've also stated before, we on Earth forget our connections with our 'other selves,' and so when we experience influences from them (their emotional energy or their thoughts), consciously or unconsciously, it may SEEM like we are receiving information, feeling, or direction from another being, rather than from another aspect of ourselves. Sometimes, our reception of energy from another aspect of us that is experiencing their life in another dimension is so intense, we become affected greatly by that energy. It may even seem like that energy is taking over our own real experiences. What is happening is that this other aspect of you is asking, begging, for you to help transmute whatever issues it cannot seem to transmute itself, in its present moment point of consciousness.

    For example, there is a part of me, an aspect of me, that resides in another version of Earth (in what you may consider another 'time' of this Earth's history), and this aspect of me is a female living in Russia who brought her knowledge of plant energy medicine into her incarnation. She has specialized knowledge of how to use plants to heal the body. This woman *innately knows* that all healing can be found within the plants and nature that surround her. She uses them for herself to maintain perfect health, and she uses them to help heal people in her community to recover from illness or maintain their health. Her community values her gifts of plant medicine and supports her with food, shelter, and companionship. This woman has dedicated space in the communal garden to specifically cultivate the plants that serve the whole, while the rest of the community grows food items in the garden. The existence of all is co-operative. People utilize their specific gifts to share with the community, and so the community lives in harmony. There is also a place of spiritual worship in this community.

    The person who leads the congregational meetings is loving. He is spiritually gifted and connected to Source, whom they call God, and the community supports and trusts him to speak when they have spiritual issues they would like to discuss. He is considered enlightened by the community, and people trust him to provide guidance. At some point, the community is influenced by religion, intensely. Like a reformation movement that is dictatorial and exerts force on the man that leads the congregation in prayer. These influencers convince the man that his people are sinful, that any use of medicine outside of the belief in God's healing power is heresy, and needs to be shut down with a powerful hand. The man is conflicted because he knows the woman providing the medicine is a loving and kind soul, and she helps the community stay healthy. However, the man does not want to lose his stature in the community because leading the community in the service of God is his mission in life, his only calling. What would he do if he refused to carry out the demands of the church leaders? They have made it clear, by show of force, that the man would be cast out of the community, and another, more compliant 'holy man' would replace him. And so, with this horrendous choice before him, feeling all the fear of being cast out, the man elects to follow the church's dictates. He convinces the community that the medicine woman is acting against the will of God, acting like a witch by casting her evil spells upon the community, and that they must cast her out of the community to be saved from the ways of her demonic spell casting. The man probably did not want to do this, but his fear of becoming alone in the world as opposed to being supported by his community overshadowed his concern for the woman.

The woman, at this point in her life, was older and less able to take care of herself when forced to live outside the cooperative community she has lived in all of her life. She fashions a shelter and takes with her the tools that some kind community members have given her on the quiet. She does know some ways of trapping and snaring animals, and so she ekes out a meager existence using her skills and tools. But it gets very cold in the part of the world where she lives. She nearly freezes to death sometimes because she runs out of wood and is not strong enough to fell large trees. Winters are long. And the woman begins to starve because the food she can obtain for herself is not sufficient. Many community members continue to seek the woman's medicines. They come to her in secret because they know if it is discovered by the church that they go to her, they will be persecuted for conspiring with a witch. They will be condemned, as heretics, and cast out or killed by the church. Their families will also be at risk of the same because each family member of the condemned will be brutally interrogated by the church. It is life-threatening to go to the woman, but they do it anyway because they know she helps them and is not evil. They take pity on her situation. They offer her food and clothing in exchange for her medicines, which she still collects in the woods. The woman is afraid, sad, lonely, and starving. Eventually, she dies from the cold and malnourishment. This is one of my aspects.

Now, those who know me understand why I prefer to live in warm climates! The warmer the better. This is the second time one of my aspects died from cold weather, that I know of! I discovered her during a swap session with another quantum healer. I recognized the woman as myself and was able to connect her trauma to the times in my life when I kept my knowledge of herbal medicine a secret because I feared being called 'crazy' for not accepting Western medicine as my primary form of healing. For much of my awakened experience, I did not speak of what I knew to be true, that plant medicine is much better for the body than chemically altered pills made in a lab.

My body has always been sensitive to Western medicines, and that is my body's way of communicating to me that it does not want processed elements put into it. Some Western medicines work very well for me when I need them, but I use the older ones, never newly released ones, and only for short periods. I have also been very fearful in the past about sharing my spiritual knowledge as it is presented to me to remember by spirit. I connected this fear with the woman in Russia. Until I became aware of that aspect of myself, her trauma of being outcast because of her practices that were not accepted any longer in the mainstream, the fear of being outcast for my 'weird' practices could not be transmuted by me. I did not know where the fear came from! On the other hand, now that I am aware of this other aspect of myself, I have healed that part of us that worries we will lose everything if other people do not like what we are saying and doing. My reluctance to speak publicly about esoteric concepts is gone. I wrote a book (*The Christ Consciousness: A Somewhat Agnostic Point of View*)! And, I'm writing this book! I participate in near-weekly YouTube video creation for myself and others because I am free to speak my truth. And guess what? Because I did the healing for me, I also healed the aspect of me that is the woman in Russia. She is not an entity attachment hanging onto my soul and making me afraid to express my knowledge. She is an aspect of my soul who sought help from me to free her.

It *is* quantum healing.

She is still very much alive in the other dimension because, as we know, there is no time. All is happening at this moment point. Using quantum fields to access that part of my soul, I was able to understand her, feel her, and remind her that there is no real death, and that she is never alone. I encouraged her to speak to God and the rest of us whenever she feels lonely, and I thanked her for coming to show me why I was so afraid of persecution for my beliefs in this lifetime. We are One now, merged in a way that our oversoul, the entirety of us, is more manifest in our minds, spirits, and bodies. We share our talents. It is a nice feeling knowing that the woman's consciousness is always with me and that we can communicate at any time. Her knowledge of plant medicine has been guiding me for a long time and I did not know it. I share with her the fiery parts of my consciousness to stand tall in her resolve, to be more accepting of who she is. And my sense of humor. She tends to be one *serious* lady. I encourage her to laugh at herself and find joy in the little things. I've also taught her how to bring higher frequency energies into her body to stay warm and be nourished when food is less available. In that sense, I have healed her as much as she has healed me by sharing her story. We have together rewritten my 'history.' The woman will not leave her body due to starvation and cold. When she chooses to leave her physical body, it will be automatic, like within a sleep state, rather than through suffering.

I will talk more about shifting your history (past/future/present) using quantum healing methods at the end of this chapter. The main point I want to make here is that at no time was I ever possessed by the soul of a Russian woman who caused me to feel fear in my life. She and I are One. If I had undertaken the swap session with a quantum healer or another regression specialist who believed in 'entity attachments,' I might have been encouraged to see the Russian woman as a soul that is separate from myself exerting influence on me. Like with the herbal remedy knowledge. In my case, the knowledge is helpful, but what if she possessed knowledge of dark ritual energy transferal and this is what I was using instead? Would the dark energy practice have come from an aspect of me? Yes! I can *channel* the information and practices of other souls. However, **the energy of others does not ever take over my body and control me unless I allow it to**. If I allow someone else's energy to influence me enough to be 'like them,' it means I have aligned my energy signature with theirs. It does not mean the other person's spirit has taken over mine.

Let's look at the example I gave through another lens. Imagine that my connection with the woman in Russia, to her energy, caused me to have an anxiety disorder, talk to myself when no one was in front of me, or close down from people altogether because I am afraid of people and what they may do to me. Say that I, as Sue, responded to my connection with her with what psychologists, medical doctors and psychiatrists would deem mental illness. I could rattle off about four or five diagnoses from the Diagnostic and Statistical Manual of Mental Disorders (DSM-5-TR) right now because of my social work training, that would fit the symptoms I propose through this lens.

If I was having one or more of these symptoms, Western healing professionals would not likely link my symptoms to another lifetime that my soul is experiencing. It's not their fault, they are not usually trained to think that way. Instead, I might be labeled as having: full-blown schizophrenia, generalized anxiety disorder (because there is no 'source' found for my anxiety and PTSD cannot be established), Antisocial Personality Disorder, Schizotypal personality disorder, Schizoid personality disorder, Paranoid personality disorder, and the list goes on. I would be chemically, behaviorally, and possibly physically treated (think shock treatments) for my symptoms, all of which would probably not work to relieve my symptoms, but could suppress them. Or maybe, because mental health symptoms can be directly tied to chemistry in the body, like neurotransmitter imbalances, I would feel better and act better with the medications. But, the true source and cause of these symptoms would not be known. This is what I think happens when people who are in close connection to the energies of their other aspects are still suffering from traumatic experiences. They are being multidimensionally affected in their energy fields, but they do not KNOW they are being affected that way in most cases, and so they are labeled by good-intentioned professionals as 'mentally ill."

    Can you see why I stopped being a social worker? It is not that social work is not a good profession. I have known many social workers who have been and still are immensely helpful to other people with their knowledge and compassion. I got to a level in social work (Master's) where, if I continued, I would be forced to start labeling people with DSM5 diagnoses (putting them into boxes) while discussing treatment for them with their doctors. When I would have a client presenting with some form of 'mental illness,' I would be expected to treat them with therapies that were approved within the confines of my social work license. If I had continued being a social worker, I would not be able to help the whole person. My soul did not want me to do that. My soul gave me lots of colorful experiences to show me that I was in the wrong profession, for me.

    What I **re-cog-nized** through my work in spiritual healing and quantum hypnosis is that 'entity attachments' are multidimensional energy influences and are only *other* parts of our soul. They feel our light and come to us for healing, understanding, and strength. They want our help. If we feel their energy and drop our vibration to meet theirs, then we can be in alignment with lower vibrational fields and it seems like we are being controlled or guided by another being outside of our soul energy. Whenever I encounter a client that believes they have an entity attachment, I structure the hypnosis session to dive deeply into each lifetime that their soul guides them to see during the session so that they can discover that they are dealing with an aspect of themself. Every single time it turns out that the client is feeling their 'other aspect' energy and has disassociated their current consciousness from that aspect. In a sense, the client's current consciousness has cut itself off from another version of their soul. A disavowment of a part of the whole soul. It's like if we say to ourselves, "I'm never angry at other people," and we suppress or disconnect ourselves from feeling anger. What we want to prove to ourselves by disconnecting this way is that we are good people. In truth, disconnecting from any part of yourself, any response to human experience, is limiting your energy. It is stuffing your energies, the ones you don't like, into areas of your physical body where they build up over time and cause dis-ease in the body. We did not come to Earth to be perfect little angels with no negative experiences! We already ARE that perfect little angel in another reality, in another dimension. We came here, focused our consciousness in an Earth-bound physical body, to have **human** emotions and experiences. It is not healthy for the mind, body, emotional body, or spirit to deny any part of the human experience.

I am not dumping on doctors or spiritual healers because they do not recognize when people are having multidimensional discord. I am trying to shine a light on the topic. Dolores Cannon spoke on this issue in-depth within her books and during her training of the QHHT method. There is nothing outside of ourselves that can take us over. We have the choice to align with the energy signature of other souls, but that is not having another soul possess us. You may ask, "What about alien abductions or people that were possessed of demonic energies and then released by a member of the church?" These are two different scenarios and I will talk about them one at a time. First, alien abduction. Yes, they happened. Maybe they still happen, but I do not know that for a fact because it does not come up in sessions with me. This scenario is always a situation where the souls of the aliens have contracted with the soul of the abductee before the abductee's incarnation. Just like we may agree to have a genetic illness before incarnating, a soul may choose to be abducted and explored, even modified physically, by aliens. Why? I have no idea why any soul would choose that. But souls do, and that is their free-will choice to have that experience.

Let's get into clearing a 'demonic' possession. This I see as similar to a client choosing a healthier version of themselves while having a hypnosis session with me. I assist my clients to become aware of their healthier versions of themselves. Religious people do that too. Not all religious healers are charlatans. Not all examples of 'ridding someone of demonic energy' is faked. Notice I said, "demonic energy," rather than saying, "ridding someone of a demon." Ridding someone of a demon would be the definition of entity attachment. Ridding someone of demonic **energy** means that the religious healer assisted the person in deciding to let go of the lower energy frequencies that were present in their reality. So it appears that the person was possessed by a demon, but what was happening is that the person was strongly connecting to and outwardly displaying the energy of another version of self, and other people judged that energy to be demonic. I'm not just throwing a wild theory at you from some 'airy fairy' higher consciousness viewpoint! I have projected words and emotions at times that some people would call demonic. There have been times in my life when I was so fearful and angry that I wanted to kill the person I felt had offended me or someone I love. My husband calls that my 'mama bear' instinct. I think, when I have this kind of response, I'm tapping into the warrior aspects of myself that do not tolerate injustice. My warrior aspects are willing to dispatch persons who do bad things to others. Some of them have extreme potty mouths and know gruesome ways to get rid of their enemies. Those are scary and appear a bit 'demonic' if you ask me!

Of course, I have never killed anyone nor tried to in this lifetime. But, if you could hear the things I say sometimes and see how angry I can get, you might think I am possessed by a demon. I am experiencing fewer of those kinds of reactions these days because I make a choice each time I witness a major injustice (my judgment), to respond as my higher self instead of my warrior aspects (ego-driven), and I choose compassion over fear. It doesn't feel good to be around a person acting like a demon. I respect my family and myself enough to go through the feelings of anger and fear privately, or to reduce my reactions with reminders that I am love and light. I remind myself that the person acting badly is doing so because of their pain, and they are not truly threatening my life or those of my loved ones. The difference between the 'old me' consciousness (very intensely reactive) and the 'new me' consciousness is that I no longer place those warrior parts of me outside of myself. I don't pretend that their energies are some bad element of my personality and squash them or deny them. I embrace them as part of who I am. If push comes to shove and there is a real threat to my life or the life of my loved ones, I know my warrior selves are on my team and I can utilize their talents to make sure that the threat stops. I am not ashamed to say that I will disable/kill another human if extreme circumstances call for it.

Do I want that to happen? Hell no! And, I do not punish myself by feeling guilty that they are a part of me, who I am. And so, when a religious "possession" is neutralized, that is what is happening. The person who appears possessed by a demon or demons is choosing to be another, higher-light consciousness form of themself. The expression of 'the demonic self' was a representation of that person's subconscious choice to align with an aspect of themselves from "the past," and bring the characteristics of that energy into current reality. The religious healer who assisted the person to choose to be the light showed their light to the client. Suggested to the client that there is another way of being. In recognition of the light, the client chose that expression of self and moved from alignment with their 'demonic' aspect. As a quantum healer, I would lead a person toward acceptance of their shadow aspects and bring them into solidarity with the personality that I am working with (like I did with my warrior aspects).

There is always a good reason why anyone aligns with their fearful aspects. Life on Earth sometimes has the effect of calling them to us, and before you know it, someone is acting just like a caveman (or woman). The base instincts that originally served survival purposes are not gone from our whole being just because we have higher consciousness now. They continue to be part of the overall energy of the soul and of God/Source. It is not a great plan to try to excise these parts of self because that denies part of God within and keeps the separation game going. I would assist the client to see their 'darker' aspects with new eyes. To help them know that they too are Source beings; and that it is okay for the client to forgive and integrate them, no matter what they are doing, into the soul consciousness energy of now. Soul aspect retrieval is not usually understood by religious healers, and so the one 'healed' using religious means continues to reject that part of themself. Using either method, the client is the one making the choice, choosing to be 'healed' from something. One method is no better than another. The method chosen is an indicator of what the client's belief system is and how they choose to heal themself.

I visualize safety in and around me at all times. And that energy is given to me by the universe because it is the energy I am putting out to the universe. The funny thing is, before I moved to Florida from New York, I was excited about the prospect of easily obtaining a concealed-carry pistol permit. I gifted my father's pistols to a friend in NY before the move because I did not want to pay exorbitant fees and go through the massive protocol to get a pistol permit in New York, to keep my father's guns. I imagined that once I got to Florida, I would get my permit right away; as in high on the 'to do' list. I am weapons trained by my father and the Army, so why not? The interesting part is that once I got here, I had no desire to get another weapon for self-defense because I feel very safe and protected by my guides, the universe, the angels, my oversoul, and by Source. My soul tells me that I have dropped the desire because I no longer feel in jeopardy of harm like I did living in New York. That is a connection to my higher self at its finest! I know it is no safer or less safe in Florida than in New York. What changed is my decision about safety, my choice to know that I am protected at all times because I lift myself to that **state of being** every day, by choice. Just like I choose to talk to my warrior selves when they want to kill someone, I tell my previously fearful selves (who have been physically harmed) that we no longer need to be afraid.

Our energy is too high to allow anything malevolent to enter our energy fields. And so it is. I am safe in this reality, a Florida resident, and do not need to purchase a weapon for self-defense that I can wear on my person everywhere I go. The other aspects of me are also healed by the new consciousness. Whatever is healed within is also experienced in the outside world. Whatever fears my other aspects may encounter in their reality, I have helped them to discern between real threats and imaginary threats. I am not suggesting that every one of them is living a utopian life without any worry. Surely there are still potential threats in every one of your lifetimes, in the lower energy dimensions, as well as mine. Knowing when to act in self-preservation and when it is not necessary to be fearful is **transcending fear**. Lifting your consciousness, and understanding more about the true nature of energy, will help you to heal your aspects so that they will join you in your consciousness. Once we accept our aspects into **our** awareness, as they present themselves, our energy becomes more and more unified with the oversoul. That means you embody more of your soul's energy in the here and now. You can say 'ascended' self if that term better suits your understanding.

Eventually, as all aspects of a soul are unified, the consciousness becomes the oversoul. We remember it all. The choice is then available to merge with Source again completely, or spread out into more aspects of the same soul and experience other parts of the hologram of Creation. In breath, out breath. Humanity is experiencing the in-breath. We are returning to Source within, who breathed us outward from itself, to experience different realities and dimensions. The best way to assimilate yourself with your aspects is to not deny them. Even if you never have a quantum healing session, you can connect and know about your other selves. You do not have to know their names and exact circumstances to connect with them. Set the intention, whenever you feel a part of yourself reaching to you, to get to know that aspect's story. Call that part of you into your conscious awareness in quiet meditation. Be **willing** to know all the gritty details of what that part of you is experiencing and doing. If you do this, you will be able to know the answers without using a hypnotist or any other spiritual connector. Meditation is not only to clear the mind of thought, it is also a conduit to make connections with energy. The intention of the meditation, the willingness to go see and know what your other aspects are dealing with, is what directs the energy that comes to you and through you.

Then accept.

Allow yourself to feel whatever it is you feel about the experience. Make peace with the things you have done or the ways of being that you are in other dimensions. You don't know something until you know it, and what's the point of being angry with yourself for behaving in an undesirable manner when you didn't know any better in that lifetime? That's like punishing a toddler for being a toddler who is having a tantrum because they are feeling overwhelmed. And if you ever did that, punish a toddler; then forgive it too. Parental and caretaker guilt is some of the most low-level energy, deep-fear dynamics in human experience. Carrying that around, even if it is from another lifetime, is a recipe for mental health issues and physical illness.

This is inner work.

This is what people mean when they encourage you to heal yourself from within.

It is work, and it does take effort and dedication.

And, it does get easier the more you do it.

As many times as you accept a part of yourself, you upgrade your vibration and eventually your frequency. Ascension does not often happen at the flick of a switch. You must be willing to shine a light on all parts of yourself. The good news is that when you do that, you are also re-cognizing the strengths of your other aspects. It's not all trudging around in a mud pit. I make it a habit during hypnosis to guide my clients to a lifetime where they feel the most powerful. Not powerful over other people, but personally powerful. Then, after garnering the details of that lifetime, I ask the client to anchor the energy of their powerful aspects into their heart space. Some people say that is part of soul retrieval. Whatever you call it, it strengthens the connection between the client and their aspect and brings their energies into cohesion. I then plant the hypnotic suggestion that any time the client thinks of this aspect, they will automatically feel the strength of them and that they can communicate at will.

You can do this for yourself through meditation and with intention. All hypnotic direction is a suggestion. When the person receiving the suggestion agrees, then it becomes their will. The person does not have to accept the suggestion. It is like taking a friend's helpful advice and acting upon it. When the advice comes, take it or leave it. Free will. A hypnosis practitioner cannot force you to accept anything you do not want. Your egoic mind will not allow you to accept anything that is not in accord with your intentions. What you see on the stage when a hypnotist suggests that a subject is a chicken and then the subject acts like a chicken is largely an act. It is an agreement by the subject to be silly for the benefit of the audience and themself.

I want to address the subject of walk-ins. This is a concept I learned about through Dolores Cannon and others that I'm not sure I agree with. A soul walk-in situation supposedly can happen when you are done with your life, or if you want out of this life earlier than your soul planned for, then another soul can slip into your body and live in your body, with your memories, while your soul moves on to another focal point of reality. Reportedly, this is by agreement of both souls on the highest level, the oversouls. Why would this happen? Reportedly, the soul coming in doesn't want to waste a perfectly good body or bother experiencing birth and childhood. They want to come in as a fully formed adult. I have experienced discord with this concept from the moment I read about it in one of Dolores' books. On the one hand, if there is an agreement between the two souls, then what would be the problem with having a walk-in situation? Both parties get what they want and I'm sure that Source would not judge it. Then, on the other hand, what about all the soul contracts that the person leaving the body has with their family, friends, co-workers, love partners, etc.? Swapping souls would be a cancellation of those contracts, would it not? It would be a different soul inhabiting your wife, for instance. Whatever connection you have with your wife on the soul level would be gone for the remainder of this physical incarnation. The silly part of me wonders if that might be attractive to some people. The serious part of me, the one that believes my word is my bond, balks at the very thought. There is a third point of view in this discussion, and it is that all truths are true. What that means to me is when someone creates something with their free will or several free wills, it becomes manifest in reality. "Whose reality" is the question. But since all of our soul energies can be focused in as many places, times, and realities as we wish, maybe highlighting this potential in the hologram is not so far-fetched. Maybe, if one soul leaves and is replaced by another, that is one timeline reality, but on another timeline of the same soul, the soul didn't leave and finished out the life plan and contracts with others.

This scenario is, without question, a quantum perspective. I can see why Dolores used to say that the information in her books, derived from hypnosis sessions, will "twist your mind like a pretzel." I am not going to commit to an answer about if I think walk-ins are real. Expanding my consciousness means that I am willing to consider all possibilities of quantum reality. I did say in my first book that I believe we can download imprints of other souls' energy for use in our lifetime. That imprint becomes part of our soul memory as a life, or experience that we had personally. Why would it not be possible to swap bodies? Here is one final piece of the puzzle on the subject of walk-ins that I heard while listening to Belinda Womak on Gaia.com. Belinda channels angelic energies, and sometimes Mother Mary. The episode I am referring to is called *Angelic Guidance to Access Your Purpose with Belinda Womak*, and she was interviewed by Regina Meredith on the *Open Minds* show. Belinda said that what we think of as a walk-in is the same soul but seems to have changed because the soul resonated with another version of itself in a higher octave. A higher octave is a way of saying higher dimension, or the frequency and sound of the soul existing in higher energy. We know this to be a frequency shift. According to Belinda, we can make these big shifts instantaneously and so it appears as if we are someone else. I do believe it is possible to shift consciousness in a quantum-leap kind of way. So, that is all I have for you about walk-ins. I have never personally worked with a client who reported to be a walk-in. I leave it to you to decide what you believe.

In conclusion, much of what people are working with now is the assimilation and unification of all their aspects of self, their oversoul's energies. There is no other soul that can take possession of you unless you agree to it, and then that is not soul possession; it is the alignment of energy. Much of what is considered a mental illness in humans can be linked to multidimensional energy connections, versions of self, and experiencing in other realities, that affect us in **this** reality. That is not to say that we cannot become imbalanced in our bodies, minds, emotions, and spirits strictly due to what we are experiencing here and how we respond to it. We must attend to our light bodies to maintain health and well-being. And, when there is a period, long or short, when you are decidedly 'not yourself,' it is helpful to go within and do some internal exploration. If there is nothing you can think of in this life that could account for a sudden change in your status, or you have been struggling with an issue all of your life that cannot be linked to an experience in this life, you may be dealing with the energy of an aspect of you that requires attention by you. Healing your aspects clears the issue for you, makes your aspects' lives better, and combines your strengths moving forward. Self-discovery and acceptance are more important than ever during this period of human ascension. We can no longer look for another soul 'hitching a ride' with us and then claim, "The devil made me do it." That is denial, and a concept that has not served humanity to raise consciousness. It keeps us stuck in the victim mentality and allows us not to take personal responsibility for our creation of reality.

Ascension to fifth-dimensional realities can be as simple as making some changes in thinking, challenging our belief systems to be rid of what no longer serves us, and aligning to our power as creator beings. We do not have to apologize or feel shame about any version of ourselves that we are not proud of. We do need to accept ourselves, our whole selves, in every evolutionary version that we are. Healing one affects all. The more you can do to heal yourself, the more uplifted energy ripples through the quantum energy fields to heal your aspects.

Believe in your ability to do this work.

Your soul believes in you.

God/Source knows you are capable of anything. It is okay to be you **and** to be human. The common joke is that none of us gets off this Earth alive. That is true when we speak of our physical form, but why not make the most of the Earth experience while you're focused here and see just how high your experience here can be? This is my intention for myself. Not perfection, only being my highest version in physical form while trying to have some fun along the way.

9

Let Go of "That Thing" Using the Quantum

Have you ever had a moment where you remembered something from your past, something you did, and you absolutely cringe at the thought of it? You've buried that memory deep in some box inside of your psyche because you simply do not want to deal with it, and remembering it is embarrassing or even painful; maybe you even go so far as to deny to yourself that it ever happened because the memory of the "thing" is so abhorrent to you? Did you have an experience where someone treated you a certain way that resulted in you feeling small about yourself, pain, or anger? When you think of that person, do you still feel angry about it even though it may have happened a long time ago, because every time the memory comes, you feel some deep level of unworthiness? Does the memory of the way you were treated cause you to feel something about someone else that is very unpleasant? Maybe every time you remember the incident; it confirms to you (in your mind) over and over that you must be some kind of weirdo or outcast from society to have anything like that happen to you. Why did it happen to you at all?

If any of this sounds familiar, then there are some energies within your physical, mental, emotional, and/or etheric bodies that are running a sort of program within you, which affects every other aspect of your life. And while this program is going on in every moment of every day, often without us being conscious of it, we are allowing those energy programs to reduce our creativity and joy in life. Why? Well, the easy thing to see is that the energetic/mental/emotional/spiritual program resulting from such incidents in our lives will tell us that we are not good people, and/or that we are not worthy of having good things in our lives because we did "X," or someone did "Y" to us.

Those thoughts are illusions, but they indicate the program is still running because you have not divined the meaning of the event which haunts you. Your mind created some meaning, and you have been believing in it ever since. If the program is still active; those negative messages about yourself, then the full meaning of the event has not been achieved.

The mental/emotional/physical/spiritual energetic program running within you is very real. But the good news is that this program, like a program running on a computer, can be rewritten and changed to work in your favor after you have taken the opportunity to understand what purpose the event came into your reality to show you. The energy of the negative incidents in life can be transmuted from pain into personal power.

You may be aware of a spiritual/psychological movement in the late 1980s and early 90s called Recovering the Inner Child, or simply called Inner Child Work. This is about therapists working to help people recover from traumas sustained in childhood. The pioneers of this technique recognized that it would be helpful to have their clients go through a guided meditation where they would visualize themselves as a child, especially at the points in life where they felt the most traumatized. Then the client was guided to visualize their adult self communicating and holding that inner child physically (imagining holding a loved one when they are hurt). It also involves the adult communicating to the inner child that they did an amazing job getting through the trauma or difficult situation, how proud the adult is of the child for getting through it, and most importantly, that the adult self would always be with the child in each moment moving forward. The inner child would know that they could make it through anything because the adult version of them was always with them, protecting them. Why did this inner child work prove to be effective? Because the adult self and the child self are the same, reaching each other energetically is always possible. The adult-self consciousness connects with the child-self consciousness and then the two are aware of and feel the connection. The child-self is infused with knowing that it is protected and watched over, even when outwardly there seems to be no one there for them to help. This is where the quantum healing happens, in my opinion. Inner child work is very needed at this point in Earth's timeline. If there is a part of you in your younger years who cringes at what they are doing or what is being done to them, then you can go to them right now in meditation and give them your love and support. This aspect of you does not have to be a child, either. You can support every part of your journey in this lifetime. This rewrites the programming.

Every single aspect of you, from every lifetime you will ever live and have lived, is very much alive in every current moment point, and actively experiencing its moment point in the eternal now (there is no time). Every aspect of you is currently alive and experiencing, but you can't see them because they are focused in another dimensional frequency (think Schrödinger's cat). But, you can meet with them and interact with them if you are willing to open your consciousness to contain multiple realities during the same focal point! Therefore, you may access every part of yourself (from this lifetime or another) to heal those aspects of you that suffer trauma. You only need to become aware of them and what the trauma is, and then you may heal it within the aspect of yourself that is experiencing it, which connects to your energy now, in the current focal point. The way to know you have healed something is when you think about it, it no longer causes a painful emotion. The memory is just a memory, neutral.

When spiritual healers assist others in healing and "recovering" parts of themselves from other lifetimes, this is called Soul Retrieval. It means that the person can become cognizant of their other lifetimes where trauma occurs. The client is usually detached cognitively from that aspect of themselves because they simply don't remember the past life and so it is not a memory in the current life. Such detachment by us from aspects of ourselves leaves us feeling incomplete sometimes, confused about phobias, and lacking self-esteem; and we don't know why. And when the injury to the aspect of us that we are detached from remains unhealed, we feel it in every lifetime following until it can be examined, understood, and healed.

Inner Child work focuses on the current physical life and the child of the current life that is you, in your conscious reality (memories). Some people can recall childhood in such a way that they remember their traumas, neglect, feeling alone, feeling weird and outcast from society, or even the times when they behaved in a way that causes them to feel ashamed. Others get flashes of memories that they suppress as much as possible, and others have forgotten all the painful parts of their childhood to protect the human psyche. I have worked with several clients that have forgotten their whole childhood up to a certain age or have forgotten big blocks of time during their childhood. It turns out, those blocks of time contained traumas that the child suppressed as a coping and survival mechanism. Our human minds are incredibly set up to protect us, to keep us "sane," to continue in life or survive. As I stated about Soul Retrieval, those parts of us that we need to heal are very much active in the quantum fields, i.e. other dimensional realities, and we may access them at any time to communicate with them and heal ourselves. You can do this on your own, through meditation and visualization (maybe record a guided meditation for yourself and use it for self-healing), or you may opt to go to any number of healers in the spiritual or psychology fields that specialize in this work. With the economy being what it is right now, and if money or time is a concern, why not try to do it for yourself first? With a little practice and allowing yourself uninterrupted time, you can be working with your inner child and other soul aspects easily and effectively! Once you get the hang of that, you can deepen your meditations to become knowledgeable about yourself, and other aspects of you in other lifetimes, and discover the "why" about the things that happened the way they did. Once you know the "why," the body/mind/emotion/spirit complex will stop running the program that calls you to pay attention to traumatic events. They will be neutralized, and you will no longer need to think about them.

    I will give you an example from my own life. There is a group of memories I have with a certain person who was an adult when I was a child and a teen. This man was a teacher and softball coach. When I was little, my sister and this man were close (not in any nefarious way). My sister is older than me by 2.5 years. As the doting younger sister, I tended to love whomever my sister favored, but that sentiment was not always returned. My sister was perfect in my eyes and the opinion of my parents. She was everything they hoped for in a daughter. I, on the other hand, was pretty good much of the time, but I also have attention deficit disorder with hyperactivity (ADHD); which I refer to now as a beautiful mind capable of holding many thoughts and ideas at the same time, and easily bored with the mundane.

    Many people found my energy and impulsivity difficult to be around. And so, one day the family was hosting a swimming party, and everyone was having a good time. People were joking around, and I very much wanted to be seen by this man that was my sister's teacher and friend. I took his leather boots and dropped them into our pool! I thought that would be funny for some reason. It wasn't, at all, for anyone. This teacher was pretty angry about it, and I don't blame him. Fast forward a few years and now this man is my teacher. I'm a little less hyper in my behavior and I still want to gain this man's approval, and for him to like me. I hoped very much he had forgotten the boots in the pool incident! But, I was not successful in gaining his favor the whole school year. He was not mean to me, but I could feel that he did not feel for me the affinity that he did for my sister. Fast forward a few more years. I had been an excellent athlete. I was a member of a summer softball team that went to the national tournament one year. None of my peers in school ever played for a team that went to the nationals. As I started my junior year of high school, I expected that I would be a regular player on the Varsity team, as I was on the junior team. But, this man was my coach for the first time. And I was not a regular player on the team that year, in fact, I was riding the bench most of the time. None of the other players that were put into my usual positions instead of me had ever achieved what I did. I was good, and very useful to the team the prior year when we won the sectional championships. I bided my time but grew increasingly upset and hurt that I was not allowed to play, other than the times the team needed someone to get a hit for them (pinch hit). I eventually lost most of my confidence and became unsuccessful when asked to pinch hit (when you don't play on the field but the coach wants you to bat). Moving now to my senior year of the Varsity softball team. The junior year is when most college scouts will notice you, and senior year is when you prove you deserve to be recruited for college softball, and possibly get a scholarship for it. In my senior year, I was riding the bench, again. I went along for about five games, hoping it would change, but then gave up and turned in my uniform. I quit one of the sports where I excelled the most and enjoyed playing since I was 9 years old.

And I blamed the man.

I hated the man.

And I hated myself because I figured the man had turned against me back when I threw his boots into my pool. I believed that. I also believed that my behavior, being rather hyper in those younger years, also prevented me from being liked by the man. I thought I had lost an opportunity to shine and possibly get a college scholarship because something was wrong with me. That is what I believed for many years.

Fast forward to today. I realized recently, when the memory of the man came to me upon waking, that this energy was still alive in me. I am 54 years of age now, and I cringed the moment I thought of him. I was angry all over again. I was angry again at myself. Having been a quantum healer for close to six years now, I knew that these feelings were indicating that I had to heal myself, or this energetic program was going to keep affecting my life. I thought I had forgiven the man long ago! This wasn't true or the feelings would have been neutral when I thought of the man, or I would not have awoken with thoughts of him in my head. My soul projected those to me to let me know the traumas were not yet resolved. The anger, lack of self-confidence, pain, and sadness I still felt were my body and mind telling me that this issue has not been healed. When something like this happens to you about a memory, you will know for sure that there is healing that needs to take place.

This is what I did to heal myself. I started to imagine myself as the child I was when I threw the boots into the pool. I could see myself very easily (me at that age). [NOTE: I've been doing this work for a long time, so understand that if you cannot imagine yourself at a certain age, keep trying and don't get frustrated with yourself. Have patience, it will happen for you too.] The next thing I did was observe myself that day. I could see how I was having fun and feeling so light, and also, I could see how innocent I was at that age. I didn't know that leather would be damaged by water! I only knew that I was trying to build some kind of rapport with the man. Being playful. Okay, good. I've forgiven myself for throwing the boots in the pool and told myself (the child self) that it's okay to make mistakes. I also told my child self that she is wonderful, smart, kind, and loving and that I will always be here for her.

Now the only thing left was for me to forgive the man. That is super important! Why? As I said, every version of us is alive in every moment that ever is, was, or will be. It's all active and going on at once. That is the quantum. Our energy signatures carry through to this moment point of reality, meaning; the version of me that is angry at the man can be felt by this man in every version of his being. So the man can feel my anger now from back to my teen years when I was playing on his softball team, and every year after that as I held the anger for him in my energy fields. It's like throwing a rock into a lake. The energy of the rock hitting the water projects outward in an ever-expanding ripple (360-degree) effect that can be felt by everything in the water. My anger is the rock, and as long as I keep throwing it in this man's lake, he is going to feel it. That is how energy works. Emotions are energy, and that energy carries throughout the dimensions. Some souls come back several lifetimes together to resolve the energy of an incident that occurred in one lifetime! It's that powerful. How do I go about forgiving the man? I started with what I think I know about him. The first thing I think I know is that the man has seemed to be very serious over the years that I have experienced his personality. I knew for a fact that he was a teacher and coach, and those positions tend to carry a level of responsibility and seriousness. I also became aware, during meditation, that this man may have been an alcoholic. Now I don't judge, but if that is possibly true, then that tells me there are some things in his life that he wants to forget or drown out emotionally with alcohol. That means that the man has some pain in his life too.

Okay. The man is human. Just like me.

That's a good starting point for forgiveness. Then I asked myself if it is possible that the man didn't like me, or didn't warm up to me, because he does not know how to deal with hyperactive children? Or maybe hyperactive children cause him stress? I asked myself if it is possible that the man being so serious all the time could be a result of his upbringing, and maybe he was rigid because of that. It would then be possible that the man saw me as being an undisciplined brat because of my behavior and being the youngest child, and simply could not see the other parts of me which are brilliant. Are you beginning to see what I'm getting at? I allowed myself to imagine many reasons why the man didn't like me that **were all personal reasons for him, and not my responsibility**. I was being who I was as a child, and he was being who he was. Neither of us was a bad person even though we did some things that were not kind. I was holding compassion for the man and compassion for myself, and in doing that, I forgave us both. The release of the anger and sadness, lack of self-esteem, and dire wish to not remember our past faded away completely. It is now a neutral feeling in my body when I recall myself and the man; my memories of those years. I finished my healing by wishing the man much love and thanking him for allowing me to learn self-love and forgiveness.

    If your memories do not allow you to know about a person and why they did what they did, I suggest you could use your imagination to consider the possibilities of why a person would do such things. People do not treat other people badly because they deserve to be treated badly. People treat people badly because they are acting from a place of personal pain. Have you ever known a happy person to purposefully do something hurtful to another human being or animal? No. Happy people don't go around doing that, they have no desire to do so. So it stands to reason that if someone is hurting you, **they are acting out of their pain**. It doesn't excuse the offender from responsibility, but it does help us to know this because then we can find ways to hold compassion and find forgiveness for the offender. Knowing this also serves you because then you do not assume incorrect ideas about yourself when you are offended (i.e. I deserved to be treated that way, I am not a good person, there is something wrong with me).

    Any stage of your life, this one or another, can be healed using your energy in quantum fields. The only barrier we have to the various versions of ourselves is our focal point. When we choose to expand our focal point to contain multiple realities (like in meditation or hypnosis), and not just look at what is in front of our eyes right now, we can then energetically connect and heal any aspect of our being that requires it. The energy of our intention to heal conveys wherever we direct it. Have you heard the saying "What you focus on becomes your reality?" It's much like watching the news. If you focus on good news, your reality is filled with more joy. You have more things to be grateful for, and more comes in to be grateful for after that because you have sent out into the universe your gratitude. If you focus on bad news (doom and gloom situations), then you remove joy from your life and replace it with fear, sorrow, anger, resentment, and so on. Reprogramming the energy of your memories of events in your life is like changing the bad news to the good news. What was once (and possibly for a long time) a sad story, can be transformed into a positive story because you re-write the meaning of the story for yourself. And in doing so, you also re-write it for anyone else involved, energetically. You've changed the meaning of the story for yourself and others from one of tragedy to personal power. And as the collective of humanity continues to heal itself individually, then the whole of humanity will heal too. It can be no other way. We heal the pain and therefore don't continue to transfer the pain to our future selves, or our families and communities.

That is, by the way, why people continue to hurt other people. They are transferring their pain onto others. It is usually the unconscious programming from our childhood that gives us our methods of dealing with pain. Some people internalize it and never pass it on to others, and some pass their pain on to others regularly. Or a combo of both. It could be conscious transference or unconscious. However, this is not about blame. It is about healing ourselves so that we can be free of internalized traumas.

Using quantum methods to heal other aspects of yourself, in this life or another, past, present, or future; are effective healing processes using a conscious focus of intention, that will free you permanently from pain and trauma, and allow you to move forward in life as the creative, confident, powerful being that you are. Compassion for everyone else's humanity is also a nice side-effect of doing this work that will ultimately bring about unity consciousness, human ascension, and a peaceful world.

10

Real Magic

Before I start sharing with you what I have learned about magic through exploring the quantum fields of reality, I want to take a moment to highlight some of my favorite mentors who are master magicians. I have had many mentors while learning about and expanding my consciousness, starting with Robert M. Bridges (aka Bob). Bob was the first mentor that I sought out intentionally, and he empowered me to see and know my light within, and begin using my magic. That is one very important key to working your magic. You must see and know the light inside of you, the God/Source spark, that resides in us all. The next mentor I will highlight is Darryl Anka, who channels an ET being (Bashar) and has provided messages from this being to help humanity ascend for more than 37 years. To live/be/manifest our highest possible realities. "Bashar describes the importance of **belief systems** and explains how to change what you believe about yourself and your world to dramatically change what you experience in your life. Bashar describes the planet as going through a major transformation now, an evolutionary leap to the next level of consciousness. Bashar's messages provide reminders of what we already know but have forgotten, and can help us experience this transition smoothly and joyfully, by expanding our awareness of the unlimited possibilities that are truly available to us in the now moment." (www.bashar.org/who-is-bashar/). Darryl's channelings highlight the importance of **belief as the vehicle of creation**.

    I wish to also highlight the teachings of Paul Selig, who is a clear channel and medium who allows 'the guides' to speak through him. Paul does not reference by name a particular being, rather he calls the beings that he channels 'the guides' (see the chapter What's in a Name). He has written many books, three that I own and refer to often, and Paul also provides workshops and free content on YouTube. Paul's work solidified for me one truth. That truth is what I have been hearing over the years about using 'I Am' statements as a form of personal transformation. I Am statements **intonate** (match) the version of you that you are choosing to be. In other words; tapping into the higher dimensional states of being creates a higher reality. The real magic, real transformation, and what we can see with our REAL EYES (realize) in our experience of now. Paul Selig's work provides methods to do this for yourself, and understanding that "holding any part of yourself in darkness only keeps you in darkness." Paul's guides speak of claiming yourself in "the Upper Room." "The Upper Room, the level of Christ mind that you embody in, is available to you." (Alchemy, Book Two: The Beyond the Known Trilogy, p. 13). My interpretation of this is that the consciousness contained within our souls residing in the monad is available to us, right here, right now. We claim and embody these consciousness realities through our thoughts, words, and deeds. *I AM* statements proclaim whatever it is you are choosing to be at any moment point. Through these words, we 'cast our spells,' and embody whatever aspect of Source we choose to be.

    I started learning about using 'I AM' statements to shift my reality through Bob's mentoring. He started me off with books by Louise Hay, which highlight personal creation of health and wellbeing specifically using I Am statements. The idea is to place whatever state of being you are wanting to experience after the words, "I am, "as if you are already that state of being and you are proclaiming it to the universe. This solidifies your agreement to that state of being that you already are in another dimension and brings it to the now moment. I started reading her books and practicing her affirmations in my early 20s. "I am love, I am abundant, I am perfect health." These I still include in my daily routine. Bob let me borrow Louise's books from his library because I did not have a lot of money to buy them in those days. You can find them at a local library I suspect, or for very little money if you buy them used. I highly recommend Louise's free online content (louisehay.com/affirmations/). It is timeless wisdom and will assist you with wielding your personal power and magic to manifest your reality, consciously. I will also mention Dr. Wayne Dyer at this time. His work has had a profound effect on my life that continues to this day. He and Louise were close friends and associates in the work of expanding consciousness/using personal power to transform (magic).

    I mention these beautiful souls and their work because they have contributed to my understanding of personal power in creation, or what we may consider 'our magic.' There are many more that I could highlight but, the key is to realize that YOUR mentors are the ones who you are called to read and listen to. The student becomes the teacher. The teacher learns from being a student. And regularly, the student teaches the teacher. This is how energy works. I use the terms student and teacher, but the broader understanding is that we are all here remembering and realizing in physical form that we are all powerful beings of Source. None of us are any higher or lower than

the others. We are in different stages of remembering (consciousness), and we are doing this together, as teachers **and** students, which is why we bother incarnating on Earth together in the first place. That's it. The only reason. By expanding consciousness through experience, we expand our wisdom. We share that wisdom all the time, whether we know it or not. An example of this is when an adult hears something a child says, or witnesses something a child does, and they hear/see the eternal wisdom in it. In this example, the child is the teacher and helps the adult remember, or realize, who they truly are, despite what lower consciousness experiences of Earth reality have taught them to believe about themselves. A shift can happen so quickly that it seems to be magical. And it IS magical when any being realizes their true self.
We, that are interested in raising our consciousness and applying wisdom to our lives, will find many mentors along the way. They are placed into our life path by the agreement of souls. We are being mentors also, in every interaction with others.

    Becoming aware of **how** we are being is key to working our magic within the highest wisdom possible. I like to give credit where credit and gratitude are due to my mentors, but the simple fact is; I am responsible for how I am being at any moment, and so are you. The information contained in all of my writing is heavily influenced by the conscious awareness of how I am being, what I have learned through quantum healing sessions and my mentors. If anything, the combination has provided proof to me that the concepts I am sharing are real and true, by application in my own life and realizing positive results. I find it impossible to separate experiences enough to pinpoint when exactly a piece of wisdom is internalized and realized. For me, it is not one piece of wisdom that has shifted my entire life, but a blending and molding process that has been going on for years. We become a projection of all of our experiences and choices. We share our magic with each other.

    I'll continue my conversation about Real Magic by repeating that **we are** Creator, God/Source beings. There is nothing nor a state of being that we are not capable of reaching and creating for ourselves. We can heal ourselves, manifest amazing technologies, art, songs, and even do things that most of us on Earth do not believe humanly possible. Expanding consciousness to gain wisdom is the key. What humans do not remember about personal 'magic' is a lot. This chapter is aimed at empowering you to recognize (re-cog-nize) your power. Many humans have physically/emotionally healed themselves and/or assisted others to do the same, even with serious or fatal conditions (i.e. the book *Dying*

To Be Me: My Journey from Cancer, to Near Death, to True Healing; Anita Moorjani). People have bent metal spoons with their thoughts, levitated themselves/objects, walked on hot coals without being burned or feeling pain...the list goes on and on. The 'magic' is within us and is being expressed by humans all of the time. We've had many examples of the mind/ body connection and changing beliefs to alter expected outcomes throughout our history. I read a story about a man whose parachute did not open after a jump from an airplane. He told himself, repeatedly, on the way back to Earth, "light as a feather, light as air." This man not only did not crush and die when he impacted Earth, he merely injured his leg as a result of the impact! What is the magic of these humans that appear to have done the impossible? Expanded consciousness. That is their magic. The real magic potential exists within all of us.

    What is the universe and what does it have to do with discovering our magic? My definition of 'the universe' when I speak of communicating with it is an energy field we set up from the monadic entity to protect and guide our soul aspects as we journey, or incarnate, within physical and etheric realities, to experience. In this sense, I am not talking about the stars, planets, moons, and suns when I speak of the universe. Those are naturally a part of it, but I am referring to universal **energy** fields when I say, "Send it out to the universe." The physical elements (stars, planets, etc.) of every universe are comprised of energy moving in such a way that it appears to take form. Universal energies are also light energies, sound energies, and thought energies. Our thoughts, words, and deeds send our energy signatures out into universal energy fields and they are 'read' by those universal energies as our intentions for what we next wish to experience. The universe responds by sending back to us matching energy to what we put out, and this is our communication system through 'the universe' with our souls. Our oversouls created this system of communication to have direct information sharing with its aspects(us), to learn about the nature of any given reality, and for us to remember to use our power to create and wield our magic.

    Whenever we are expanding our consciousness, 'the universe' can be counted on to guide the path no matter what we are focusing on. I use the example of a baseball pitchback. It's a net that players use when they do not have someone to throw a ball with. For instance, when a pitcher is practicing in the backyard, they throw the ball at the pitchback, towards a square target on the net, and the ball is returned to them. The pitcher can gauge their accuracy by how the ball comes back to them. This eliminates the need to chase all over the yard after the ball once it is pitched. Your intention (your energy) is the ball, that you send out into the universal energies (the pitchback), and the universe sends you the ball back (feedback about your intentions). Sometimes you get physical manifestations like; a change in health, getting that job you want, finding your next place to live, or meeting a person who helps you in some way (direct feedback). Other times you get synchronicities. For instance, how the lyrics in a song you listen to seem to answer a question you are thinking about, a conversation overheard provides insight into a dilemma you are experiencing, something you hear on the radio or social media gives you an idea to do something. Synchronicities are indirect feedback from your soul. Direct and indirect feedbacks from the universe are NOT accidents, nor coincidences. They are reflections of our states of being and how we are creating. They are also mirrors of our energy. To wield our magic consciously, we must decide to become aware of the messages by 'tuning in' to our experiences more thoughtfully, otherwise, we think whatever comes is mere coincidence or luck. I assure you, there are no coincidences in this world and we make our luck.

You may receive a 'gut feeling' about something with no reasoning attached to it. That is the universe sending you a message from your soul through your body! These messages inform you when your intentions are for your highest good, or that they are 'off the mark' with your soul's purpose. If you do not receive a message about one of your intentions in some form, then you may look at your intention as neutral. Do it or not, your soul isn't commenting because whatever you are intending with a neutral response is not going to take you off-course from your soul's plan. But, if you get a super positive feeling or message when you state your intention or think about it, then that is a message that you are moving in high accordance with your soul's plan. I suggest grabbing those with both hands because those intentions will bring you the most joy in life. Following those exciting ideas will unleash your magic to create the reality you will most enjoy experiencing. Hence the saying, "Follow your joy."

Whatever you are realizing (manifesting), you have put out into the universe through your thoughts, words, and deeds. If you don't like what you are receiving, then it is time to evaluate what you are putting out. When you evaluate what you are putting out, then you expand your consciousness. And that is when you discover, or remember, more of your creative magic. Expanded consciousness. This is the first place to start when you want to work your magic. There is no great secret here. In fact, it is so obvious, that we would automatically know about it if we did not go through the veil of forgetting as we came to the 3D or 4D realities (Earth). The soul had to reduce part of its consciousness (memory that we are Source, we can manifest whatever we wish) on purpose to have the experiences it wanted to have as separated from Source.

Social conditioning has reinforced our amnesia. Everyone in our lives from our birth seems to tell us what our limits are because they also have forgotten that we can manifest any reality. No problem, our souls planned to forget. Some do remember from birth on, and we call them awakened or enlightened souls, like Jesus. Those individuals have a special mission while on Earth and their souls chose not to diminish their consciousness when first arriving in human form. They had to be taught how to live in human reality, but they did not forget their divinity. The reason the rest of us are awakening now and starting to remember is because we have already experienced what our souls intended in lower consciousness realities, and now we are ready to embody our souls' consciousness energy to have more evolved experiences. Our superhuman 'magic' is being activated. We can fast-track this process with the intention that we will **pay attention** to universal guidance by noticing what manifests in our realities. How can we be more conscious of what we are intending, being, and what we tell the universe that we want to manifest?

Let's start with the magic of thoughts and emotions. Thoughts and emotions are part of our soul's communication to us and from us, using quantum fields of energy (universal energy). You could say that thoughts and emotions coming from us are part of the song of our soul. Is the song being played at a high frequency? Are the notes melodic, or are they sometimes scrambled? What are we telling our soul about our current status? More on that in a bit.

As we discussed the four light bodies, thoughts, and emotions given by the oversoul **to us** are a guidance system to keep us moving in the direction we set up in our life plan. An example is when you are going about your day, you hear a bird singing, and it causes you to feel joy. The soul is sending you positive reinforcement of whatever you are doing through universal energy fields that attracted the bird to your vicinity. If you experience the bird and it is making a racket of irritating noises, your soul may be trying to warn you about something, or disagreeing with whatever you were thinking about just then. Is it possible you were thinking some negative thought about yourself that the bird was sent to scramble the thought out of you? Were you feeling angry about something someone did and the bird is mirroring your annoyance? Too many people ignore the signs and symbols around them when their soul is trying to communicate. We were never taught by society that this is how the soul often communicates. Another example is if you go out in public and witness a family fighting (verbally). Do you question why you witnessed that? Is it possible you are trying to work something out within your own family and the one you just witnessed is showing you what not to do? Awareness. What is your environment communicating to you? That is your soul's message.

Our emotions are also generated from the thoughts in our human minds. When we speak of emotions generated by the human mind, these happen as a result of our Earthly experiences and the thoughts we have about those. Their energy goes out into the universe to our oversouls rather than coming to us from the oversoul. So, we have thoughts and emotions as humans because of what we experience, and how we are being, and those are communicated to the oversoul. Then, our oversoul responds with direct or indirect feedback.

If I do something and I feel guilt or shame about it, it is not because my oversoul is sending those emotions. I feel shame because I have a belief that tells me what I have done is shameful. The oversoul will send me a higher thought about myself. My human aspect might then choose a better action in the future than what I did before because I choose to be more like the self the oversoul communicated to me. In this example, I feel guilt or shame because I have not yet learned to accept the truth. On Earth, I will not always behave as my oversoul would, but my oversoul is always guiding me to know it better. It will never leave me out in the cold nor condemn me. Once I accept the fallibility of my human nature, the oversoul's reminder will be received and integrated. These reminders are not judgments. Humans judge themselves, not oversouls. Oversouls communicate unconditional love and reminders about our true nature. The whole communication between soul and aspect is flowing constantly, and it goes both ways.

There are two emotions that all other emotions stem from. Love and fear. Love can be witnessed in many forms. And so it is with fear. The way to tell the difference between all of the designations is if something makes you feel good, or not. If something causes you to feel good, it is love. If you feel anything else, then it is fear-based. Unconditional love is the highest frequency of vibration. It is the energy of Source. Source is unconditionally loving. Souls begin to experience fear the further we journey away from Source in density because we forget our true nature, which is always unconditional love, God Spark. If you consider that kindness, compassion, peace, forgiveness, courage, generosity, acceptance, and other similar models of behavior are states of **being loving**, then it is easy to see the emotion they start with and result in, are love. For example, I decide to be kind to my friend, not critical. I practice kindness to my friend as she processes (thinks about) an experience she calls 'a mistake.' Something she did and now regrets doing. I suggest the benefits that could come from the experience, rather than adding to her distress by stating all of the potential negative side-effects of the 'mistake.' In this example, I am **loving** my friend who is evaluating an experience she had. We describe that state of being as kindness. But what does showing kindness do? Kindness uplifts the vibration of energy. It is one expression of love. Kindness, compassion, forgiveness, courage, generosity, acceptance, and many more are states of **being** love. I put 'mistake' in quotes because nothing we do is either good or bad in the eyes of Source, it is all experience. Since humans are oft to judge experiences, we can attach a good or bad thought about them, and we usually do. We judge our experiences rather than using them to shape how we wish to **be** during the next experience.

Experience allows us to make choices. Are we going to see the experience as good, bad, or as merely an experience that helps us know our true nature more? Are we going to be like our highest self during difficult experiences, or are we going to be some other way? Our soul came here to have experiences, to remember that we ARE Source, and explore the unlimited ways we can be Source while we experience. Our challenge is not to judge the experiences, it is to remember who and what we are. Once we fully remember, then we will act as our oversoul would and as Source would, with unconditional love, in every moment. We will transmute negative emotions (fear) and live in loving ways naturally. Moving from one polarity to the other is how our soul expands its consciousness, its wisdom. Life on Earth is one focal point of reality with the illusion of time, not a competition to see who can fully remember and be more like Source first. We have as many lifetimes to experience different versions of our soul's energy and make these choices, as we wish to have. We are not likely to go from forgetting who and what we are completely (3D consciousness) to remembering it all in one moment. To do that, humans would need to release all judgment of everything, let go of labels of any kind, and stop being interested in outcomes completely. Basically, you would have to become a tree or snail. All joking aside, if you did shift from not remembering to suddenly remember it all, that would transform your aspect immediately from physical to non-physical. I suppose it is possible, but I have not done it and so I will keep discussing the steps that I have used in my own life toward remembering my true nature, my magic.

I have talked about how higher vibrational emotions are expressions of love. Now let's cover the lower vibrational emotion, hate (extreme anger), and why exercising fear keeps you from expressing your magic. How is the emotion 'hate' a subcategory of fear? I will give an imaginary example. Say I bought a house and the bank has foreclosed on it because I cannot make my mortgage payments. I do not technically own this house because I did not pay for it in full when I made the purchase agreement. I made a contract with the bank to pay for it in installments. When I get the foreclosure notice, I think I feel hatred for the bank. I might blame the bank for me not being able to live in the house much longer. What is going on is that I am in **fear**. I fear the judgment of others about 'losing' the house, I fear not having a place to live, and maybe I also fear that I am stupid for buying a house that I can no longer afford. Are these fearful thoughts true? Well, I'd say they are true for me if I **choose** to believe in them, and not choose other thoughts about the experience. What other thoughts could I choose? Here are some suggestions. Maybe I can afford to rent an apartment or stay with someone until I get my finances back in order. What if I choose *not* to think at all about what other people think about my situation? What if, at the time that I entered into the purchase agreement with the bank, I had enough money and could easily afford the payments, but I lost my job and this is the cause of having to find alternative living arrangements rather than the bank doing something to me that I should hate them, or myself, for? What if I think I spent my money unwisely, and my next thought is that I've learned from the foreclosure to be a better money manager in the future? Will I still hate the bank if I choose one of the higher thoughts? **Reframing** our thoughts about an experience is usually helpful after the initial fear has passed. Reframing fearful thoughts expands consciousness enough to learn from an experience, drop the fear, and move forward more positively than blaming someone or something. Maybe I gambled my money away and that is the reason I cannot afford my mortgage. In that case, do I need to hate and blame myself, the bank, and the people I gambled my money to? Or, can I choose to learn from it, forgive myself, and not repeat the experience?

If I make alternative choices from the initial fear-based thoughts, then my fears are not real. They are emotions created by the **illusion** that I would have nowhere to live and people would judge me for it because I am a bad person. Of course, we humans also have a habit of feeling fear when something happens that alters any reality of what we believe to be stable. Most of us do not like change because what we currently know *appears* to be more comfortable than some unknown reality. Most humans have been taught to fear to change (social conditioning). There is also a very real survival element, to resist change, that we carry in our DNA, and it comes from generations of ancestral experience where change could mean serious discomfort or even death. There is nothing wrong with feeling fear. As we expand our consciousness to reframe our experiences within modern realities, we can feel LESS fear. To reframe the experience of losing my house in my thoughts is to decide if the fear is somewhat justified (I must leave my house soon, action is needed), if the fear is a socially conditioned response that can be discarded (everyone is going to think I'm stupid because I let this happen), or if the fear is not useful and I can let it go (I have enough resources to obtain a new place to live). Once the initial thoughts are reframed, I will shift from hate/fear and change to more loving emotions/thoughts, going forward. I have shifted from creating my next reality in fear to a new reality inspired by personal power and energy. Just like magic.

Our brains are like computers with partial DNA drivers. Some of what is stored in our DNA is about biological imperative, while the rest is programmed through social conditioning and ancestral experience. It does take time and effort to reprogram your thoughts and brain, and your soul is communicating through universal energies and your light bodies to help you do it. Each person will get there in their own time. Be kind to yourself, reframe experiences with broader views about them, and positive results will happen. This is your magic. You get to choose your reaction, the thoughts that frame your beliefs for every experience that you have.

When you change your thoughts and beliefs, emotional states follow suit. The more you choose the higher thought about an experience, the more you will feel your **vibration** is higher, and your beliefs will be altered toward higher consciousness beliefs. And then the universe will send you more positive experiences to be happy about, more to love. Your oversoul and every higher self in between you will cheer your progress! You will feel more love for yourself and others. The thoughts you will put out into the universe will get pitched back in the form of better future experiences.

I think we need one more example. How is sadness (or long-term sadness, which is called depression) fear? Let's say I was bullied as a child. Kids didn't usually like me, for whatever reason, and they pushed me around, said nasty things about me, and pulled pranks on me that hurt my feelings. During these incidents, I felt sad because I feared that something was wrong with me, that I was unlikeable, and/or that this would always be my experience in life with other people. Over the years and into adulthood, I carried these fearful thoughts around with me in everything I did. New jobs, relationships, and family interactions. I continued the fearful thought that something is wrong with me and that people wouldn't like me, no matter what I did or how hard I tried to be likable. This stretched out so long that I am diagnosed with depression, and medicated. The problem is, the medication might make me feel better for a while, but the underlying fear that causes me to feel depressed has not changed, so I keep increasing the dose of my meds or changing them, with little lasting results. Maybe I go for counseling to see what the root cause of my depression is. I do this for a long time and start to feel less sad. My thoughts about myself and others start to shift to higher thoughts. I then realize, while in counseling, that my views of being bullied were skewed because I remembered that there were, in fact, a lot of people that did like me when I was growing up. I also make lists of what I like and don't like about myself, and realize that I am judging myself very harshly most of the time. My list includes judgments about myself that are not based on fact, and I drop those thoughts. I continue the counseling sessions and notice that I feel better and better about myself. I've even learned what motivated me to do things that I am angry at myself for. My consciousness expands and I decide to study counseling techniques and apply them to others. To share my knowledge to help people find more understanding of themselves. Years later, I have a hypnosis session to raise my consciousness even more. I start meditating and practicing yoga, and these practices raise my consciousness further. Turns out, I realized that my fearful thoughts about being bullied as a child were causing my sadness. And then, as my consciousness grew to know myself more truly, I was able to release those fearful thoughts. A nice side effect of the whole process is it led me to a career that I love.

        To recap the magic, depression causes me to be willing to open my consciousness and discover that I am afraid. I allow myself to open the door to self-realization because I did not want to be afraid anymore. Yes, it hurts all over again when I recount my experiences. But, this time I am viewing the events through the eyes of an adult, and with someone who supports reframing the thoughts about the events. As an adult, I can see much more about the bullying events than I could as a child. I can see that many of the children that bullied me were going through problems themselves. Maybe I also realize that I was a bright, shiny kid that found joy in the little things, and this is probably another reason why others didn't like me (more re-framing). They did not want me to shine brighter than they did, so they bullied me to reduce my shine. The old saying, "Misery loves company." I also identified a part of myself, as a child, that for whatever reason didn't feel worthy of love, and so I attracted people that would be unloving towards me (the pitchback). That issue is really common, by the way. You might be surprised how many people have that fearful belief rolling around in their subconscious, creating havoc in their lives! So where am I now in the process? I have decided to look for the root cause of my depression (introspect), I've made steps forward to do that (take action), and I am now reprogramming myself and my childhood experiences with different thoughts (re-framing). What's next? This is where I use my magic some more. First, I tell my child-self that I love her. If no one else does, I love her! That is the most powerful spell that I cast. Second, I remind her that she made it through all of that, and she is very strong to have done so (reinforcement of positive vibration). I list for her all the things I love about us, the way we are. This process is called inner-child work. Inner-child work uses quantum energy fields to reach a part of yourself that is very much alive and affecting your current emotions (shared consciousness). In this whole process of self-discovery, I also identify ways that I have allowed my fearful thoughts to invite vulnerability to people who are attracted to someone with low self-esteem, and I start setting boundaries with those people. I might even reduce exposure to those people who contribute to my fears if they do not respect my boundaries and start treating me the way I know I deserve to be treated. I eliminate people who intentionally try to play on my fears after setting boundaries because they do not deserve any more chances to exert their power over mine (exercise personal power).

    Wow. I feel so much better! I feel excited about my future because I value myself. I love myself! It starts as small steps, but the more I perform this magic, the more powerful I feel personally, and at some point, I notice that my reality gets better and better. The people in my life are supportive, even if it is only one person, me! I am willing to risk being alone now because I enjoy my own company, not because I am fearful people won't like me. Friends can be beneficial and I prefer having them, but if push comes to shove, I am only going to invite friends into my energy fields that have the best intentions for our relationship, or I am not having them at all.

If you have guessed by now that this last example is from my own life experiences, then you are correct. I discovered some of my magic. I put the work in to know myself and expanded my consciousness, which shifted my reality in what I can only say is magical ways. And, I continue to do so every day of my life. I highly recommend it. My life feels more joyous and happier now that I have dropped the fear that I am unlovable. The long-term sadness has gone away. The new emotions brought about by the new beliefs about myself are not some constant stream of positivity, excluding lower emotional states. But, the joyful emotions, the love, does occur more often than I ever thought possible as a 21-year-old. And this is why I continue to expand my consciousness every day. To challenge and alter my beliefs in ways that bring more joy to my life. I am a work in progress. If I could feel this much better, then why not keep going?

I have discussed utilizing your thoughts and emotions to expand consciousness and know your soul's calling, which unlocks your magic. We can change our whole reality with our magical ability to know ourselves, see things in new ways, and transform into new ways of being. We have choices. We are not stuck being the way we learned to be in childhood. The magic you realize within yourself starts with awareness of your thoughts and emotions, and what they are telling you about yourself. **Emotions** change according to the **beliefs** that we hold about something; some experience of the world we live in, or what we believe about ourselves. Let us now focus on beliefs about the world and what is possible, and how they shape your magic.

Dr. Masaru Emoto was a Japanese researcher and held a Ph.D. in alternative medicine. He conducted a series of experiments with energy and water in the frozen state; his ice crystal work. What Dr. Emoto discovered is that water molecules (in ice crystal form) display differently depending on the energy that was given to them. The test subjects were vials of ice. The influence on them (the test) is the energy given to the ice crystals, provided by people speaking to the vials of ice. When a person would speak negatively close to some ice vials over time, the ice crystals appeared distorted when viewed with a microscope. The ice crystals that were spoken to kindly displayed beautiful patterns. The water in all test subjects (the ice) came from the same source in each trial. Dr. Emoto conducted many studies of this phenomenon with repeated results. He used fresh water, salt water, water with additives in it, etc. He concluded that the energy vibration of the speaker physically changed the presentation of the molecular structure of the water in frozen form. I'm simplifying this but the bottom line is; positive vocalizations (tones) carried the energy of well-being to matter. Negative vocalizations resulted in the distortion of matter. I learned about Dr. Emoto's experiments when I was studying quantum healing. I use these concepts in my life and practice. The relevance of magic is that we can **transmute** any negative element in our environment based on how we think about it, and how we speak about it, and those depend on what we **believe** about it. If we say and think good things about our food, water, air, homes, cars, jobs, relationships, and everything in our environments; the energy given will transmute negative energies that are in their fields and transform the environmental element into something that you desire more to experience.

The more you practice it, the more energy is given, and the more transformation you will see.

We give more to get more.

The exception is when people are involved. We can shift the energy of our relationships with other people when our thoughts, words, and deeds are of a higher vibration than usual. But, if we do this for a while and the other people involved refuse to shift, then it is time to wave goodbye to them. Release them with love and gratitude (you wish the best for them, and are grateful for the experience because it taught you something about yourself).

Add gratitude for anything you are enjoying because being grateful is some of the highest vibrational magic you can wield. It seems like a huge leap of faith to believe that just thinking about something positively could result in a positive outcome, and yet, isn't giving energy to the objects around us going to result in a pitch-back from the universe? Does the universe send us more of what we send out? Thoughts, words, and deeds are energy. The vocalizations to the ice crystals in Dr. Emoto's experiments were energy projections. When you tell your body good things about it, it will respond with good health and appearance. We are the true conductors in the symphony of our lives. What notes are we playing? Do you like the music, or would you like to change it? You can. We all can if we start being aware of the notes we are playing. The notes we play about our food/water sources can change their energy, and that changes the effects on our physical systems.

As an example, a friend of mine traveled and stayed in Mexico for vacation about 35 years ago. She told me that she bought bottled water during the vacation to avoid drinking any Mexican tap water, to avoid getting sick. My friend believed that drinking tap water in Mexico would make her sick, even though millions of Mexicans drink tap water every day. She told me that back in those days (35 years ago) the Mexican people fertilized their crops with human feces rather than animal feces, and so Americans had been known to get sick from drinking the tap water because their bodies were not used to consuming human bacteria on that scale. I have no idea if any of that is true, I'm sharing my friend's belief. She was having a grand time and drank the bottled water in perfect health for the first four days/nights. On the fifth night, her roommate asked her if she purposefully brushed her teeth using tap water to wet the brush, or was it by accident? My friend did not realize that she had done it, and went into a panic about it. She told me that wetting her toothbrush with tap water is a habit and she probably did it every night without thinking about it. Sure enough, my friend had manifested a full-blown stomach issue (including diarrhea) the evening her roommate posed the question, and it continued into the following day. When she told me about it, I asked her if she thought the cause was the tiny bit of tap water she used to wet the toothbrush. She replied "Yes." My friend studied to be a nurse. She had a big fear of germs and bacteria in those days. I asked her directly, "Did you wet your toothbrush with the tap water the previous nights?" After some thought, she responded "Yes," and then she attributed the illness to have resulted from a cumulative effect of doing that. I asked her then if it could have been her *discovery* of the fact that caused her to become ill (the belief that the water would make her sick), rather than the water causing the illness. She maintained belief in the cumulative effect, using the tap water over several days. I do not claim to be knowledgeable about how much human waste in tap water will make a human sick, but I do know that our stomach acid destroys a lot of bacteria ingested with our food. I think my friend convinced her body to become ill because her belief in the water's toxicity was so strong. Can I prove it? No. Is it *possible* that my friend had transmuted any negative effects of the water the first four nights because she was simply not aware that there was anything wrong with it when she wet her toothbrush? Yes.

    This is a probable example of the placebo effect. The placebo effect is well documented in the scientific community, although scientists cannot explain it. It usually means that people given sugar pills in a trial/study of medication experienced the same healing as those who got the actual drug being studied. I've always suspected that the placebo effect is what happens when the mind directs the body to do something. It happens, in my opinion, because we are expecting a certain effect and we believe it will happen because we are taking action that we believe will cause the effect we are expecting. The mind is the governing agent of the body, and the body does what the mind tells it to. I wrote extensively about the body-mind connection and how our beliefs affect our health in my first book.

Energy is energy.

Thoughts are energy and form our beliefs.

Beliefs affect our future thoughts and therefore direct our energy. A belief about the body is the energetic directive for the body to be a certain way. Therefore, if I take medicine (even though I don't realize it is a sugar pill) and believe it will heal my illness, then my body will heal. The body registers this energetic directive and heals, even though it received sugar which is not supposed to cure anything by medical standards. The placebo effect means that you are curing your body with your thoughts, and, as the above example with Mexican water illustrates, you may also make your body sick with your thoughts. There is scientific documentation that people in drug trials that received the placebo experienced 'side effects' to the non-drug because they expected that all drugs have side effects.

Disclaimer: for this next conversation, I am not speaking about foods you are allergic to. Food allergies usually have a deeply rooted cause that is mental, emotional, ancestral, or even a past-life scenario, speaking metaphysically. Food allergies in mainstream society are legally considered a medical issue, and I am not a medical doctor, nor am I giving medical advice. The following discussion about food intentionally exempts cases of food allergies.

If you consistently believe that a certain food is bad for you, your body will respond negatively when it receives the food. It may not process the food at all if your beliefs are strong enough. Then your body may pass the food unprocessed, or feel sick when you eat it. If you tell yourself that everything you choose to eat is good for you and that your body will process it effectively and easily, you will have that result. Unless you do not believe what you are telling yourself. You cannot "fake it till you make it" with the body/mind connection because your body knows when you are lying to it. But, if you do change your thoughts about the foods you are eating, then you will notice a change in your overall beliefs, and in how your body responds to those foods. It's like flipping a switch, magic.

Let's consider for a moment that all of our food sources are not of the same quality. Cows, chickens, fish, and plants have different levels of health, and they have different nutrients/chemicals fed to them. How are we to know we are ingesting the best possible food for our bodies? Outside of reading labels and picking food sources you feel comfortable with, I suggest using Dr. Emoto's methods to think and speak to your food, to transform it to its healthiest state using energy, before eating it. One can also give thanks to the animal or plant while cooking the meal because gratitude honors the soul of the food and the energy of gratitude is of high vibration. It will transform food and water to its healthiest state.   Plus your body knows you are doing all of this and accepts the food as being good for you. The food is then processed easily.

Speaking of the body's reaction to your thoughts and beliefs, if you tell yourself everything you enjoy eating will make you fat, guess what will happen when you eat those foods? Your body-mind connection is just *that* powerful. I have used my thoughts to create the state of being 'thin' without changing my diet. Without additional exercise. That sounds like magic, and it happened. God knows the fad diets and weight loss "miracle" pills did not work at all for me! Do they work for anyone? 'Thinking myself thin' worked for me for years until I accepted the fear-based belief that I would put on weight when I hit menopause. I've lost most of the weight that I gained when I first went into menopause, but I wish I didn't let that thought slide into my brain because once a belief is settled there, it takes countermeasures and effort to stop believing it.

Think about it for a minute. Why do societal forces work so hard to tell women they will get fat, especially in the belly, when they go into menopause? I know about the hormone change thing, but I think that's just an excuse because not all women gain weight during menopause! If the cause of menopausal weight gain were only about hormones, wouldn't **every** woman gain weight at that time in her life? I think it is a fair question. Moreover, I suspect that society drills these messages into our heads (women) because there is a decided benefit for others when we believe it and manifest actual weight gain. The gyms get more older women signing up ($), doctors get more business ($), pharmaceutical companies get more sales ($), and herbal remedy companies get more sales($), the list is endless. Wardrobe changes alone could sink a girl into depression and then there she goes to the doctor for some antidepressants or weight control medication ($$$$)! It is maddening to me the way societal forces try to manipulate our beliefs for their own gain. I spoke about a woman's issue, but men are far from out of the target zone. They worry about their appearances just as much as women do. Take hair loss for instance. I'd like to have 1% of all the sales from hair growth products, chemical or natural, and I'd never have to work another day in my life.

Let's please stop taking outside advice about what our bodies will do, dictated by advertisements and other sources, and start directing our bodies to be healthy and to look the way we want them to. Let's stop imagining that one bite of anything you like to eat is going to add 5 lbs. to your hips. Eat the damned cake and tell your body it is good for you. You will process it easily, and the cake is providing nutrients for your body. Enjoy the cake after you give your body its directives! Do not, for one second, feel guilty about eating it. Imagine it is just as good for you as a pile of steamed carrots. The cake does have flour, eggs, oil, sugar, salt and vanilla in it. Or chocolate. Sometimes it has fruit! What's better for you than some eggs and fruit? See what I mean? Remember what I said about allergies, we are not discussing those. Obviously, you are not going to eat something you know your body has seriously reacted to in the past and jump to believe it will be good for you now. For every other food, YOU decide how it will affect your body.

You can direct the appearance of your body by your thoughts and beliefs about it alone. Food changes and exercise are not necessary, nor are chemicals and pills. Don't look for evidence of this in the mirror the same day you begin changing your thoughts. It takes a bit of time in our 3D and 4D reality when we start because energy moves more slowly in lower densities. I avoided the mirror and the weight scale when I began shifting my thoughts from overweight to thin and strong. The evidence came firstly in the way my clothes fit. I was losing fat reserves, and my clothes were looser. When I did start looking in the mirror again, I noticed that the areas where I imagined fat melting away from me were slimmer. Then I worked on the tightness of my skin. Every day I imagined my arms and legs were firmer, I could see my muscles more, and my skin was smooth and soft. Next, I worked on my hair. I have naturally curly, thick hair. I've been told all of my life that this type of hair is difficult to keep hydrated and healthy looking. I was told that I might lose clumps of hair when I hit menopause. I experienced fat gain and hair loss because I believed they would happen. Then, I shifted my beliefs again because I got tired of fighting with my body. I decided to work with it again, to have the reality of it that I want. What are your beliefs about your body? Do you think you will be overweight no matter what you do? Have you tried everything you can think of to lose weight and it didn't work? Is your hair falling out because someone in your family has male-pattern baldness and you believe you are destined to lose your hair too? Well, if any of these things ring true for you, then you have nothing to lose by trying to change your thoughts.

It costs nothing but your conscious attention, the upkeep is nothing because once you change your appearance for the better, the only thing that can stop it is choosing a different thought. You may need to buy new clothes or stop wearing hats! I did that, shifted it again to what I wanted, and none of that cost a dime because I held onto my 'thinner' wardrobe. I tell myself **every day** that **I am** in perfect health. If there is a day when I do feel not perfect health, I may get some exercise, go out into nature and absorb some energy, or maybe take some herbs. Those actions are programmed into my psyche as signals to my body "We want perfect health, let's have it now." Then I follow it up with more thoughts of perfect health. It works. You can also say "I am always returning to the state of perfect health" on the days when you don't feel so good. Louise Hay hit the bull's eye when she wrote about how to cure any dis-ease and create health/beauty in your body. She spelled the recipe out in black and white. Others have copied and built upon Louise's methods because they work. Using quantum energy fields, we can link up to the version of ourselves that we desire. He/she/it already exists in quantum fields! Remember? There are many versions of yourself on different timelines. Healthy versions, sick versions, muscular, athletic, smart, confused, attractive, not attractive, and so on into eternity. What version are you choosing? How would you like to be? Use your energy, your magic, to make it so creator-being!

Somebody is going to write a comment to me about making themselves taller, or about growing big boobs when they have been an A-cup since puberty. That's fair, and I'll deal with the creation of any "body reality," now. The simplest answer is that you can change your body in any way that you want, but **you must believe it to be 100% possible**. Remember what I said earlier, the body/mind connection is so complete that you will not be able to manifest something, any state of being if you have even the slightest doubt about your ability to do it. This is why I chose to exclude food allergies from the above conversation. Back in my 20's, I had hefty food aversions to chocolate and corn. I asked Bob about transmuting it, and he said to me what I just said to you. I had to 100% believe it to make it manifest. Well, I didn't believe then in my ability to do it, but at times I would eat corn products or something with chocolate in it, and I would suffer the consequences! After much attention to change my thoughts about corn and chocolate, now, and for the past 10 years, I do not suffer at all when I eat corn or chocolate. I have reprogrammed the messages from my thoughts to my body about them, and my body accepts both without issue.

     These days I'm working on changing my belief that once an adult tooth is pulled, it cannot grow back. I've had several removed, and I'd like to grow them back instead of getting a bunch of expensive, and possibly painful, dental work done. I take good care of my teeth, but I've spent way too much time in a dental chair. I discovered through hypnosis why I've had these problems with my teeth. No pun intended, but I found the root cause. Turns out, I have had many periods in my life where I had difficulty making decisions. I didn't trust myself to make the right choices. And so I 'chewed on' options obsessively, sometimes without deciding at all. The physical cause of tooth loss stems from my anxiety about making decisions. I grind my teeth at night, just like I 'grind on' decision-making. I had massive fears about the future during certain periods of my life, and this caused the grinding and breakdown of my teeth. I developed TMJ syndrome when I was working as a Child Protective Case Worker because I worried so much about my cases, and my own family, while I spent time away trying to help my clients. TMJ syndrome includes jaw tenderness, headaches, earaches, facial pain, and also tooth deterioration because the stress from grinding affects all of these areas. Once the surfaces of the teeth become cracked or chipped, they are open to bacteria that get inside the teeth where you can't brush them out, and mouthwashes do not penetrate. They decay over time. The pressure that human jaws put on teeth is amazing, and that is just chewing food. Imagine a person grinding their teeth all night and there you go! Once I discovered the root cause of the TMJ, I consciously managed my stress, reduced concerns for things I could not control, and with regular awareness of managing my fears; I will not re-experience the issue. These days I include my teeth in my thoughts about perfect health. I'll let you know if I do in fact grow back the adult teeth I had pulled recently. I was trained in dental science when I was in the Army, and so this is a big challenge I am giving myself. Changing my beliefs about regrowing adult teeth goes against everything that science told me is possible. But I also know it is possible. Others have done it. I need to shift my belief about it, that it is not possible. If I can do that, then my energy signature will match the vibrational version of me that has all her teeth intact. Even Charles Darwin suspected a link between plant growth and vibration. We all know that talking to our plants lovingly helps them to grow, right? Why would it be any different for humans? And there is that guy that jumped out of an airplane at high altitude and didn't die when his parachute failed to open. If he can do that, then why can't I grow back some teeth?

An article in The New Yorker magazine; "Persuading The Body to Regenerate Its Limbs," written by Matthew Hutson, discusses the work of a developmental biologist at Tuft's University named Dr. Michael Levin (PhD, Genetics, Harvard Medical School), who gave a presentation in 2018 for the Neural Information Processing Systems (AI) conference. Michael Levin discussed reprogramming a worm's body to regrow cut-off parts using electrical impulses (energy). Levin also compared the human brain to being like a computer because of its trillions of neural interconnections. He posited that the human body can be manipulated with electrical charge to regenerate parts as he did with frogs and growing their legs back after amputation using electrical impulses. He even coaxed tadpoles to grow eyeballs on their stomachs. Yes, gross, I know. What's even more fascinating to me is that Dr. Levin said, "You may not know that human children below the age of approximately seven to eleven can regenerate their fingertips." My brain immediately asked the question, "Why only below the age of approximately seven to eleven years of age?" If one human can do it then why can't we all? Is it social programming that sets in at a certain age that convinces us it is not possible? At what age do we start believing what we are told about the human body's capabilities? Is there evidence that what we are told is true in all cases, every time, or are the 'facts' we are told about the body theories? By the way, whenever a scientific experiment is done, the conclusions are almost always theoretical, not "facts" proven. Why? In science, something is not considered proven (fact) unless the results are repeated many times and the results are consistently the same every time. If there is one case using the same procedure where the results differ, there must be a variable that is unaccounted for in the experiment. Once a variable is discovered, studies must continue until the results are the same with no variables before the conclusion can be considered fact. Think of how many possible variables there can be in human studies. It rarely, if ever, happens that something is proven about human physiology. In essence, what we are often told about the human body is a series of correlations made because 'in most cases' something **appears** to be true. What you get from studies are guidelines for future studies, not facts. Suppositions. You may do enough studies to show that something is true for *most* test subjects, but there are usually exceptions.

Let that information sink-in the next time you consider taking a new drug approved by the FDA that has been fast-tracked (fewer studies done before approval for human use). If science understands only a small percentage of the human brain's capacity, then think of what it does not know about the whole body's potential. What are the potentials of the human mind that we have not discovered yet? And what if we add the energy of the oversoul through the light mind-body to the energy of the physical mind? Do all things become possible? I think so. Quantum healing techniques alone have rendered many instantaneous healings and transformations. Many other forms of energy work render healing results that are not explained by science. Quantum healing and other modalities for healing are put down by people of science as "pseudo-science," like with Dr. Emoto's work, but the results cannot be dismissed outright. A lot of medical professionals are starting to incorporate alternative medicine practices into their businesses to provide overall wellness. These pioneers have figured out that health and healing consist of treating all facets of the human, especially the ones that pills and surgeries cannot, to bring balance to the human body.

    Let's slide away from science a bit more and turn back to metaphysical concepts. What about the people with severed spinal cords who were told by doctors they would never walk again, and yet they walked again anyway? Did that person use their mind-body connection to heal themselves? Maybe the mind-body connection and exercise (physical therapy)? What about people in a long-term coma that wake up and are functioning again normally? Did their body need time to heal itself? Was their consciousness having a life review and deciding if they wanted to stay in this life? Was there a conscious decision by the soul to come out of the coma and live again, and so spontaneous recovery happened?

    How? What? So many questions.

    My take on Dr. Levin's work is that electrical impulses seem to be the key to regeneration. Brain waves are measurements of electrical impulses. Is it possible that your thoughts are directing your body to do something or be some way? If we tell our body to walk, it just does it. We usually don't even think about walking. We have the intention to go somewhere, and our legs walk us there. It is accepted by our belief system that we can walk. Babies watch us walk, and when they are strong enough, they begin walking too. Babies do not wonder if they can walk, they see us doing it and just start trying until they do it also. After a spinal cord injury, if the person believes it is possible, and they focus thoughts on walking (intention), practice this focused attention on that specific outcome, the mind directs the body to walk again. It sends electrical impulses to areas that were injured, restores the pathways of communication from the mind to the legs, and boom! The patient that was told they will never walk again, does. Energy must **go** somewhere, it is never static. Directed energy toward a desired outcome will bring the outcome IF you have no thought or belief that it will not happen. If you do have a contrary belief to the state of being you wish for, then that presents resistance to the energy of your creation. All thoughts are creative and light up parts of the hologram. Which version of you are you lighting up? Continued belief in any illness keeps that illness in place in your reality, until you choose another belief. Why not shift to another thought about yourself? Why stay stuck in one state of being when there are so many to choose from? Keep your intention and focus so directed to the new belief about yourself that it has no choice but to become your reality. You will see, the transformation will be magical.

Consult Louise Hay's books if you do not believe me. She cured herself of stage 4 cancer by changing her thoughts! Countless others have done it too, recovering completely from illnesses and bodily damage that medical professionals thought could not be cured.

One final story about the magical regeneration of body parts. A colleague in the quantum healing community told a story on our Quantum Healers forum. I do not have validation of this story other than my gut feeling that it is true. She said she became aware of a boy living in a remote part of the world. He lost part of his arm in a farming accident. He grew the arm back without medical intervention besides his mother cleaning and dressing the wound after it happened. The boy's arm grew back! My colleague said that when the boy was asked how he grew his arm back, he didn't understand the question. The boy thought it was a normal thing that happened. He had not been told by anyone that it isn't possible, and so his body just did it. Like breathing air. We **can** just do it. The saying goes within the spiritual community, "You have to believe it to see it."

Our beliefs about our environment and how healthy it is for us can change how our body responds to the environment. For example, toxic chemical trails that reportedly come from airplanes (also called chemtrails), are intentionally released to make people sick by some nefarious group that wants to reduce Earth's population by poisoning the air. *Lots* of people believe this is happening. They are called "conspiracy theorists" and largely dismissed by mainstream society. However, for the ones who do believe, the effects can be devastating to their bodies. Some report having been tested, and the tests show toxic levels of metals in their bloodstreams that cannot be sourced to anything in their houses or foods. Water testing also comes up negative for the metals in these folks, or so they say. It is a phenomenon that has some medical doctors scratching their heads again. Of course, these folks believe that the metals in their blood come from chemtrails.

Which came first, the chicken or the egg? Did these people hear about chemtrails, go into fear about it, and manifest toxic levels of metal in their blood? Or, did this phenomenon start happening because of water contamination with metals and people latched on to the belief that a nefarious cabal released toxic levels of fine particle metals into the air to kill us? Wouldn't doing that also kill the cabal members too? Anyway, I'm not calling these folks liars. Somehow, *some* people are experiencing high levels of metal in their blood. It may be an alternate reality that is occurring in another timeline version of Earth, where an evil cabal exists. That is possible. Sometimes we can see what's going on in an alternate timeline when it is energetically superimposed on our own (Earth). Earth has many timelines and many layers. That does not mean we have to join with others and live their version of reality! We can see another version of reality playing out and not be **of** it. The choice is ours, free will. I suspect that believing in some nefarious group dumping metal into the air with airplanes is probably not going to improve my health. I have never had a blood screen come back showing that I have excess metals in my system. I have had numerous blood screens for annual wellness exams, before two operations, and before giving birth to my two children. I was a regular blood donor for years and also had blood screens done before and while I was in the US Army. I've lived in four states and visited more since 1997, so I have drunk from multiple water supplies over extended periods. I think *something* would have shown up if I was bombarded with heavy metals from chemtrails. Or maybe my body got rid of the heavy metals from chemtrails and water supplies on its own if they exist. Either way, I've been in good health all of my life. I lived for 14 years close to an airport. I saw tons of *contrails* from airplanes that form when the warm/moist exhaust fumes from an aircraft mix with the cold ambient air, producing ice crystal clouds that we can see. I **believe** that contrails are all I am seeing in the sky when an airplane goes by, not evidence of some rotten conspiracy to poison people. Some people believe that chem. trails are causing them to be sick. They have the blood tests to *prove* that heavy metals are present in their systems. Okay, keep believing that. It is your free will to do so. See if you manifest health while doing that.

I don't mean to sound like a jerk, but this is exactly what *not* to do.

We are manifesters. The beliefs we have about our environments become manifest in our bodies. You may say to me, "Sue, there are pollutants in every part of our environment and they affect our health, it is a proven fact." I will direct you to the part of the discussion where I told you that studies/experiments rarely prove anything. Once you agree to something, the energy of that agreement brings it into your reality. People and frogs that do not 'know' we cannot grow back severed limbs do it. Someone forgot to help them agree that they cannot in-fact grow back their limbs. Check your beliefs. Are the sources of information that helped form your beliefs trustworthy? Are they in fear? Do they want YOU to be in fear with them? Is there something in your body or mind that does not agree with what you have been told about your environment, but you have been afraid to let it go, 'just in case' the information might be correct?

Fear, fear, and more fear.

It is the largest enemy of good health. A close second is anger. If you love Mother Earth and feel angry a lot about humanity's impact on the Earth, you are projecting to Mother Earth your anger as well as holding it inside you. You project lower energy when you think she is incapable of healing herself. Mother Earth has her ways of dealing with humanity. She infuses us with love and absorbs much of our fear with her beauty. That helps us to value her more and take better care of her. It may seem that what happens with extreme weather is retaliation by Mother Earth, but extreme weather is caused by the accumulation of human anger around the world, not by Mother Earth's wrath. She cleanses human damage to herself energetically. She does it with love, not anger. An example is what happens when a huge load of crude oil is spilled. The ecosystem sustains damage, some animals and birds may die, and then several years later, evidence of total recovery is found. The oil is transmuted by Mother Earth, which is also what humans do with everyday pollutants in the environment. There is so much that we consume and are exposed to that could theoretically kill us. Yet, we do not, and our bodies handle these contaminants with ease if we let them. Dr. Emoto's work shows us that we can transmute, and transform, the energy of anything if we put intention into it.

PAY ATTENTION to your thoughts. Reframe or let go of beliefs that do not serve you. Your environment is what you light up in the hologram, what you give energy to. Mine is very healthy, beautiful, and supportive of my health.

Another example of environmental beliefs and how they affect us is when I was a teen, we had a friend drop by our house on Halloween night to show off his costume. He sat in our living room for about an hour, talking and joking around with us. No issues. Then, one of our cats decided to make an appearance. When this guy saw the cat, he became visibly upset and asked how many cats we had. He immediately began to sneeze. Once we told him we had three cats, the sneezing became constant and our friend left the house. He stated he is very allergic to cats. If I hadn't witnessed the event, I would not have believed the sudden massive change when the cat appeared. None of our cats touched our friend. One came into the room, and that was it. Our friend was physically and emotionally at ease until he saw the cat.

What happened there? I strongly suspect it was my friend's belief in his cat allergy that derailed the visit. There was no more or less cat dander in the room before the cat appeared. Cat dander is believed to be the cause of cat allergies and the cat was not cleaning herself when she came into the room. Our cats typically perched themselves all around our home, including the chair that our friend was sitting in for an hour.

What changed? I contend that our friend's belief about cat allergies was so strong that he did not realize the dander in the environment was unchanged by the presence of the cat. It was there the whole visit.

There is one more thing I want to tell you about that I think is magical. Do you remember how I keep telling you that everything is going on in the eternal now moment? There is no past and no future? Some say that depression happens because we stay mentally stuck in past moments, reliving the dramas, having regrets, feeling angry, feeling victimized, and wishing there was something we could do to change the past. I agree. What if there is a way to sort of re-write the past, energetically, using meditation or hypnosis? What I am about to describe is a process to **re-write** your **energetic reaction** to past events without changing the physical events themselves. The effect is transformative, and I have applied the process many times with clients during quantum healing sessions.

Imagine there is a trauma in your 'past' and you go 'there' during hypnosis. I do not have to guide you to it, you connect to the traumatic event naturally when your thinking mind quiets and I ground you to see where your consciousness has traveled. You are consciously in the space-time continuum with the energy of the trauma, and you are now able to witness the events again. You will not re-live the trauma, because I am trained in techniques to keep that from happening, but you will be able to view the events once more with a different perspective. You now have access to the perspectives of the other people involved in the trauma, and your higher self or guide team, who can inform you about why you were traumatized by the events if the reasons are not obvious. With your higher self there, you also can ask your soul why the events happened in your timeline. What was the reason? What were you supposed to get out of it? How did it affect the people you are concerned about? If you did something to someone else, what are the reasons why you did it? In the hypnotized brain state, there is no question I cannot ask you. You will tell me right away if you do not wish to answer, but you will not be upset that I asked the question. I will have ensured that you are emotionally safe to hear the answers. You will be physically safe because the events that you are viewing have already passed.

This is where the magic happens.

You will be presented with a choice after gathering the information about the event(s) that you are witnessing. After all of your questions are answered, and you may even be able to get some answers from the perspective of other people involved in the events, you then get to choose if you still feel traumatized by the event, or if you choose to see it as something else. Did you interpret the events in a certain way when they happened, but now you see that there is information you didn't have at the time, and it changes your reaction? Traumatic experiences can be transformed through understanding, forgiveness, and conscious choice not to allow the energy of the past to affect your present moment. The shift is immediate, in most cases. Some scenarios do require more contemplation on the part of the client. I have conducted sessions where clients discovered the reasons why their souls agreed to experience certain things, and that was all that was needed to release the energy of the traumatic energy associated with them. Listen to other quantum healing sessions on YouTube and see if I'm being honest with you! I recommend anything by Dolores Cannon, of course, and Alison Coe is a very compassionate practitioner too. Malka Ahern is one of the most effective practitioners I have ever had the privilege of receiving sessions from (https://www.malkaahern.com). And, I will recommend one more person besides me if you are interested in having a session. Her name is Erika Furuzono, and she uses multiple techniques in conjunction with quantum healing to assist your transmutation of whatever issue is bothering you (https://www.angeldustproductions.com).

The reason quantum healing works to resolve depression is it can shift the energy of a situation if the client is willing to do that. The personal power to do it resides with the client, however, going through quantum energy fields allows us to access past events with a perspective that is broader vibrationally and more complete with information than our memories ever can be. The reactionary energy to the history of one person is limited compared to experiencing quantum perspectives of history. This process is real magic. It is possible to access quantum perspectives by yourself using meditation. I do it for myself, and the process always helps me to know more about events.

In conclusion to Real Magic, I have discussed that we are of Source, creator beings, with no limits besides our conscious beliefs about ourselves, and our beliefs about the nature of reality. We have **infinite** potential to create and manifest in our realities, and I refer to this as our magic. Our magic is within us, not something we need to study outside of us. Our souls set up universal energies to guide us as we set intentions to light up parts of the hologram of Creation. We must expand our consciousness beyond our five senses and our social conditioning to become great magicians. Expanding our consciousness will assist us with letting go of old beliefs. Which ones are helpful? What needs to go? Being open to taking on new beliefs. Our beliefs dictate where the magic goes, and what it shows, and can assist us to create beautiful realities for ourselves. Are we creating the life we wish for, or are we creating unconsciously? As with everything I write about, the personal power to decide is always in the hands of the individual. Reading and listening to other people's work can provide mentorship as you journey towards expanded consciousness, to unleash your magic. Social conditioning can be reprogrammed. Using your emotions as a guide for transmuting is a powerful method to cast-off societal programming/beliefs that you have adopted as your own.

Know thyself.

Introspect.

Take action to resolve the personal destructive beliefs that exist in your energy fields and warp your creations.

Be more of your oversoul's essence, meaning; the best version of you. When the choice to be love or to be fearful happens, choose love, because it is the greatest gift to yourself and you will get more of it back from the universe. Finally, don't be in a hurry as you are open to new methods for using your magic. You are here to have experiences, and there is help available to you. Why rush yourself or judge yourself as you experience this Earth reality? You can't get it wrong; you can only expand further.

11

Abundance!

The world's definition of abundance is shifting to include much more than money. Love, time, health, peace, creativity, friendship, animals, nature, problem-solving skills, energy, and guidance from etheric beings...these and more are now being counted as objects of abundance as much as food, shelter, clothing, cars, and money. And that proves one thing for sure, our consciousness is expanding.

Gratitude deserves a mention because as I have stated before, the more gratitude we have for what we have in life, the universe will send us more, and more. Universal energies will send us stuff and experiences that we never knew we wanted to have once we get on the gratitude train. You don't have to know where it is coming from, only that you are grateful for it, whatever it is. I am hearing more people say that they are grateful just to be alive. How is it that we forget to be grateful for being alive? These are not all doddering old people either. Although doddering old people do tend to get towards the end of their lives and realize how precious it is, more so than young people do. Perspective is a beautiful thing. But seriously, I hear young people saying it too. I have heard that there are souls out in the galaxy that would like the opportunity to have an Earth incarnation, but there are already so many incarnated now and the others must wait for the opportunity to be presented to them. In other words, someone has to physically die before another can come in. I have no clue if that is true. But, before you give away your ticket to be here on Earth at this time, consider this. There has never been a timeline of Earth where the collective of humanity is shifting consciousness the way that we are now. We have golden tickets to witness and BE present while the shift is going on. We will be the ones who carry the experiences of humanity's great shift in our souls long after Earth humans have fully oriented to the 5D reality.

You may think that you would be happier if you turned in your ticket and went on to some heavenly realm now, but I think you'd be wishing you hadn't the moment you crossed over. Gratitude. I'm not going to lie, there are times when I wanted a full, fat refund for my ticket to Earth. I was very angry about the 'unfairness' of life. If you have **never** been very angry about something during your life, some massive illusion of injustice, then you truly have a lot to be grateful for.

Earth life is HARD.

And it is also mysterious, beautiful, exciting, buzzing with energy, and alive! There is no other place where souls can get the variations of rich experiences they can right here on Earth. At least not that anyone has heard about in this universe. Why am I making such a big deal about us being here on Earth? If I can coax you for just a few minutes to feel grateful for being alive, that means you will no longer take life for granted, and then you can be grateful for all the experiences in life. Not just the good ones. One thing I heard when I was conducting a hypnosis session with a friend of mine is that Earth's density allows us to experience things more in-depth, more viscerally, and from more perspectives than within the higher dimensional realities.

Is that a good thing? I think so, and here's why. If your consciousness is in spirit and you are working on grasping some piece of wisdom, you might have to observe other souls having the experience of whatever you are trying to grasp because you are not experiencing it. You are watching other beings experience it. It may take observation of hundreds of lives to grasp a concept that can be known through one human life on Earth. This information is not mine. I received it from a higher dimensional being, one of my friend's higher-selves, who called himself I Am One. I Am One was focusing on creating a planet (illuminating new parts of the hologram) when we dropped in through hypnosis to ask him some questions about the nature of reality. I Am One did not have to stop what he was doing to answer our questions. Talk about phenomenal cosmic power! By the way, when you talk with higher dimensional consciousness beings, it is good to know that they do not usually identify as being him or her. Most of the ones I have encountered do not have physical bodies, have balanced masculine and feminine energies, and if they do have bodies they are asexual (do not reproduce the way that humans do). That's a whole other book that I am not going to write.

If I am given the choice, which I am because I am here incarnated on Earth, I will take this opportunity to experience things once or twice 'the hard way' over watching someone else suffer for lifetimes for me to learn something. "Rip the bandage off quickly, please." Let the expanded consciousness happen sooner rather than whenever. That's my preference. And I feel more grateful than ever to be here, now. Gratitude can be a type of acknowledgment that we are not victims of anything. It means that we have taken responsibility for being here; a feeling of personal power and creation. Even if we don't know why we are here, but we are grateful for just being, then we are making the most of our potential within the consciousness that we now hold. It is a definite step towards remembering the truth of what we are.

Along with practicing gratitude, it is essential to feel worthy of receiving abundance. You may want to manifest a boat or a shiny new house for yourself. If you do not feel worthy of receiving the boat or house, you won't get them. It is the same with love. To feel worthy of receiving love you must first love yourself. The good, the bad, and the stupid. The more loving you are with yourself; the more love will flow to you. That's abundance! This is actually the way other people learn how to treat you, by watching how you love yourself. Love is an absolute reciprocal energy when it comes to giving it away (i.e. the more you give, the more you receive from the universe). This is not the same concept as; I gave my wife all my love, why does she not love me the same way? The latter would be called dependence and expectation. Love is only balanced when you love yourself first, and then you do not expect someone else to give it to you in return. It will flow back to you naturally because energy matches energy, not because you made someone the object of your love. However, if you attach an expectation to the love you are giving someone else, then you are adding resistance to the love that you are giving and it will return to you with resistance. Love will return to you no matter where it comes from.

Some Eastern spiritual practices speak of letting go of attachment to anything and anyone to manifest whatever you want. Even attachment to all your identities and names, titles, and property. The teaching goes that it is not wrong to have desires in the material world, but attachment to the things we desire causes resistance to receiving them. This sounds kind of Abraham Hicksy to me, in a good way. My mentor basically said the same thing. He was teaching me how to manifest, and he instructed me to hold what I desired in my mind and imagine it is already with me. Feel it, **know it**. Then, he said to let go of whatever I was thinking about and get on with my day. The key ingredient in my mentor's training is the knowing part. Knowing is having faith that something is true, even when the evidence has not become apparent yet.

If you followed my hologram of the Creation model, you remember that just thinking about something lights up a part of the hologram that was previously dormant or a potential. How does it come to us and at what point does it come to us? I'm going to roll with what Abraham (Esther) Hicks teaches to answer that. Whatever we are wanting manifests for us when we are an energetic match to it. I think the energetic match is key because matching energy lights up the whole piece of the hologram that we want to have in our reality. The Eastern philosophy piece, to give up all of your identity, adds the icing to the cake because when we do not identify with any aspect of our life on this planet, we are then just beings having an experience like the rest of humanity. This puts us all on the same level within our minds, we feel free to manifest anything we want to, not because of some family name, a pile of money, a job title, or the role we play within our community. It does not mean we must give up all those aspects of ourselves; tell the world we have no name, give away all of our worldly goods, quit our jobs, and stop caring for our families. The **attachment** to these identifiers is what we give up. Eastern philosophies suggest that we view ourselves as parts of Source, the All, having experience from lifetime to lifetime. Suffering is caused by attachment to what the lower mind thinks we should have instead of flowing with what is and being grateful for it.

    We manifest reality every day. I suggest that when we do not like some of our manifestations, we are all powerful creators who can change them. Be grateful for how life supports you and reflect on whatever energy you are holding onto that is causing the manifestation of what you do not like. Similar energies attract. Energy matches manifest. The parts of the hologram we illuminate are in agreement with what we are being.

12

Finding and Honoring the Essential Self

I have written many words about raising vibration and frequency, being the best version of you, asking for higher energy assistance to help heal what ails you, bringing in abundance, and so many other concepts related to expanding consciousness. At this time, I write the most important thing I can say to you. You are 100% perfect, just the way you are right now. I have stated many times that you, me, everyone, and everything are parts of Source. This final chapter is intended not to make you think otherwise, but to help you know the difference between the essential self and habitual behaviors. The old saying is that "humans are creatures of habit," and I agree with that. Habits form for each one of us in a combination of personality, social conditioning, and sometimes for survival reasons. Habits can be shifted to higher states of being or dropped completely if they no longer serve us in any way. The essential self is the nature of who you are and how you tend to respond to life events, people, and your environment.

The aspect of your soul pie that is you on Earth has a distinct essential nature. In other words, you carry your oversoul's essential nature, however, you may not express all of your oversoul's consciousness within one lifetime. You are a slice, not the whole, expressed in human form. Your oversoul has chosen certain parts of its essential nature for expression here, to have whatever experiences it wishes to have. For example, some people 'live life out loud.' They externalize most of their thoughts and feelings, are boisterous, and everyone who knows them understands that this is the way they are (the music artist PINK comes to mind). Other people are contemplative in their essential nature. These folks tend to investigate concepts, observe, keep to themselves, and not speak to issues that they are not informed about if they speak at all in social settings. I could list many more types of essential nature, but you know that what I am speaking of is called "personality." Most of us exhibit several essential natures that are enacted when circumstances call for us **to be** that part of our personality. It is the way we interact with the world seen by the people that truly know us. Social conditioning suggests that some personalities are favorable, and others need to change. I suggest that changing your essential nature requires a quantum leap, at which time you would be shifting to another version of yourself, a different vibrational aspect of you. It can be done, however, it seems to me that gentle shifts made over time as consciousness expands are easier paths to travel. I also think that trying to force yourself into a quantum leap can be harmful to you. It is more a submission to society's goading, 'be the person we want you to be' when anyone fights their essential nature. Do not give in to any voices that tell you that you need to change who you are. Instead, listen to the voices of the ones who love you if you engage in bad habits that harm relationships or your well-being.

There is a big difference between the essential self and habits (habitual behaviors). For example, if I yell over to another room in my house to ask my husband for something to drink, two dynamics are going on. One dynamic is that my essential nature is loud, and the other is that I have a habit of asking my husband to get something for me, instead of getting up to get what I want for myself. If asking my husband to get things for me bothers my husband, or he resents performing the service when I ask, then continuing to ask him to get me things is a bad habit that I may want to stop doing to keep our relationship healthy. He does not resent my loudness. My husband knows that I have a loud personality, I usually speak my mind no matter who I keep company with, and this element of my essential nature 'loud' is respected by my husband. If I cared what other people think of my loudness, I might try to change that part of me, which is my essential nature. Eventually, I would resent the people that encouraged me to be quieter. I would resent myself because I am trying to be something that is not in my nature to be. Can I be quiet in environments where loudness is not appropriate, like visiting someone in the hospital? Of course! It is respectful to honor the recovery needs of people in the hospital. The only time I am loud in a hospital is when someone recovering needs something acutely and they are being ignored by the staff. Even in those situations, I am not the same kind of loud as when I am laughing with friends. Can I change the fact that I am *not usually* shy, pensive, and introverted? I do not believe that I can. Is it possible for me to be shy, pensive, or introverted sometimes? Yes. My soul essence came into this body, and it likes to be loud. Loud is simply a descriptor I am using for ease in this conversation, it is not a judgment.

I suspect that many relationships fail, in large part, because one or both parties do not know the difference between bad habits and essential nature. I also think people have generally forgotten about the art of intimate communication, and therefore it becomes more challenging to suss out the differences. We have expectations within relationships with each other. Some expectations are reasonable (i.e. respect), and others are formed by judgments of what a person *should be*. The roles we play within relationships can be much more flexible if we are mindful of our expectations of others. For instance, being female does not preclude me from being an independent thinker who shifts states of being. I am a wife and mother, and these facts do not automatically add up to some contract that I also need to cook, clean, and feel comfortable with other mothers; scheduling play dates with our kids. My kids are grown, but when they were little, I found several other mothers whom I felt comfortable scheduling play dates with. I did not enjoy public centers where moms and children got together. Sometimes I cooked or cleaned. Sometimes my husband and the children did the cooking/cleaning while I went to class (I studied graphic art and design). Roles within our family were not static because I refused to step completely into the female roles; of caretaker and nurturer. To put myself into those boxes all of the time would have been a denial of my essential nature, which is more dynamic.

The contract I speak of is linked to societal beliefs about what a wife and mother should be. You can rattle off similar expectations of men, children, groups, and so on. It seems like humanity is becoming aware that cooperation within any unit is preferable to forcing people into roles that they must play due to some factor of their beingness. Relationships go much smoother when people can feel free to be who they are. What does any of this have to do with exploring the quantum? As humanity becomes more aware of the multidimensionality of consciousness, we also come to understand that the labels and expectations we have placed on ourselves and other people have limited that consciousness expansion. Whatever our personality is (multiple possible iterations), there is some form of experience that fits it. Or many. We can drop bad habits to improve relationships as long as we are willing to have discussions with each other, look within, and be willing to let go of harmful behaviors. We cannot so easily keep denying who we are inside. As consciousness expansion happens, who we are inside will also expand because we link to the other aspects of our souls. For me, I have opened up to; the warrior, the observer, the artist, the scientific mind, the philosopher, the lover, the caretaker, the herbalist, and so many more aspects of my whole soul. I often joke that I never know which of my personalities is going to show up in the morning, it depends upon the day. All of my personalities work together instead of vying for dominance, as I honor them instead of trying to limit them. I know that any part of my essential self is a gift that can be called upon as situations require it. It would not be useful to maintain a submissive demeanor if I find out that someone has stolen my credit card information. Similarly, my tendency to say what is on my mind would not serve my relationships if I did it all the time without using some filters. That kind of brutal honesty is not helpful in many situations. If I did go around spouting my truths to everyone, in every situation, that behavior could be thought of as a bad habit. Just like I know it is bad manners to belch at the dinner table, I do not go around spewing my truths to everyone. Situational and self-awareness are key.

One last discussion about relationships and quantum realities. The dynamics of a relationship will change from where it started. Everything changes. It is the nature of reality. When people can grow together, and respect one another's growth and independence; the relationship can become a much richer experience. The relationship may not look the same as when it started, but the counterparts are respecting one another's essential natures. When people within a unit grow independently and do not respect each other's essential nature, or the attraction to being in the relationship is no longer there, that is when the relationship needs to end. Blame is often tossed around, for example; "you are not the same person that I married" or, "When I met you, you were so much fun and now you spend so much time doing _____ that we do not spend time together anymore." Relationships are not always *intended* to be maintained for a lifetime.

When looked upon from the soul perspective (soul contracts), many unions occur for brief periods, and this is the plan of both parties. We come together with other people because there is something we wish to experience as a unit, be it a friend, group, lover, spouse, teacher or student. It does not matter why a relationship ends, however, endings can be experienced more peacefully if we can accept that the energies of the other individual(s) and ours no longer match up, without blame. Love is love, in its many forms. It does not go away nor become neutralized because the person you shared that love with is no longer in your physical experience. They remain in your etheric experience (the dimensions without form). Once energies connect, they can always be felt. Since we are all connected at Source level and through all the quantum fields in-between us and Source, there is no real loss. The illusion of loss feels debilitating sometimes on Earth. I know that feeling. Allow the feeling to move through you until it seems less debilitating, and then I suggest imagining your reunion in the afterlife with the ones you have separated from in this brief physical existence. You will be with them again. Just thinking about the other soul brings that soul's energy closer to you. It lights up their essence within the hologram. I make a practice of sending loving feelings to the ones I have been close to and no longer see. Saying a prayer for someone is doing the same thing. And, hold the highest version of that person (or persons) in your thoughts. Imagine the best outcomes happening for them, and you will be assisting their journey because that energy conveys, it is felt by them, even if you do not speak another word to each other.

     Finally, look within and identify the pieces of your personality, your essential self. Bring back the ones you have banished from experience. Love every part of you. This is bringing together and honoring all aspects of your soul. It is freedom. You are not meant to put yourself into boxes nor be certain ways for the sake of others exclusively, and without question (by the expectations of others). You do have the *choice* to be certain ways *for* others; like if you become a caretaker for someone, love someone unconditionally, stop bad habits, advocate for yourself, or choose to take on a leadership role within your company. These are choices. Before you call me out and say, "I had no choice, the role was thrust upon me," think again. Somewhere you made a soul contract with someone else or a group, and at that level, you have made the choice. Roles thrust upon us can be thrust back. You can refuse to play a role. There are no victims here on Earth. All of our experience is free-will based, even if you do not remember making a choice. Actively choosing in this 'now consciousness' is powerful, indeed. Accepting that we are the ones who choose what roles we will play for others is empowering.

13

What Happens In A Quantum Healing Session
A Brief Overview

Quantum healing hypnosis starts when the practitioner assists the client to relax the thinking/analytical part of the brain, the left hemisphere (left brain), using breathing techniques, relaxing the body, and meditative visualization. Before it begins, the practitioner has taken whatever time is needed to get to know the client's history, questions, health concerns, and past methods for maintaining well-being. We also explore the client's belief systems; if they have spiritual beliefs and what they are, because it is important for us to be in accord with the client's beliefs when accessing higher consciousness beings residing in other spaces within the quantum. The client does not need to be given knowledge ahead of time about higher energy beings if they do not believe in them. What will happen if there is no belief in beings other than the ones we experience on Earth is that the client will experience higher energies as part of their subconscious mind. And that is as much a perfect experience for the client as are other clients meeting their guides, a deceased relative, Jesus, Buddha, or an angel.

    Practitioners of this process are taught not to judge what a client believes, but to work with those beliefs because doing so will provide the best possible result for the client. Everyone's consciousness will perceive higher energy beings in a form that is in accord with each person's belief system. For example, I may experience a higher energy being as Jesus, while you may experience that energy consciousness as Thor. We could be communicating with the same being, and you see Thor because your beliefs are consistent with the Norse beliefs about gods. A QHHT/BQH practitioner does not judge nor argue about what you are experiencing, we acknowledge all. It is not the identification of who you are communicating with that is important. The content and meaning for YOU is what we strive to achieve. This has never been a problem for me as a hypnosis practitioner. While being a social worker, was able to meet my clients wherever they were in consciousness because I strive not to judge anyone else. Judgment of another keeps us in 3D consciousness/separation reality. I do my best not to be there.

    Once the client has reached altered states of mind/consciousness, the practitioner begins working with the right side of the brain. The right hemisphere is open to all experience without analysis, receives images, knowing, feeling, audio communication; and sometimes a combination of all four; assisted by other dimensional beings who have come into the session. Higher energetic beings (HEBs) assist the client to illuminate parts of the hologram where their other aspects reside. We call this memory or past-life memory. Sometimes it is a future life the client is shown. The importance of the HEB assisting is that it or they are sometimes another soul aspect of the client, and know the client's intention for the session. It makes HEBs expert guides for the session. They know exactly what part of the hologram the client needs to see to resolve their issues. Helping the client consciously connect with HEBs is what the hypnotist does. Practitioners are regularly affected by the energy of the beings of higher light and consciousness during sessions. It raises our vibrations and frequencies along with the client's.

Once the client begins to receive impressions of a reality other than the one we are currently maintaining, this is an indication that they are beginning to illuminate another part of the hologram of Creation where their soul energy resides. Before this illumination, the client's consciousness is usually not aware of the other aspect of itself. The practitioner then suggests that the client move closer to the illuminated energy until he/she becomes merged in the reality (grounded within it). Once the client grounds into this foreign reality, we can ask lots of questions of the aspect that resides in that reality. We find out if the aspect has a body, what period of Earth it is if they are on Earth, or another planet, if the aspect is male/female/both/neither, what the aspect is doing at this point in its life, and if they have family or community.

Sometimes, a client's aspect does not have a body at all or the body is in a form that is alien to the client. It can take a while for the practitioner to tease out this information. We must be patient during the process, as the client becomes acclimated to what they are experiencing. Often, the client's left brain consciousness will jump in and try to tell them what they are experiencing is not real. I invite the client's analytical mind to join us during hypnosis, but, ask it to take an observational role rather than a protective role. The analytical mind is the part of us that protects us from harm. I believe that inviting it to come with us during hypnosis allows the client to relax and feel protected while all this weird stuff is happening. And here is something for other hypnosis practitioners to consider. If we do not help the client to feel safe, they will not allow themselves to go deeply into hypnosis. And, if we do not protect them from becoming re-traumatized by what they see, feel, hear, or touch; they will snap out of hypnosis very quickly because the left brain never really 'goes away' during the process. Even if the left brain goes to sleep, it will snap back awake and pull the client right out of hypnosis if the client feels threatened. This happened to me while I was the client. My practitioner did not guard against re-traumatization, and I snapped out of the hypnotic state rapidly. The left brain will always protect the self. The experience did teach me to be very aware of my clients' states of being. I watch over them to ensure what happened to me does not happen to them. I suggest to other practitioners to work in tandem with your client's analytical brain for that reason alone, and it will allow them to remember much more of the session afterward.

Once the client is grounded within this alternate reality of self, they often become aware that this reality is another 'lifetime' of theirs. They begin to provide accounts of what the aspect is experiencing, feeling, and knowing. Every element of that lifetime is available to explore, and the client gives these descriptions easily. The practitioner must look for reasons in this alternate lifetime why the HEB brought the client to this particular lifetime to review. It seems to me that the HEB always knows which lifetimes the client needs to know about to heal from current issues they experience in this lifetime. I may guide the client through several alternate lifetimes before one of the client's guide team shows up to answer questions about them. In many cases, the client does understand the meaning and connection of each lifetime to this current one. However, once the guide team shoes up, one or many, we get to dig into the larger questions the client has discussed with me before hypnosis. I think of this part of the session as 'the main event.' If one member of the client's guide team does not have the answer to a question, I call in another member who has specialty information about the question. Sometimes what I call an angel comes into the session for the client, or a member of their family here on Earth that left this physical reality and moved on to a non-physical reality. Other times a galactic being shows up.

Whoever comes in for the client, I know they possess the highest intention to assist the client to heal and expand their consciousness. That intention is set before anything else happens. And so, lower energy beings cannot access the session. Once the client has their questions answered, I call in the client's highest self, the oversoul, to ask if there is anything else they want the client to know, and to provide any healing the client has asked for. Because every being in Creation is energetically connected, it is possible for ones other than the oversoul to assist with information and healing. I do prefer to call on the oversoul of the client though, because I want the client to feel the enormous power that they have, to know that they are always connected to this power and can access it at any moment point. To further empower my clients, I provide suggestions of the oversoul energy to be anchored to the heart space of the client. It is always there anyway, but doing this during hypnosis helps the client to be consciously aware of the fact. I do not mind conducting multiple sessions for the same person. But, I do try to connect them in a way that they only need one session, in the tradition of Dolores Cannon. The finale is when I ask the oversoul to heal any physical conditions the client wants healing for. Sometimes the healing requested is emotional in nature, or mental. The oversoul already knows the client's intentions for healing and so it provides it for them. During a quantum healing session for myself, I could see what was happening as my oversoul healed my heart. I was not aware at the time that my heart needed healing! The experience cannot be adequately described in words, however, I will compare it to having an energy ray, like the sun, move through my body, which is healing/benevolent/love energy. Tears rolled down my face as I experienced it.

After obtaining every bit of information and healing that is possible for the client, I count them out of hypnosis and ground them back into this reality. That's it, folks! The hypnosis process is not the big scary thing that stage hacks make it out to be. I can no more make you do **anything** within the hypnotic state than I can make monkeys fly. Everything that happens or does not happen within the session is agreed upon by the client and monitored by the client's analytical mind. I am skilled in this process with techniques to prevent a client from re-experiencing trauma from an event that they are witnessing. Sometimes a client needs to remember a trauma their soul has experienced to transmute the energy of that trauma for all aspects of the soul. Seeing it again, and thinking of it again are possible without *feeling it* again. I can help mute the feelings to where they are manageable if it is important for the client to identify them. Quantum Healing Hypnosis Technique and Beyond Quantum Healing have big, scientific-sounding names. I'm here to tell you that these techniques are not scary in any way if you allow yourself to trust that you were encouraged by your soul to have the experience. The soul wants you to heal, enjoy life, and expand. Having a session can help you do that.

14

Starseeds and Galactic Assistance
Exploring the Quantum With Pier

Pier Bené is a friend and fellow quantum healer whom I had the pleasure of meeting and working with since 2020. We have been discussing topics regarding Earth's changes/shifts and ascension ever since. The year 2020 of this version of Earth seems to be the 'kickoff' year in my reality where starseeds began truly finding their human 'star family.' Sometimes the term finding 'soul family' is used to describe when souls suddenly come together in life. These two terms; soul family and star family, are interchangeable in my opinion, because it is the focus of the lens we are using to look at a relationship that seems to imply the use of one or the other term. In a recent discussion with Pier, he indicated that he prefers to describe soul attraction as a function of two or more people with similar frequencies, and this is the reason people come together. Pier stated, "It is the alignment of frequencies that causes two or more souls to meet." Viewed through this lens, souls coming together are not family, instead, they are energetic matches. His description transcends the human definition of 'family.' I think Pier's understanding is an expansive, energy-based viewpoint. If everything is consciousness, and consciousness is energy, and we are energy beings, Pier's description makes sense. I am aligned with this description. After all, every one of us is a Source being, and so any merging of our energies can be considered 'familial.' For ease of understanding in this dialogue, I will continue to use the terms 'soul family' and 'star family' because they are more commonly used in spiritual conversations. I will be inserting more of my discussions from quantum hypnosis with Pier as we go along. First, I need to define what I mean using the term 'starseed.'

    It is my opinion that a 'starseed' is a person who, on the soul level, from one or several galactic focal points of reality has been called upon by humanity to come to Earth to assist with the ascension of human consciousness. The difference between a starseed and a 'galactic being' coming to Earth to help is that a starseed incarnates as a human to assist, bringing with them part of their galactic knowledge (consciousness), while a galactic being may remain in its current form from another dimensional reality to locate their energy and focus close to Earth, by ship or energetic portal, to assist humanity's ascension. Dolores Cannon has gifted some great YouTube videos that describe the 'call for assistance' that humanity put out into the universe, and she describes the 'volunteers' (starseeds), who incarnate on Earth to answer the call. Some starseeds have prior experience with human incarnations on Earth before they answer the call, and others do not. The starseeds who have not focused on Earth before this Earthly lifetime have other incarnations (focal points of reality) within galaxies other than this one; incarnations within our galaxy, but not on Earth; and have accepted special 'missions' to bring their consciousness, their light, to Earth by incarnating here to help humanity expand. These 'first-time' Earth experiencers find the density of Earth reality difficult to operate in. The first-timers usually go through the veil of forgetting because they must reduce their consciousness, as every other soul must, to relate with the Earth experience. One cannot come from a totally different reality and adjust to being a human without experiencing what it is like to BE a human in limited consciousness. Starseeds, the first-timers, must approach their mission like any other soul (with amnesia), to be able to have compassion for other humans while completing their mission. Some first-time starseeds remember their galactic heritage at some point in human form. These brought more of their higher consciousnesses (light) into the human mind complex (light body of the mind plus the physical mind), or they adapt quickly to the density of Earth and transcend human social conditioning. You will know them to be the ones who do not fall easily in line with social norms. When a first-timer cannot remember why they are here, their mission, and where they came from; they may become desperate as a result of their dealings with the harsh circumstances of Earth. Sometimes unconscious first-time starseeds feel that Earth is not their home, feel depressed about being here, and they want to remove themselves from the Earth incarnation before their missions are complete. Starseeds know the harsh experience of the density of Earth may result in permanent amnesia to who they are is a distinct possibility, before accepting the mission. This is the reason codes have been implanted into our DNA to find one another. We help each other cope on Earth. We also act as a beacon to each other. Like one torch lighting another. Each torch also lights up the rest of humanity. Before long, the original call to galactic beings to raise humanity's consciousness will result in torches lit up all over the world. Humanity will experience at some point the light of each individual more than any shadow, one big bonfire if you will, and we can see this bonfire as the result of 'ascension.'

Ascension is how we will experience more unity consciousness (amplify/merge higher frequency transmissions), resulting in more experience of preferred realities. As I have stated several times, humanity is done with wars, greed, suffering, hunger, power games, and generally feeling like each one of us is on our own in this world. We, as a collective, want to be unified to co-create an Earth reality that is supportive of **All** who come here to experience it. Starseeds are here specifically to light up the consciousness of others, to remind others that their highest light has always been within, no matter what the Earth's experience has been thus far.

Not every soul experiencing on Earth is a starseed with this mission; however, every soul on Earth is experiencing other incarnations within galactic realities, in different dimensions. This goes back to the concept 'everything is happening in one eternal moment.' And so, soul recognition due to galactic origin is also happening in that respect. This is another example of quantum realities. For instance; I am Sue on Earth, and I have three parallel lives (incarnations) that I am aware of happening within the Pleiades. Two of my 'other selves' (soul aspects) within the Pleiades are focused on student-like dimensional reality experiences, and the third is considered an Elder. The Elder "me" sits on an advisory council. He is wise and knows a lot about increasing consciousness, and he monitors Earth's timelines for analysis of how we are progressing. My soul aspect, Sue Beckley, brought the energy of the Pleiadean Elder, along with other energies of my wiser galactic aspects (Sirian, Arcturian), and merged them with other aspects of my oversoul into the personality of Sue, for the mission of raising human consciousness on Earth (starseed mission). This is NOT my only purpose for being here. I am also assisting both of my family lineages to heal from generational traumatic patterns, but the starseed mission is of great importance to my oversoul and one of the primary missions I came for. I also came back to Earth because I love the beauty here, enjoy merging energies with the animal kingdom, and want to have some fun while I complete these other missions. I love humanity! Many aspects of my soul experience as humans, and so why not come back and visit one more time?

I think of it also as a training program to become a guide at some point in my soul's evolution. I am already a guide, as one of my higher selves, AND, I am in-training from this point in my consciousness to become a guide. I know that is confusing. Remember, each soul is focused within infinite dimensional realities. This aspect of my soul is still in training to be a guide. My soul energy is focused many times on Earth, since the beginning of Earth's formation. These other focuses include incarnations as a human, and non-human. I remember, through hypnosis, being an air elemental working to form the Earth's atmosphere. My soul is heavily invested in the Earth experiment. One of the reasons I accepted the starseed mission to help raise human consciousness on Earth is due to my love for Earth, and desire for Earth's progression. That would make me a starseed with multiple galactic and human heritages, who, fortunately, remembered these heritages despite going through the veil of forgetting. The humans on Earth that recognize my energy may share an incarnation on another planet (Pleiades, Sirius, Arcturus, others), but they may or may not be starseeds sharing my mission. We will enjoy meeting one another, having discussions, and maybe participate within groups of similar interests (i.e. helping animals, protecting nature, discussing channeling, connecting consciousness, etc.).

Pier is a starseed (by my definition) who shares my mission to raise consciousness in humanity. We planned to meet when we did before we incarnated here. We met and started to work together as our consciousnesses began to remember who we are. Sometimes I shed light on a concept he is working on, other times he does that for me. The familial feeling we have for one another is a result of other experiences together and, as Pier stated, "the resonance of our individual frequencies." Our frequencies are in accord, and this alignment has drawn us to one another to explore quantum realities to gain insight and share it with other people searching for answers regarding consciousness. We express our understandings a bit differently sometimes, but largely, the information we receive while working together is helpful to both. Pier writes about our discussions and sessions, and I write about them too. The more our awareness of concepts grows, the more detailed our descriptions become. This is our contribution to humanity's ascension, together.

Fun fact, according to one of our hypnosis sessions, we have "traveled" together many times. One of Pier's 'higher-selves' goes by the moniker *I Am One*, and does not use the term 'incarnation.' I Am One describes the coming together of souls in various lifetimes as 'traveling together,' flowing energy. I Am One identifies as a male in a starship, assisting in the creation of a planet with two moons. He spoke to us of the love he feels for the developing planet, matching frequencies, and how the activation of light within others works. I Am One said to us that the love he feels for the creation of the planet is Source's love, which we will be infusing into our writing. He spoke of the beauty of the light as he looked upon the planet. It can be felt by all who see it. I think that what I Am One was saying is when we create with love, all can feel that love while experiencing the creation, whatever it is. When I asked him if he is Pier's higher self, I Am One responded, "There are no higher selves and lower selves, we ARE." So I asked him, "What do I call you?" "I Am One" was the response. This is how I Am One describes his relationship with Pier; he and Pier are one being, as are all the aspects of their soul, and therefore, no hierarchy.

No *one* aspect of a soul is higher or lower than another. I, and the quantum healing community, use the term "higher self" to indicate levels of consciousness; higher light frequency, and that is the only reason for the term. It is important to make this distinction because, as I Am One stated to us, there is no version of anyone that is better than another. I was searching for a name during the session because human language requires labeling to be comprehensible, or so I thought. Humans like to sort and define who and what we are speaking to when channeling higher energies, but I have come to know that it is not required to garner their wisdom (see the chapter What's In A Name). It is the energy of the session, and what is being conveyed, that is important. Not the name. And, as I came to see, Pier is indeed all of his other aspects and One with his soul. Pier has shared with me the connections he has made in meditation with other aspects of his human journeys. They are in communication now consciously, co-creating together, toward healing and unifying humanity. As I said, Pier and I do not always relay information using the same terms, but our hearts work together nicely. The most important concept for me from talking with I Am One, as he answered our questions; is, the love I Am One is infusing into the planet he is creating is Source energy, the energy we will use for our writing.

Anytime we focus love on something or someone it is felt, and that is the energy that causes recognition of Source energy within others (lighting the torch). I feel intense gratitude for meeting Pier and for our time together. We share a starseed mission, and so much more. Our friendship, and energy flow together transcends Earthly and Galactic experiences right to our origin, Source. The fact that our energies are flowing here on Earth now highlights how important it is for humans to work together at this point of Earth's shared ascension. Starseed or not, you are **just as** important to the Ascension of Earth and its people. You will meet, or flow energies with, other people you are aligned with. Try to be bold and see where that goes. Pier was a 'stranger' to me as a human when he first contacted me. However, I felt his energy and so I went with the flow and we enjoyed fabulous conversations before we ever decided to work together, exploring quantum fields. If he had not been bold enough to contact me, and I had not been bold enough to grab that opportunity, well, I shudder to think of missing out on all that we have shared. It has not been the way of humans in recent generations to trust 'strangers.' We have been taught to do the opposite because humanity was not operating within intuitive energy, we were operating in fear. People have even gotten so fearful that they will ignore a stranger who greets them as they casually walk past, and pretend that the person never spoke to them. What kind of nonsense is that? Saying "hello" to another human being is some kind of offense? Common… you know that is not the loving way to be. There is nothing to be fearful about saying "hello" to a stranger. If you go with your internal knowing about a person, that 'gut feeling,' you can trust it. Your internal feeling about another person knows if you are in danger, or not. Especially if you meet someone online, and a dialogue starts. You will know by the tone of that other person's words, and you can feel safe if you are attracted to their energy. Please do not miss out on an opportunity to have an experience like Pier and I share because you are shy or do not trust 'strangers.' You can always decide to block a person from your social media if you no longer wish to communicate. No one is truly a stranger in the grand scheme of Creation.

Starseeds have, within another dimensional reality (timeline), risen above Earth's frequencies, but agreed to focus here again to show other humans how to rise above Earth's frequencies as well. Most people will not do this in quantum leaps. They need to rise through the levels of Earth's frequencies, like climbing a ladder, before consciousness in human form can surpass the highest level of frequency in each Earth reality (3D-5D). Starseed or not, we are all on the ladders. The ones who are higher on one frequential ladder reach the person closest to them, to rise also. Like what Tim McGraw sings about in the song *Humble And Kind*, "When you reach the top of that ladder, reach down and help the next one up." The thing about frequential ladders is that we never stop climbing because we go past Earth, all the way back to Source. We are actually already at the top, and everywhere in between. The aspects here want to **re-member**, through experience, what it is like to climb the ladder consciously. The whole movie is set up by our agreement to experience that together. And we are each playing our part to do just that.

"Way showers," is another term used for starseeds on the mission to light up humanity. Because you are human, like me, you may think I am implying that some humans have a bigger purpose here on Earth than others. Nothing could be further from the truth. Every soul here on Earth has a purpose, a gift to give all of humanity, and each one of us are all-powerful beings. Earth is considered to be an "experiment" of consciousness for souls to learn from. Whether a soul ever incarnates to Earth, or not, every soul in our universe observes the Earth experiment and learns from it. Earth people focus here many times, or one time, to support the 'raising consciousness' experiment. There is so much to be gained by experiencing it and by observing it. And, we do it by expressing many versions of the soul's frequency. There is no 'hierarchy of importance' according to which role anyone is playing at any point on the timeline of Earth. My soul's energy is focused here in some "darker," low consciousness roles for sure, if we want to place judgment on my other soul aspects! I do not judge them. My alternate Earth aspects provide experience for others on Earth. What being here has to teach me is for the expansion of my soul. Judgment of your role in this moment point of focus is not necessary and will cloud understanding of what you came to get out of the experience. All roles are necessary for the experiment to work. The souls that chose to be human want to know what it is like to have very limited consciousness to the point where they forget they are Source beings and then move back to the consciousness where they remember again. That **IS** the Earth experiment. It plays out in all the ways it was intended to. Like Dolores Cannon has said, "It is a play, a movie." Each of us is the director of the play/movie. We pick our roles, play the roles, and obtain wisdom from playing and directing. Each role is important in contrast to the others, and interchangeable. One lifetime you play the bad guy, the next lifetime you play the good guy. Also, there are **many** timeline versions of the Earth experiment. This is the quantum nature of Creation, and why some people remember the history of Earth differently than others do.

The phenomenon of humans remembering history differently has been dubbed "The Mandela Effect." The ME is being discussed more deeply in many circles these days. Quantum realities and shifting timelines explain the ME in my opinion. How could souls experience variation in timelines as being real if soul aspects were not willing to forget their other memories, forget alternate experiences of Earth, and then use current experiences to remind themselves that all versions are true? What is happening is that we know a variation of truth as we move from 3D consciousness to 5D consciousness. Once you shift your timeline, the details of what is agreed upon by the collective may change. I am old enough to have been alive when the version of Earth that included Nelson

Mandela dying in prison happened. I clearly remember seeing the news when his death was broadcasted in my twenties. And, I also remember that he was liberated from prison and has spoken for human rights ever since. Both realities are real and true but they exist in different dimensions, on alternate timelines. The ME is known when some people **do not** forget the details of the prior timeline that they have shifted from, but the events have created new realities in the current timeline, so those people are maintaining **both** sets of memories, multidimensional memory (bi-location). Until they talk to other people who also hold multiple reality memories of Earth's timelines, these timeline variances may cause a person to think they are crazy in some way. The ME is less 'weird' when it is shared by many. Can you see why it is SO important for humans to have honest conversations about their experiences? It is time for humans to let go of the fear of appearing weird. Who cares if you are weird? You are not hurting anyone by sharing your weirdness. I spent many years not expressing my weirdness for fear of being judged. Now that I do not care what people think of me, I am free to share an entire book filled with weird stuff with you.

It's very liberating.

Every soul that focuses in reality on Earth is essential for the other souls doing it too, no matter what 'role' they are playing. Soul contracts are mutually beneficial to the parties agreeing to them. Contrasting roles are what bring us to unity consciousness at some point on the timeline. The old saying goes, "How can you know the light if you have never experienced the dark?" The good news is that we get to be it all; exchange roles, revisit a lifetime and do things differently, incarnate as another aspect of the soul, as many times as we wish! The dark, the light, everything in between. Starseeds have already ascended their consciousnesses on Earth or within other realities. They are not 'better than' any other soul, they merely want to help brothers and sisters of Source by providing mirrors during the process. And some of us are in training for other roles also (wink wink).

Galactic beings that come to Earth to help humanity ascend are our brothers and sisters of soul if they have a 'gender' at all. Galactic beings do not always have a gender. The point I am trying to make is; galactic beings, known by us as Extra Terrestrials (ETs), ARE versions of us in other forms. The **higher-dimensional** versions care what we are experiencing because what we are experiencing affects them. They add water and sunlight to the plants (us) because they care about nurturing themselves. They know we are them. The plants (we) will eventually flower and grow fruit (become them). It does not matter when the fruit develops, benevolent galactics will care for the plants during every stage of their development. There are non-benevolent galactic beings (also us) who interfere with the growth of Earth's plants. These lower-dimensional beings enjoy power and control over humanity and do not want human consciousness to expand. They are important actors in the separation games/movie.

As above, so it is below.

We grow both ways, through contrasting experiences.

Non-benevolent galactic interference is as important for humans to expand consciousness as other humans playing dark roles are. However, after a long period of experience with these opposing influences going on, humanity wanted **all** of its galactic brothers and sisters to back off and let us ascend on our own. "Go away, and let us grow our consciousness," we said. By soul agreement, planet Earth was placed "off limits" to galactic intervention for a long while. We could only reach the higher galactic beings during this period through consciousness connection; using meditation, hypnosis, alteration of physical states of being (i.e. drug use, herb use, and extreme physical stress), or raising our vibration (tapping into psychic abilities). Humanity largely misunderstood the individual teachings of beings like Jesus and Buddha, or their teachings were intentionally distorted. Too many humans did not see that Jesus, Buddha, and other high-frequency beings (enlightened humans) were endowing us with the means to be as they are. Instead, we put them up on pedestals and worshipped them, calling them divine beings, while ignoring **our** divinity. As Dolores Cannon described, the souls of humanity were not seeing much change in collective consciousness even with some individuals using consciousness expansion techniques, before humanity called out for galactic assistance again. Wars, power, and control games; all of the circumstances resulting from limited consciousness continued following the ban on galactic interference. Humanity began to cry out for help. Doing that permitted higher energy beings to assist humanity once again. And they are. Benevolent galactic beings are relocating the lower frequency galactic beings from our reality because we are finished with the experience they came to give us. The higher energetic beings, HEBs, (see Neale Donald Walsh) are also healing our damaged, manipulated DNA, which was limited by lower energetic beings, by providing light codes to the collective. I listened to a 9D Arcturian Council (channeled by Daniel Scranton) state that light energy is being infused into our food and water sources. Light carries coded information that transforms damaged DNA and activates dormant DNA. This means that just taking a bath or shower is helping us, lifting consciousness to where we can see issues more clearly and make better choices.

Galactic interaction with Earth is not the demonic takeover of Earth that Hollywood movies would have us fear. Hollywood movies about alien invasion are representative of other versions of Earth's reality, not what we have to look forward to or be afraid of. The important piece of Daniel Scranton's channeling that I want to highlight is; we no longer have to be concerned about the quality of our food and water sources with this light from the galactics. It was the case when people were awakened spiritually but did not know about the energetic transmutation of impurity from food, water, and processed foods (Dr. Masaru Emoto's process). They worried when they could not afford high-quality foods, had to drink tap water, and basically felt subjugated to the food industry's standards. Feeling subjugated by anything, including tainted food sources, is not aligned with higher consciousness. What about the people living where the water source is naturally dirty and this is all they have to draw from? According to Daniel's channeling, the galactics help humanity by infusing light into every element of our environment. Food, water, trees, oceans, lakes, animals, and flowers; projecting it through the sun to our atmosphere. Go outside and bask in nature. See if that doesn't increase your vibration. Again, this galactic assistance does not violate the law of free will because humanity asked for help, and they are us anyway. It's not like HEBs are directly shifting your mind to a higher state of consciousness for you. They are not flipping a switch in your brain to make you be something that suits their agenda. Instead, the galactics are helping you switch your brain by feeding your body more light contained in every element of existence. It is strikingly similar in my mind to starseeds lighting torches (infusing their energies with the energies of other humans).

Now I want to share with you more in-depth excerpts from my sessions with Pier and I Am One. When I first began to have a conversation with I Am One (Pier was under hypnosis), I Am One described being in a ship, looking at a planet with two moons. He described what he was seeing as a view through a panoramic window, an observational perspective. When questioned further about his circumstances, I Am One said that there were others on the ship with him, but he did not have any family with him. A little while later, I Am One stated that he, the ship, and "all of it" **is** him. There is no one with him, he is it all, as described. Imagine my confusion hearing this, at the time! I later heard my friend Erika describe a similar situation in a session where she was viewing scenes on a ship, and she is the ship. Their energies are One. So, these descriptions lead me to think that in higher states of consciousness, each one of us is aware that we **are** everything that we are experiencing. By imagining other people on the 'ship' Earth, it gives an awareness of 'others' being present, even though the others are also you. Thought and intention create the reality. Thought and intention (consciousness) light up the other parts of the hologram of Creation and bring them into our experience. In this sense, we are they, and they are we. Unity consciousness. We may think about soul contracts while looking at life from one perspective, and they are real. Aspects of Source do come together for experience by agreement. The quantum element about it is; beyond being aspects of the soul, at the same **eternal** moment point, each of us is the whole and includes the *illusions* of others within our realities. They **are** us because we are Source. Are the others in your reality actually there? Yes! Are the others in your reality there because they agreed to be there, or because they are projections of your consciousness? Also, yes! If you remove the "or" in that last question and replace it with "and," you begin to understand what quantum means. When we look at life on Earth with a lens that is energetically close to the Earth experience, we get soul plans, soul family, soul contracts, starseeds, and all of those other labels because everyone **seems to be** individual. If we look at life through an energetic lens closer to Source, we are all of everything in Creation. The difference between these two perspectives is the level of consciousness being applied through the lens.

    The final thing I want to share with you from my sessions with Pier is about seeing God/Source in other people. Every person makes choices about how they will express their soul's energy within any reality. Some step closer to knowing that they are God/Source, and others move further away from that knowledge. Expanding consciousness for you includes knowing that no matter how far away another appears to be from Source, you can still see the light in them. You may not choose to interact with someone who is behaving offensively, but you can 'hold space' for them as an expression of Source, and love them for that reason alone. Condemning another is condemning a part of the self. I Am One made it clear that the light Pier sees in me, what made him decide to work with me, is FELT by me, and helps me see it in myself. Every time I can see the light in another, even when I do not like what they are doing, the energy of recognition is felt by the other. It helps light their torch.

Some in the spiritual community call that dynamic 'holding space' for another, but I suggest it is more than that. Recognition is energy transference. Projecting anger towards, or damning another being, is aligning with separation energy. It does not feel good. You may think you feel better after 'putting someone in their place,' or acting in retribution towards others whom you perceive have wronged you. In the recesses of your heart, you know that it does not bring relief to the situation.

The only relief humanity has for the feelings of separation is **to be** love.

Forgive.

See Source in everyone.

Know it is all that you are. Anything else is an illusion, part of a movie that you are working your way through. Like all movies, there is an end to the illusory nature of reality on Earth, and we go home afterward. We are capable of bringing 'home' here if we choose to.

15

Not Goodbye...See You

This concludes the sharing about my quantum explorations, for now. There is no beginning nor end to our journey together, so I will not name this recap of key concepts "conclusion." Pier and I like to end our conversations with "See you." This means several things to me. One is that I see the essential nature of Pier, and he sees mine. The other thing it means is that as eternal beings, we will always see each other again, in this incarnation or another. Acknowledgment of our eternal beingness. I feel that way about all of humanity, and so it is my farewell to you for now.

  Raising your frequency of vibration will help you to be even more receptive to the energy of Source, your oversoul, and other monadic beings; some of whom we refer to as angels. Opening your mind to the possibility that we are so much more than we first thought, is the first step. Much of what has been labeled 'occult' can and has been described in scientific terms. Unless you want to get an education in quantum physics and math, you may try using your intuition instead to decide if the models I have provided resonate with you. If not, let the concepts contained in the book percolate in your consciousness and compare them with what others are saying at this time to derive your models of understanding. I am one of many humans speaking about and writing about the soul's journey and what it means to transcend the third dimension. People explain concepts in their way according to their understanding, and that is a good thing because it is unlikely that one person spreading the message of unity consciousness will be in accord with 8 + billion people on Earth. The more people that light their torch, the closer we will be to the bonfire of enlightened collective consciousness. To me, ascension means that we come to a beautiful experience of life on Earth, together, and individually. Each experience of this is important to the collective. If your primary concern is to improve your daily life, which does help the collective tremendously, consider what my mentor Bob would tell me, "if you don't know what to do, do the loving thing." That bit of advice has served me well from the moment I heard it. If I feel something and it is not loving, I do not berate myself about it because that is an experience of being human. I do avoid other people while I am feeling lower emotions, so as not to pass that energy to them. Or, I work through the feelings with someone willing to hold space for me. We all need a good 'time out' once in a while. After that, it is easier to come back to other people and be my essential self again. The advice to do "the loving thing" means for yourself, and for the people you encounter. Care about how you feel so much that it becomes improbable you will do anything unloving, even when you feel something else besides love.

This is my goal too.

Are you ready to fully step into the power that is you? To create all that you wish to experience in your reality? You have been lighting up parts of the hologram of Creation all along. You will do it more consciously now. The time has come to know that you **are** Creator/Source/God, to know that everything that has happened before this moment has been by your divine design, and when you opted to read this book, you knew there is even more of your soul to experience with an expansive view. Step further into your light, your energy, as it is safe to do so again. The 'past' is another dimension of your soul's journey. Reach within, from time to time, to your inner child that you know in this Earth reality, and let your child-self know you have done a fantastic job together in this life! Tell the child that you are always there for him/her/it, and together, there is nothing you cannot create. When you do connect consciously with your other aspects, in other dimensional realities, you form collaborations to heal all lineages. Build your strengths together in oneness during this lifetime.

You can step into a state of consciousness where everything that has happened in your life makes sense, and you **know** where your soul wants you to travel next.

We are not alone at any time in our lives.

We have each other, we have our all-powerful oversouls, and we are One, God/Source.

Source by any other name is still the Creator.

Brightest blessings of love and light from me to you.

I have a running blog which is available on my website: www.quantumexplorations.com

I will be posting more there in 2023 as well as adding videos to my YouTube channel, Quantum Explorations: @quantumexplorations3283.

You can follow Quantum Explorations on Facebook by searching the name.

www.ingramcontent.com/pod-product-compliance
Lightning Source LLC
LaVergne TN
LVHW021713060526
838200LV00050B/2644